American Women in the Twentieth Century

Series Editor: Barbara Haber, The Schlesinger
Library on the History of Women in America,
Radcliffe College

Pulling together a wealth of widely-scattered primary
and secondary sources on women's history, *American
Women in the Twentieth Century* is the first series to
provide a chronological history of the changing status
of women in America. Each volume presents the
experiences and contributions of American women
during one decade of this century. Written by leading
scholars in American history and women's studies,
American Women in the Twentieth Century meets the need
for an encyclopedic overview of the roles women have
played in shaping modern America.

Forthcoming Titles:

American Women: 1900-1920
Nancy Sahli

American Women in the 1920s
Dorothy M. Brown

American Women in the 1960s
Carol Hurd Green

Mothers and **More**

American Women in the 1950s

Mother and Child, San Francisco, 1952, by Dorothea Lange. Exhibited in
The Family of Man photography show, Museum of Modern Art, 1955.
Courtesy of The Dorothea Lange Collection, Oakland Museum, Oakland, Calif.

Mothers and **More**

American Women in the 1950s

Eugenia Kaledin

Twayne Publishers
Boston

Mothers and More
American Women in the 1950s

Copyright © 1984
by G. K. Hall & Company
All Rights Reserved
Published by Twayne Publishers
A Division of G. K. Hall & Company
70 Lincoln Street
Boston, Massachusetts 02111

Book production by Marne B. Sultz
Book design by Barbara Anderson

This book was typeset in
10 point Janson with
Harry Heavy display type

PRINTED ON PERMANENT/DURABLE
ACID-FREE PAPER AND BOUND IN
THE UNITED STATES OF AMERICA

Library of Congress Cataloging
in Publication Data

Kaledin, Eugenia Oster.
Mothers and more: American women in the 1950s.

(American women in the twentieth century)
Essay on Sources: p. 249
Includes index.
1. Women—United States—History—20th century—
Addresses, essays, lectures.   2. Mothers—United States—
History—20th century—Addresses, essays, lectures.
3. Feminism—United States—History—20th century—
Addresses, essays, lectures.   I. Title.   II. Series.
HQ1420.K35   1984   305.4'2'0973   84-15656
ISBN 0-8057-9904-4 (hardcover)
ISBN 0-8057-9907-9 (paperback)

To my students in the Programs for Adult Women:
Northeastern University, Burlington Campus
1964–1967

Contents

About the Author

Eugenia Kaledin, a Mellon Fellow at the University of Pennsylvania in 1983–84, is the author of *The Education of Mrs. Henry Adams*. She is currently executive director of the Alliance of Independent Scholars, Cambridge, Massachusetts.

Preface

This collection of essays attempts to present a view of American women in the 1950s that modifies the dominant myth of their victimization. Although I intend to clarify the impact of attitudes that defined women primarily as bearers of children during the 1950s and kept them out of positions of power in every institution, I also want to suggest that women continued to cope with discrimination in ingenious ways. In assessing the achievements of a decade notable for a lack of organized feminism, I attempt to catalog the many ways women with some choice managed, in Gerda Lerner's words, to play a role in history *on their own terms*. I believe that women's overall contributions to the decade were humanizing and important.

The period after World War II was a time of value upheaval. Fear of communism, increasing military-industrial organization, sharpening awareness of civil-rights inequities, and growing affluence challenged American women to remain a moral force. The family, women were told over and over, was the core of a free society. The ambivalence that most new mothers felt about going out to work was steadily reinforced by a society that did not want them competing with returning veterans for the best full-time jobs. And the role most were urged to play, the traditional nurturer, the guardian of culture, often seemed—even to the most radical—preferable to the struggle for success in organizational worlds that openly discriminated against women.

Ultimately, we may find the either/or issues women continue to face much more complex than work versus children. When women are discouraged from competing as equals with men they seem to evolve, perhaps to invent and reinvent, a set of values designed to confront or assuage their powerlessness. We find them during the 1950s working in a number of ways to enhance the quality of life so that more of their voices might be heard. What they had to offer, even when they were successful on male terms—as a few women always were—was a way of regarding the world often overlooked or undervalued by men. Their priorities were often different.

If opportunities for power were indeed scarce during the 1950s, what may be of more interest is that visible women sometimes even refused such positions. Eleanor Roosevelt, who worked all her life to stir up women's political awareness, refused to run for Congress; she insisted that barnstorming for the United Nations, and also for Adlai Stevenson, was more important. India Edwards turned down the chance to be Chairman of the Democratic National Committee; Marya Mannes refused to take over a television talk show; in 1953 Dr. Leona Baumgartner quit her job as Assistant Commissioner of Health in New York City to dramatize stultifying restrictions and inadequate salary schedules. Whether men would have made similar choices is worth the consideration of future feminist theorists. The different ways women have to assert themselves in social situations must be examined with more sophistication. We need to refine our means of assessing how women view their decisions in historical perspective. It is too easy to allow traditional definitions of power to diminish women's achievements as they have similarly limited women's opportunities.

The women of the 1950s who put home and family first found strength, I believe, in a growing awareness that their achievements need not be measured by the same standards as men's. They cherished the "separate but equal" idea, which would be challenged by political activism on another level before the decade was over. But their insistence on *difference* became absorbed into the culture in an androgyny that would have a deep impact on the generation to come. Many women attempted to extend the traditional values of nurturing and caring into other spheres of activity.

Middle class women took satisfaction in working on their own terms as volunteers—in projects that would be inadequately understood by more professionally oriented reformers at the end of the 1960s—in what appears to be a recurrent pattern in American life. Fifties women set up libraries in poor school districts; they organized to make more people aware of nuclear holocaust; they led school children around art museums, and, before the decade was over, they sat in at lunch counters with blacks to emphasize the importance of the new civil rights movement. The League of Women Voters, a significant force during the decade, provided useful political training in middle level management for women who would later enter the "real" world of party politics.

Another aspect of women's satisfied awareness of their difference appeared to the women at home through the new productivity of older women at work. If it was at first hard to find women pursuing full-time careers while raising young children, it was easy to find women going back to work as the children left the nest. Many women appeared to be incredibly active beyond the retirement age of men. That women often play different roles at different stages of their lives is one fact I hope this book illumines. Studies of such "new old" women may eventually help to reassess the way we have wrongly measured women's productivity in the world by male stages of life. In the 1950s, in a culture that tended to identify all achievement with youth, it was encouraging to discover older women in the work force even if their jobs were unequal to their abilities. Talk of extending education and retraining older women became a primary part of the undertow of feminist expression at the time. Women college presidents, particularly, urged educated women—as individuals—to keep their intellects active, even though there were still few institutional changes to help them. As an example of mature accomplishment on her own terms, Eleanor Roosevelt towered over the scene.

The few brilliant young women like Rachel Carson and Hannah Arendt who succeeded on male terms in gaining public recognition for work that was considered somewhat unconventional by the narrower professionals in their fields were by no means "feminists," but they remained inspirational for other women who needed to keep being reminded that women's minds were never inferior to men's. Margaret Mead also remained a controversial presence in the 1950s as she attempted over and over to reconcile women's dual biological and cultural roles.

Another conventional source of pride for women during the decade was their impressive creativity. There could be little doubt about women's high level of achievement in the worlds of art and literature. In photography, painting, sculpture, drama, and the dance, women excelled. And if their work was not always representative of what was most fashionable it nevertheless was able always to hold its own. Much of the writing of the period that concentrated on inner life did reflect women's own sense of isolation, but even the writers did not mirror just one point of view. Interviews with artists and authors often stressed the particular satisfactions of being able to work at home, or in being able to set their own work hours. Yet artists, almost by definition alienated from the mainstream of American life, managed to share the intellectual challenge of the period; they did not give up their work when they had children any more frequently than performers did.

Writing in every sphere became a source of strength for women during the 1950s. Words became a way to explore the mystery of nature against technology. And words remained a means to cope with a world that had narrowed women's opportunities at the same time that it urged them to develop their potential. Like graffiti artists making dazzling marks on the walls of buildings with locked doors, many women attempted to speak to the society as a whole. A few achieved remarkable eloquence in their search for identity in poetry; others wrote lasting fiction; still others, as social critics, prepared the way for the ideological feminism to come.

The conservative role assigned to women by society permitted a few women to identify with the heritage of alienation that ultimately enriches mainstream culture; they turned their frustrations into creative energy. That many women during the 1950s were damaged or lost is surely true; but that many others also found genuine satisfactions in a number of ways is undeniable. Like Josephine Herbst who sought identity with the eighteenth-century horticulturalists, the Bartrams in *New Green World* (published in 1954), many women grew aware of a long tradition that saw the gains of progress as a severance from the wholeness of things. When the activities of these women eventually become incorporated into linear American history, the decade of the 1950s will seem more worthwhile.

No decade can be characterized neatly by the ten years that confine it. The feminism of the 1950s, as I see it, begins in 1946 with the publication of Mary Beard's *Woman as Force in History*, a vision for intellectuals, and extends to the appearance of Betty Friedan's *The Feminine Mystique* in 1963, a popular book that freed great numbers of women to redefine their needs in a world that was ready for change.

Because my background is in American Studies, not in history, I have attempted to look at the richest variety of experience representative of this period rather than to focus simply on the political activities of the group of women coming of age, or on the statistics involving education and work. The attitudes of culture critics have been more important than have government records in my struggle to understand how women saw themselves. And the unrecorded personal histories of dozens of women have contributed to the way I understand these times. Any book dealing with women's minds in this period could easily become a series of intellectual atrocity stories.

To Barbara Haber of the Schlesinger Library I owe ongoing gratitude for her steadying faith and commonsensical advice. The staff at the Schlesinger Library deserves a note of appreciation for making scholars feel so welcome. To the librarians and the research resources of the town of Lexington, Massachusetts, I also extend special gratitude. The women's book-finishing group of the Alliance of Independent Scholars provided both emotional support and valuable criticism. Carroll Smith-Rosenberg's gift of a quiet place to work must never be undervalued. My students at Northeastern University, Burlington, over many years taught me more sharply than any statistics about the losses of the 1950s. And the bravery and resilience of a number of inadequately rewarded friends who also came of age in the 1950s continue to remind me of the best that American women are capable of.

Grace Clark must be cited for her vigilance in helping prepare the manuscript, and Fran Opher for her Philadelphia sensibility. Arthur Kaledin provided frequent historical consultations. To the children of the decade, Nicholas, Jonathan, and Elizabeth Kaledin, I am finally grateful for having expanded my world in ways I never could have predicted.

Eugenia Kaledin

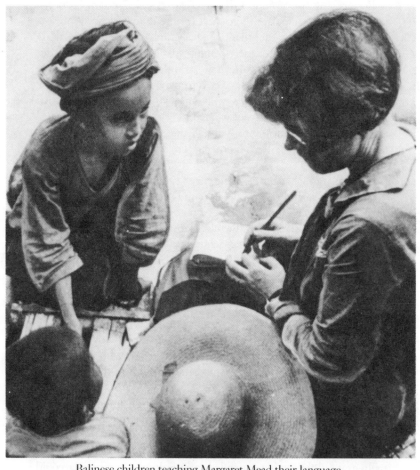

Balinese children teaching Margaret Mead their language.
Reprinted from People and Places *by Margaret Mead,* © *The World Publishing Co., Cleveland, 1959.*

Chapter One

The 1950s: Global Awareness and Domestic Change

When witty, articulate Adlai Stevenson lost the 1952 presidential election by more than six million votes, a professor at the University of Utah echoed the way many educated people felt: "It's not just that a great man has been defeated," he said; "it's that a whole era is ended, is totally repudiated, a whole era of brains and literacy and exciting thinking."[1] Although historians to come would be kinder to the Eisenhower administration, which looked so painfully dull at the time, many would find it hard to describe the 1950s as a period of creative risk or political vision. The Eisenhower age, more complex than the consensus ideology it attempted to reflect, did little to discourage the fears and anxieties underlying hopes for a new democratic community on American soil. Changes in the world economy began to affect us all.

"The great fear" as David Caute so brutally and extensively defined it in his book on the anticommunist purges under Truman and Eisenhower—the fear of communism that extended through the decade and touched almost every kind of contemporary behavior—reached back to the economic insecurities of the 1930s.[2] We lived with an unconscious sense that New Deal economic policies might never have overcome earlier failures without the incentive behind the incredible industrial organization of World War II. Although Eisenhower's programs legitimized many of the "socialistic" reforms of previous Democratic administrations, his failure to understand the importance of civil liberties in civilian life intensified other anxieties.

America had created a great number of jobs and many new kinds of social security, but World War II left us much less innocent. Not only had we witnessed the horrible success of the Nazi holocaust as a realistic example of totalitarian technological efficiency, but we also experienced tremendous anxiety about Russia's acquisition of atomic weapons. When we could not see ourselves, theoretically responsible democrats, as the sole possessors of the atomic bomb we grew hysterical. In 1954, pleading for a return to sanity, Lewis Mumford, a long-standing student of American civilization, commented: "In the name of freedom we are rapidly creating a police state; and in the name of democracy we have succumbed not to creeping socialism but to galloping Fascism."[3]

Ironically, our technological superiority, instead of providing a sense of complacency, often became a prime source of new anxiety. The 1950s became the decade of the airplane, which made the whole world smaller than a lingering isolationist spirit wanted it to be. And the development of television suddenly made instant communication visible across the nation. By 1956, Americans were buying 20,000 TVs a day and there were more than 500 stations; by 1960, fifty million sets had been sold; and by the mid-1960s, 94 percent of all homes had one or more television sets.[4] We became instantly aware of many places in the world far from our hometowns that seemed to have an impact on everything we did. By the end of the decade, moreover, few Americans even had hometowns; a vast new highway network and a glut of automobiles made us more than ever a nation of movers. *On the Road* was an apt title for a novel describing the lives of the nonconformist Beats, but it might have applied equally to the upwardly mobile conservatives pursuing corporate success. Rootlessness and restlessness were built into our way of life. The 1950s exaggerated the freedom to seek better economic opportunities and richer experiences, at the same time that the decade nourished the organization man and the "other-directed" citizen who rejected the insecurities of traditional individualism.

The decade was far from being monolithic; after the 1954 congressional censure of Senator Joseph R. McCarthy for excessive Red-baiting, the vision of consensus developed into a more self-critical ideal. Many serious thinkers attempting to reassess and analyze what was worthwhile about American life included areas that needed improvement. If the fear of losing whatever was stable in America shaped many attitudes, much may be said for the concern for values that accompanied that fear. Few decades have produced a more interesting array of self-analytical social thought.

What Was Happening in the World That Made It Seem Essential to Justify American Institutions?

In 1950 India became a free nation, one of the "new" democracies at the edge of the Communist world to which we would feel morally and economically committed. In 1950 also, Harry Truman initiated the Point Four Program as a constructive way to fight communism with technical aid. In June of that year, when North Korea invaded South Korea, United Nations forces, dominated by Americans, joined in the defense, fearful of appeasement—of allowing another Munich. But in 1951 Truman fired General Douglas MacArthur for wanting to extend protective intervention too far. Many Americans, believing that we had "lost" China with the overthrow of Chiang Kai-shek in 1949, showed great sympathy for MacArthur, the old soldier who faded away almost at once.

During that period, as part of our commitment to the North Atlantic Treaty Organization, American troops were stationed all over Europe. When Gamal Abdel Nasser became head of the newly independent United Arab Republic in 1958, we were reminded of yet another area of the world where Communists could intrude on our economic interests. "Isolationism" had become a term that belonged to the New Deal; but Eisenhower ignored Nixon's pleas to intervene in the ancient wars of Vietnam, and he quietly disregarded the Truman Doctrine of commitment to help smaller nations when, in 1956, the Russians brutally put down the Hungarian revolt. He also persuaded our allies the French and the English not to embroil themselves in a crisis over Egypt's nationalization of the Suez Canal. At the same time, however, John Foster Dulles proclaimed a new "massive retaliation" program—the beginning of the stockpiling of nuclear weapons—and boasted of "brinksmanship" as the core of our foreign policy. The inability to understand that most of the world lacked the economic security and the political experience to participate in our kind of democracy was propelling us toward a new kind of imperialism.

By the time the Korean armistice was signed at Panmunjom in 1953, over 54,000 Americans had been killed; and American casualties amounted to over 165,000. That same year, Russia announced its successful development of a hydrogen bomb.

The Republic of Ghana, founded in March 1957, inaugurating an Africa of independent nations, was not as threatening as the Russian orbiting of *Sputnik* in October; that year a second *Sputnik* carried a dog into orbit. Because our own Vanguard rocket exploded disastrously in December, a general alarm rang out among American educators. Afraid of being surpassed by the Russians in the technology race, we began to reshape our entire system of education, with the help of the 1958 National Defense Education Act, to stress math and science.[5]

In 1958 China bombarded Quemoy, and Nikita S. Khrushchev became premier of Russia. Richard M. Nixon, then vice president, was heckled and attacked on a goodwill tour of Latin America. But there was also a moment of cultural accord in the Cold War when the Russians awarded the Tchaikovsky musical prize to Van Cliburn, a Texan. That June Imre Nagy, the leader of the anti-Soviet Hungarian resistance, was executed. At that time we were paying for all the costs of the South Vietnam army, and 80 percent of its government expenses.

When Fidel Castro overthrew the Cuban government of Batista in 1959, we greeted his immediate success with enthusiasm but subsequently turned against his radical economic and social policies. That was also the year of Nixon and Khrushchev's "kitchen" debate; Khrushchev, on a visit to the United States, was refused permission to visit our commercial utopia, Disneyland, for security reasons. He had proclaimed that communism would bury us. Although the opening of the Saint Lawrence Seaway, also in 1959, suggested the rare possibility of a satisfying international venture, by the time the 1960s rolled around we had to confront the French atomic bomb, the loss of Cuba's friendship and its subsequent trade pact with Russia, the reality of war in the Congo, and the independence of seventeen new African nations. By the end of the decade most of us accepted as fact that we would never again be able to sustain the myth of an uninvolved, self-sufficient America. Our economic interests were global and our moral commitment to "freedom" seemed clear, even if our confusion about self-determination for others remained. We worried that Khrushchev's prediction might actually come true.

How We Behaved

The 1950s stand out politically not as a decade when we challenged injustice on an international scale, but as a period devoted unrealistically to ferreting out Communists in our own backyard. How did we go about protecting ourselves from dangerous neighbors?

When Alger Hiss, apparently the epitome of Ivy League respectability and achievement, was indicted for perjury in his second trial, on 20 January 1950, people began to think twice about Senator McCarthy's snide remarks about "Reds" in the State Department. It seemed momentarily possible that the laundry list McCarthy waved about on 9 February might contain the names of "205 card-carrying Communists" in government.[6] Part of our American heritage, the naive innocence so neatly captured by Herman Melville in the character of Captain Delano in *Benito Cereno*, demands an astonishing gullibility. Conditioned to the pursuit of happiness, we have often had a hard time coming to terms with the flaws that remain in our society and have been quick to look for outside conspirators when things go wrong. McCarthy offered an easy explanation for everything in the world that was causing us problems. Ridding our country of Communists at home seemed a panacea. That McCarthy never attempted to collect the $25,000 Senator Millard Tydings offered him if he could convict one person in the State Department of being a Communist, remains a fact.

If the 1950 purges were relatively harmless compared with similar hunts for subversives in fascist countries, it must be recorded that suicides occurred among the blacklisted, that a number of responsible people lost their jobs, and that many essentially innocent individuals—like Owen Lattimore, who retired to England—once accused, were never again able to overcome a sense of suspicion. The Civil Service Commission actually fired 2,611 "security risks" and reported that 4,315 other government workers resigned when they learned they were under investigation.[7] Character assault is a particularly vicious kind of hostility; its wounds, even if healed, leave terrible scars. The damage to American civil liberties remained.

In June 1950, *Red Channels*, an official blacklist of entertainers, appeared. Because people who influenced public opinion were considered particularly dangerous, entertainers and teachers found themselves suddenly as significant as the people who shaped foreign policy. Many talented artists and writers lost their jobs; and the shame of people denouncing each other for survival or for "patriotic" reasons became a painful moment in our history. As late as 1980, Lillian Hellman and Mary McCarthy would still be redefining their own integrity in terms of their behavior in the 1950s.[8]

By the end of September 1950 we had passed the McCarran Act for Internal Security, to register Communists and to strengthen espionage and immigration laws, as well as to set up detention camps for spies and saboteurs in time of emergency. To speak out against such extreme protective measures at the time was almost equivalent to identifying with the "enemy." Yet the cartoonist Herblock and the syndicated columnist Drew Pearson, who was actually physically attacked by McCarthy, stood up as consistent opponents of the anti-communist hysteria as also did the maverick I. F. Stone. At such moments the free press becomes an essential source of strength for minority opinion.

In Pasadena in 1950, a "progressive educator," Willard Goslin—later defended by James Bryant Conant, president of Harvard, in a front-page *New York Times* book review—was dismissed from his post for no good reason.[9] In many parts of the country progressive education, designed to encourage thinking rather than learning by rote, became an easy scapegoat for educational incompetence. That same month Harry Truman gave the go-ahead to build the hydrogen bomb. And the government published a pamphlet, *You Can Survive,* a "how-to-do-it" booklet suggesting that it would be possible to resume normal living after a nuclear holocaust. The government also published lists of what might be included in improvised homemade bomb shelters.

Popular books like *Washington Confidential* asserted that "where you find an intellectual you will probably find a red."[10] Harvard was labeled "the Kremlin on the Charles," but Conant's record of ignoring McCarthy was good, and Nathan Pusey, his successor as president of Harvard in 1953, had earlier resisted McCarthy's inquisitions at Lawrence College, in Appleton, Wisconsin. Sarah Gibson Blanding, president of Vassar, emerged as a heroic defender of academic freedom when many untenured professors lost their jobs for unpopular opinions and many others were denied passports essential to their academic research. At the time, even nonacademic intellectuals became defensive. In 1953 William Phillips and Philip Rahv described the ideal reader of the *Partisan Review* as someone "concerned with the structure and fate of modern society, in particular with the precise nature and menace of Communism."[11]

With Eisenhower's landslide election in 1952, the Republicans captured the Senate and made McCarthy head of his own committee on government operations. "He seemed to have proved what a politician respects most," Eric Goldman wrote, "an awesome ability to affect votes."[12] He had been reelected in 1952 by a majority of more than 140,000. Exploiting his power, McCarthy promptly sent Roy Cohn and G. David Schine on a whirlwind tour of overseas information services, which cost many conscientious public servants their jobs and ended with the banning of "books, music, painting, and the like . . . of any Communists, fellow travelers, et cetera." Needless to say, "et cetera" included some extraordinary types like Henry David Thoreau and Foster Rhea Dulles, an anti-Communist professor cousin of the secretary of state. Librarians were ordered to remove the writings of such dangerous thinkers at once; some really did burn the books. Although Eisenhower, in a speech at Dartmouth in June 1952, openly criticized the outrage ("We have got to fight [communism] with something better. Not to try to conceal the thinking of our own people"), he did not countermand the directive.[13]

In 1952 also, we destroyed an entire island with a hydrogen bomb test and began to pour money into the B-52 bomber.

By 1953, the government instituted a more extensive loyalty check—by executive order—of all federal employees. And on 19 June 1953, in spite of pleas for clemency from forty members of Parliament, and even from the zealous anti-communist Pope Pius XII, we executed Ethel and Julius Rosenberg as "atom Spies," a warning to anyone with access to even the most remote state secret. The quality of the evidence used against the Rosenbergs, and the extremity of the judgment, led Jean-Paul Sartre to denounce the Rosenbergs' execution as "a legal lynching that has covered a whole nation with blood."[14] Whether such an execution contributed finally to America's sense of security, or merely aggravated our national anxiety, is worth considering. The intense mania for ferreting out Communists would last for at least another two years.

When Charlie Chaplin, pursued by the FBI, gave up his reentry permit in 1953, deciding never to return to the country that had fostered and enjoyed his talent for many years, he reflected on the loss of civil liberties:

America is so terribly grim in spite of all that material prosperity. They no longer know how to weep. Compassion and the old neighborliness have gone, people stand by and do nothing when friends and neighbors are attacked, libeled, and ruined. [15]

But Joseph McCarthy's downfall began when he took on the army on national television. The power of the new medium to expose extremism should not be underestimated. After eight years of irresponsible and destructive use of senatorial authority, McCarthy was, in December 1954, finally condemned by the Senate—67 to 22. By 1957 he would be dead of acute hepatitis. But the uneasiness about communism remained. In 1954 also, J. Robert Oppenheimer, the distinguished physicist who helped develop the atomic bomb, was deprived of his security clearance, ostensibly for much earlier associations with Communists. And as late as 1958, after Richard Rovere published an anti-McCarthy article in *Esquire*, three hundred subscriptions were canceled. Funds for the House Un-American Activities Committee continued to pour in. With the founding of the John Birch Society in 1958, anticommunism would indeed be institutionalized. Douglas T. Miller and Marion Nowak, the radical historian authors of *The Fifties*, are right to insist that "it is impossible to understand United States history since World War II without comprehending the pervasive nature of the anti-Communist phobia." [16]

If the 1955 admission of Harvey Matusow, a witness against many leftists, that he consistently lied for money, disillusioned some people, others were heartened by the presence during the 1950s of the Kefauver Commission to expose organized crime. Dishonesty, we were learning, paid well. In 1958, Charles Van Doren's appearance on "Twenty-One," a rigged TV quiz show, reminded Americans again that the best and the brightest are not always the most moral. The handsome Van Doren had wanted to overcome the general public's hostility toward "egg-heads." Rigged quiz shows were after all nothing but simple entertainment. "Rarely, in the long history of public confessions, had anyone revealed an episode of more thorough-going fraudulence," protested one historian. [17] In 1958 also, when Sherman Adams, one of Eisenhower's closest advisers, admitted taking bribes, people numbly accepted the cheating as part of a long heritage of indifference to the law. Forgetting that Melville and Mark Twain had withstood many nineteenth-century confidence men, John Steinbeck wrote to Adlai Stevenson as a contemporary voice of conscience: "I am troubled by the cynical immorality of my country. It cannot survive on this basis."[18]

Liberal Satisfactions and Concerns

When Earl Warren, the former governor of California, was made Chief Justice of the Supreme Court in 1953, few people expected the court to champion the liberties of minorities and radicals. But Warren surprised his original supporters: "biggest damfool mistake I ever made," said Ike.[19] Later that year Eisenhower also created the Department of Health, Education and Welfare, an important tacit acknowledgment of the need for government to play a role in areas the private economy was neglecting. And in 1954, the year Irving Howe founded *Dissent* magazine, the *Brown* v. *Board of Education of Topeka* decision was handed down, marking the beginning of the end of the "separate but equal" idea in American schools. "Separate educational facilities are inherently unequal," the decision read. It was the start of a great new movement toward black equality that took fire in the 1960s; liberals condemned separatism of any sort at that time. In 1957 Martin Luther King, Jr., helped to create the Southern Christian Leadership Conference, which became an important force for justice for blacks. And some women involved in these civil-rights actions would begin to wonder about extending the concept of equal justice to themselves, just as they had done after the Civil War.

In 1955 the Salk vaccine was acknowledged as an effective preventative for polio; one source of public anxiety was about to disappear. And scientists by 1959 had achieved the mass production of synthetic penicillin, which began to save many lives. The development of antipsychotic medications during the 1950s would enable the populations of mental hospitals to dwindle from 550,000 in a 1955 census to 190,000 by 1977.[20] Approved for a vast consumer market by 1960, the birth control pill appeared to promise women the end of unwanted pregnancies—simple control over their own bodies that would have an impact on all their choices in life. Technology also began to give us the computers that would liberate many human beings from tedious jobs and restructure the nature of thinking as well as the definition of unskilled work. Xerox was about to become a new verb as well as a process that speeded up every level of communication.

In August 1957 Congress passed the first Civil Rights Act in eighty-two years. But the achievement of any degree of civil rights for blacks has not been easy. In 1955 Emmet Till, a fourteen-year old boy, was kidnapped and murdered for whistling at a girl; his two white murderers were acquitted. That same December Rosa Parks was jailed for refusing to move to the back of the bus in Montgomery, Alabama, initiating the fifty-four-week bus boycott that brought Martin Luther King, Jr., to national attention. In September 1957 the president sent troops to Arkansas to protect the constitutional rights of the black students who wanted to go to Central High School. On a happier note, before the decade was over a black American made world news in the realm of sports. Althea Gibson, the first black allowed to play in the United States Lawn Tennis finals, won the championship twice and went on to triumph at Wimbledon.

The AFL and the CIO merged in 1955, giving big labor tremendous bargaining power. After the National Defense Highway Act was passed in 1956, ostensibly to build roads for escape during atomic attack, the automobile took over as the decade's main means of ground transportation. "By 1958, over 67.4 million cars and trucks were in use, more than one for every household (nearly 12 million families, mostly in suburbia, even had two or more cars.)[21] "The Volkswagen company sold 200,000 beetles here in 1958, a period of minor recession, while American car manufacturers, careless about future shortages, glorified the *big* car. Tail fins suggested flying, at the same time that the Edsel, a flamboyant Ford, became symbolic of a new kind of failure. A general indifference to alternative means of travel led to the tearing up of many railroad tracks and the disintegration of many urban transit systems.

In 1959 we gained two new culturally varied states, Alaska and Hawaii, signifying that distances and differences might indeed be wiped out by the plane and TV. And the launching in 1958 of *Explorer 1*, from Cape Canaveral, America's first successful space satellite, did much to raise national self-esteem. That same year a "Ban-the-Bomb" movement began to gather momentum, and a group of early environmentalists managed to prevent the building of a nuclear power plant alongside the San Andreas fault. When we chose the first seven astronauts in April 1959, America felt confident about the technological conquest of space.

It seemed clear when 10,000 students marched on Washington in a Youth March for Integrated Schools both in 1958 and in 1959 that many young people were not ready to accept the end of ideology. The student auxiliary of the National Committee for a Sane Nuclear Policy was founded at Cornell in 1958, and a student Peace Union was created at the University of Chicago in 1959, at the same time that Wisconsin University students also began to publish *Studies on the Left*.[22]

TV shows of the 1970s trivializing the 1950s concentrated on trends like rock music, hula hoops, and hot rods, but the comfortable small house stage set may have been what was most characteristic of the decade. For the first time in history more Americans owned their own homes than lived in rented premises. William J. Levitt, whose picture adorned *Time* magazine in July 1950, became the inspiration for the 1.4 million houses started that year. With help from government-supported mortgages for veterans and more subsidies for the roads leading to suburbia, the number of American homeowners increased during the decade by over nine million, reaching an incredible 32.8 million by 1960.[23] The fulfillment of this material aspect of the American Dream for so many people would be too easily disparaged by the children who grew up in these houses aware that they were already part of a broader world community. If some variations on Levittowns were made of "ticky-tacky," they were nevertheless cleaner and pleasanter than the crowded city tenements many Americans continued to flee. Being able to own a home frequently did bestow a measure of dignity on people who enjoyed working to keep it. Cultivating even a tiny garden provided some satisfaction when nine-to-five work remained dull. The vast production of plastic flowers during the decade did not necessarily rule out a greater interest in gardening, any more than the invention of the TV dinner discouraged greater interest in gourmet cooking. "Levittowners," as Herbert Gans described them, were far from "apathetic conformists ripe for take-over by a totalitarian elite or corporate merchandiser"; Gans found them to be more "inner-directed" than many upper-middle-class Americans.[24]

That the government was not simultaneously concerned about what was happening to the cities' cores, or with saving ethnic neighborhoods, or with the ultimate environmental damage that might re-

sult from a spreading megalopolis appeared years later to be a
mistake. But an economy that has tended to favor speculation rather
than long-range planning had learned to live with such flaws. With
the building of many different kinds of family-oriented suburban
communities, often labeled "gilded ghettos," some ethnic values remained, but the isolated nuclear family remained the main social
unit. During the 1950s in suburbia there were few visible homosexuals or families with lodgers; communal living arrangements were
rare; and even grandmothers were hard to find. "Togetherness," a
key advertising word of the decade, meant mother, father, and three
or more children.

Many people threw their energies and imaginations into "do-it-
yourself" home improvements. In 1954 it was reported that "70 percent of all wallpaper was hung by novices."[25] The credit card, the
fiscal invention of the 1950s, permitted more extensive spending on
home embellishment as well as on personal needs. What this greater
freedom to spend plastic money meant to the whole economy was
not yet clear; it seemed easier for Americans to believe at the time
that buying things produced jobs. Consumerism was no longer the
prerogative of the rich, nor was indifference to the powerless and
destitute. Urban poverty could be ignored in suburban prosperity.

Yet even the more creative aspects of consumerism would not be
satisfying to a nation with a religious tradition as deep as ours has
been. The tremendous turn to organized religion during the 1950s
reflected both spiritual need and underlying anxiety. Not only did
we perceive our national mission to be a spiritual leader vying with
the godless communist world, but we also felt driven toward personal religious aspiration. Norman Vincent Peale, Billy Graham,
and Monsignor Fulton J. Sheen dominated the decade; Joshua Loth
Liebman, author of *Peace of Mind*, found thousands of readers outside
the Jewish community. By the late 1950s, over 63 percent of the population were officially enrolled in churches. For two years in a row—
1953 and 1954—the Bible was on the best-seller list.[26] And by 1955
The Power of Positive Thinking had sold over 2 million copies; Norman
Vincent Peale was included in a tribute to the best salesmen of the
year. In the 1950s, unlike other periods in American history, religious enthusiasm involved every class and social division: "Protes-
tants, Catholics and Jews, rich and poor, old and young, intellectuals
and illiterates, suburbanites and city-dwellers, farmers and small
town people, blacks and whites."[27] A 1954 survey revealed that four

out of five people would never vote for an atheist for president, and 60 percent would not even permit a book by an atheist to remain in a public library.

In spite of the fact that most of the religious fervor of the 1950s concentrated on individual salvation, there were a few important religious dissidents, like the Quakers and the Catholic Workers, who believed in action for social justice and intervention against the politics of nuclear armament. Both Billy Graham and Norman Vincent Peale, however, made specific statements *against* social activisim. The popular religions of the time reflected the vision of consensus and conformity and served finally to justify the status quo.

Will Herberg's *Protestant-Catholic-Jew: An Essay in American Religious Sociology (1955-1960)* characterized the dominant spiritual mood as "religiousness without religion." He saw the new affiliations not as "a way of re-orienting life to God," but rather as "a way of sociability or belonging."[28] Whether providing social communities for a nation of uprooted individuals has not always been as valid a function for American religion as providing doctrinal commitment may be debated. What might ultimately be more disillusioning about the spiritual fervor of the 1950s was the degree to which religion also became a big business.

Every aspect of American life seemed involved with the problem of self-justification. We were driven to examine American culture both critically and creatively. In fact, the 1952 *Partisan Review* intellectuals' mourning over the end of the "great" period of twentieth-century writing had, by the end of the decade, proven premature. Critics praised remarkable new talents. James Baldwin's *Notes of a Native Son*, William Styron's *Lie Down in Darkness*, Ralph Ellison's *Invisible Man*, Allen Ginsberg's *Howl*, Saul Bellow's *Seize the Day*, Vladimir Nabokov's *Lolita*, Norman Mailer's *Advertisement for Myself* and J. D. Salinger's *Catcher in the Rye* were all books of the 1950s-strong assertions of individuality in an organization world. The "alienation" held against these writers was nothing new; the American writer has more often than not taken an adversary stance.

What may be more significant in connection with 1950s writing is that the creation of the quality paperback made such good books available to many people. Between 1952 and 1961 the sale of books actually doubled.

Although it was then easy to ridicule the giant abstract expressionist canvases of Jackson Pollock and Willem de Kooning, their work remains a legitimate creative reaction to the materialism of the age, another sign of the strong individualism totalitarian countries could not tolerate in their own visual artists. It would have been hard to deny that New York in the 1950s was becoming the center of world art. And much of America followed the leader when George Meany, then head of the AFL-CIO, insisted that by a higher standard of living Americans meant "not only more money but more leisure and a richer cultural life."[29]

Art museums and opera companies and symphony orchestras all multiplied in the 1950s. Long-playing records became the musical counterparts of quality paperback books. "Americans spent greater sums on tickets to classical concerts than to baseball games, and more on records and hi-fi equipment than on all spectator sports."[30] Art movies sprang up all over; one of the best aspects of the new internationalism became cultural exchange that imported classical foreign films like *Rashomon, La Strada, Wild Strawberries, Bridge on the River Kwai,* and *The 400 Blows.* If the mediocrity of television troubled intellectuals who did not always appreciate the native vitality of Elvis Presley or Buddy Holly, or the slapstick enthusiasm of "I Love Lucy," they might have seen in our own movies—in spite of the blacklist—a number of films that did credit to the remaining social awareness of the American film industry. Films like *Born Yesterday, Twelve Angry Men, On the Waterfront, High Noon,* and *Rebel Without a Cause* were as much criticisms of American life as the distinguished *Three Faces of Eve, A Streetcar Named Desire,* and *Singin' in the Rain* were distractions from its immediate pains. We had more choices than Cecil B. DeMille's 1956 fantasy version of *The Ten Commandments* or the 1959 horde sensation, *Ben Hur.*

The banning of D. H. Lawrence's *Lady Chatterley's Lover* from the mails in 1959 appeared to be a last-ditch stand for a censorship over which commercialism would soon triumph. In fact the first issue of *Playboy* magazine appeared in 1953. Periodicals critical of American society, *Dissent* and *Liberation,* also 1950s creations, offered more serious fare. The comic-book industry, which hit a high point in 1953–54—with 650 titles in print and a monthly circulation of over 100 million—responded to Frederic Wertham's criticism of their violence in *The Seduction of the Innocent* with a self-imposed censorship code that actually led to some commercial decline.[31]

The *Partisan Review* intellectuals' survey "Our Country and Our Culture," published in three issues in 1952, was not merely the continuation of a tradition of looking at ourselves with European eyes, it was also a continuation of the self-critical stance that often characterizes American thinkers. If, as Morris Dickstein asserted in *The Gates of Eden: American Culture in the Sixties*, the culture of the 1950s was "European in its irony and sophistication,"[32] it was also intensely American in its simultaneous willingness to look critically at all its institutions. The adversary position many intellectuals cultivated may have been "of the age" insofar as it was apolitical, but intellectuals could be proud to identify with a more ageless "tradition of critical non-conformism going back to Thoreau and Melville," which may indeed be, as Richard Chase insisted, "our *only* useful tradition." Thoughtful Americans were still looking for usable truths, ways to relate to an unsympathetic establishment. If "dissidence from within sounds like an unheroic mission," Chase continued, "we have only to ask in what other mood has the American mind ever been creative, profound, fresh or promissory of the future."[33] To criticize the minds of the 1950s—as some historians have done—for being paralyzed by a sense of tragedy is as meaningless as to celebrate the 1960s for a belief in progress. In any vital culture such attitudes continue to nourish each other. And writers and social critics invariably provide the incentive and rationale for political acts.

Mrs. George H. Davis, Mayor of Washington, Virginia, 1951.
Reprinted from The Revolt of American Women *by Oliver Jensen.*
Courtesy of the Schlesinger Library, Radcliffe College.

Chapter Two

American Women: Images and Acts

W riting about what women were doing or how they were changing in the 1950s must be more complex than describing political and cultural events. In her 1946 book *Woman as Force in History: A Study in Traditions and Realities*, Mary Ritter Beard insisted that women must be celebrated behind the scenes as well as pitied for anonymity, or admired for obvious accomplishments. The high marriage and birth rates after World War II, appeared to intertwine naturally with "the feminine mystique," the idea that woman's place was in the home and nowhere else—convincingly documented by Betty Friedan from 1957 questionnaires.[1] But most women of child-bearing age did not believe that having babies would limit their access to other social roles.

"Never Underestimate the Power of a Woman" was the slogan of the *Ladies' Home Journal* during this decade in which women had almost no access to power in the institutions that shaped American life. Yet the over five million women who subscribed to the *Journal* in 1955 would surely not have felt the slogan ironic—any more than they would have taken it entirely to heart. In a world in which few competitive opportunities existed for women because the best jobs and training were given to war veterans, the family provided many women with a sense of importance by offering both responsible work and the satisfactions of intimate companionship. Precarious as the American family may have always been as an institution in an upwardly mobile society, it was not solely the creation of Madison Avenue.

The feminine mystique was not even then the only attitude available in the culture; a number of active women also called attention to different values outside the home. The McCarthy era even produced a few women like Mary Stalcup Markward and Berenice Baldwin, who made the news as undercover agents for the FBI. And there were nuns organizing to support the Wisconsin senator, whose research staff included Phyllis Schlafly, as well as women's groups circulating petitions to try to prevent McCarthy's ultimate censure. Perhaps the most talked-about woman of the decade was Ethel Rosenberg—involved in an international spy episode that led to her death in the electric chair, a fate that history would not condone. The other most frequently mentioned public woman was Oveta Culp Hobby, former head of the Women's Army Corps, who became the first Secretary of Health, Education and Welfare. Like the FBI agents Markward and Baldwin, Hobby remains an example of the women whose values become completely identified with men's; hers is often the only female name listed in indexes of historical surveys of this period because her power was politically conventional.[2]

Yet Rosa Parks stands out as another woman whose name belongs in every history of the Eisenhower era. Parks's quiet defiance of the Jim Crow habit in Montgomery, Alabama, in 1955 not only led to the long bus boycott that brought Martin Luther King, Jr., to national attention but also demonstrated anew in America the power of organized passive resistance, which would influence the civil-rights movement in the decade ahead (see chapter 8).

A number of women, including Senator Margaret Chase Smith and playwright Lillian Hellman, also emerged as defiant spirits against McCarthyism at a time when timidity characterized many of their masculine peers. Women entertainers like Judy Holliday, Katharine Hepburn, and Lauren Bacall, refused to cooperate with the House Subcommittee on Un-American Activities in extending the blacklist of movie personalities; Marilyn Monroe, never as dumb as she pretended to be, helped to get the passport of her husband, Arthur Miller, restored. Agnes Meyer used her influence as part owner of the *Washington Post* to denounce McCarthy's Red-baiting: "The very life blood of democracy," she insisted, "can be pursued now only at the risk of one's reputation as a loyal American." And a few serious women scholars, including Professor Helen Markham of the Harvard Medical School and Rosamund Tuve of Connecticut College, openly protested the loyalty oaths that were being forced on teachers everywhere. "Adults must be certified conformers," Tuve, an authority on the Renaissance, objected, "before they can teach other adults." A number of women lost their jobs because of whipped-up hysteria. "Nothing I have done has been inconsistent with the true ideas of American democracy," said Eleanor Maki, a forty-two-year-old art teacher in Detroit; yet she saw herself subjected to "the most vicious kind of persecution." Even after her clearance Esther Brunauer, an international-affairs expert, was dismissed from her State Department post.[3]

With all the political limitations, however, the 1950s sustained a small but lively group of women social and cultural critics. If there was a moratorium on organized feminism there was no shortage of women writers concerned with the need to change institutions as well as with the reports of what was going on in the world. Marya Mannes contributed regularly to the *Reporter* magazine and published a collection of her social thought significantly labeled *More in Anger*; Aline Saarinen's *New York Times* art and architecture criticism was exemplary for intellectual breadth and human awareness. Jane Jacobs and Betty Friedan began to publish sections of the books that would awaken Americans in the next decade to new areas of concern, as Rachel Carson would make the entire world conscious of the need to save the complex patterns of nature from technological destruction. Freda Kirchwey, concerned with peaceful uses for atomic energy, remained editor and publisher of the *Nation* until 1955; Elizabeth Hardwick, Mary McCarthy, and Diana Trilling produced social criticism that revealed the range of values of the liberal imagination in America, while Janet Flanner continued to jolt us with trenchant descriptions of how we appeared from Europe (see chapter 6).

Journalists flourished. Marguerite Higgins became the first woman foreign correspondent to win a Pulitzer prize for her account of the Korean War in 1951; Flora Lewis and Claire Sterling reported news from Europe; Doris Fleeson focused on Washington, while May Craig extended her influence on the television talk show "Meet the Press"; and Sylvia Porter's investment advice was syndicated everywhere. Throughout the decade Gertrude Samuels's and Edith Evans Asbury's bylines appeared regularly in the *New York Times*. And Eleanor Roosevelt remained an active journalist both in her "My Day" column and in two women's magazines. More outspoken than her husband had been, Roosevelt did not hesitate to connect a reluctance to support Jack Kennedy with his refusal to condemn McCarthyism.[4]

Margaret Mead, in the public eye almost as long as Eleanor Roosevelt, continued to make Americans aware that women, even old women, in other societies often had roles of significance and power. If her 1950s audience picked up the side of her message that accepted women's biological function, it was not because Mead herself ever neglected to talk about cultural conditioning as the source of women's self-images.

And she had some allies among the more radical psychotherapists Karen Horney and Clara Thompson. Although the more conventional Freudians Grete Bibring, Helene Deutsch, and Therese Benedek (along with Marynia Farnham) may have dominated the decade with their insistence on biological destiny as the source of happiness, it is important to realize that there were dissident voices as well. Mabel Newcomer in 1959 published the monumental *Century of Higher Education for American Women*, unconsciously demonstrating the falsity of Farnham's assertion that spinsters should be barred from teaching because they were "incomplete" human beings. And Eleanor Flexner gave us—also in 1959—the indispensable *Century of Struggle: The Women's Rights Movement in the United States*, describing a number of heroines who, by Marynia Farnham's standards, would be labeled hopeless neurotics. As early as 1953, the same year that the Kinsey report on *Sexual Behavior in the Human Female* appeared, American women also had a chance to read in translation that key document of modern feminism, Simone de Beauvoir's *The Second Sex*. Kinsey's statistics—derived from interviews with nearly 8,000 women—became a solid foundation for women's new sexual liberation. When Ashley Montagu, the anthropologist, published his double-edged thesis on *The Natural Superiority of Women* in 1952, asserting that women's superiority was so self-evident that society need not encourage them to compete with men, we were fortunate to have Eve Merriam point out how this proclaimed "the natural superiority of the minnow that can exist on less food than the whale." Montagu, she concluded, managed to love the life out of women. At a period when discrimination against women was built into every institution, it was satisfying to find a few critics demanding deeper consideration.[5]

Creative writing was a source of power for the women of the time. Many writers of the 1950s turned inward more than the generation preceding them and the polemicists who followed; there is no question that they also exploited their regional backgrounds as representative reality. Yet to criticize such conscientious artists as Carson McCullers, Flannery O'Connor, and Eudora Welty for narrowness is to overlook the authenticity of the range of feeling embedded in their work. It need not be a blot on the 1950s, as Morris Dickstein implies in *The Gates of Eden*, that the "elusive mysteries of personality" dominate the writing of the period, or that the writers are intensely concerned with "craft, psychology, and moral allegory."[6] Perhaps these are the qualities that continue to fortify the human spirit most strongly. How should we deal, after all, with Emily Dickinson's reluctance to mention the Civil War? The appearance in 1955 of the definitive volumes of Dickinson's poems—with all their variations—left people astonished at the range and riches available to an apparently isolated mind. To denigrate the work of Jean Stafford because her main concerns are psychological, or to dismiss the imagination of Elizabeth Bishop because her politics are oblique, is to impoverish a rich literary tradition in the search for ideology.

And to ignore the more socially involved writings of Harriette Arnow, Kay Boyle, and Tillie Olsen is even less understandable. If women writers were not committed to the more visible political conflict of the times, they nevertheless wrote critically of different social realities. Lorraine Hansberry and Gwendolyn Brooks reminded us that black women were becoming vital contributors to a literature of conscience; Muriel Rukeyser created poetry out of social tension; Adrienne Rich and Denise Levertov, if predominantly apolitical during the decade, were finding ways to extend their concern for human values into more active worlds. The disciplined craftsmanship they were forging, the complex humanism they cherished, would make their later polemical work all the more powerful.

Although some popular writers, like Phyllis McGinley, carried the celebration of women's domestic role to fulsome extremes, others, like Shirley Jackson, expressed more complex realities at the same time as they conveyed the moments of pleasure with their children. Motherhood was far from simple. Even the fiercely angry Sylvia Plath could write of her little son, in "Nick and the Candle Stick," "You are the one / Solid the spaces lean on, envious. / You are the baby in the barn."[7] The satisfactions of mothering could be as real as its frustrations. And if there were no strong female writers at the time speaking as leaders among the Holy Barbarians, the Dharma Bums, the Beats—who dropped out of society in the late 1950s—an important value of this group of dissidents was their acceptance of femininity as a positive force in the world.

The Beats worshiped—as Norman Podhoretz claimed in his terrified essay "The Know-Nothing Bohemians"—primitivism, instinct, and energy. Their open celebration of homosexuality at one extreme, and "unisex" at the other, suggested a growing desire to include female principles in the dominant male culture. Jack Kerouac even appeared to be restoring "Mom" to a position of respect; "Mémère" plays an important role in the background of his life on the road. In 1954 Lawrence Kubie first presented an important paper, "The Drive to Become Both Sexes," to a far different group, the American Psychoanalytic Association, at Saint Louis. And in the same year even Norman Mailer acknowledged that homosexuals could be depicted as human beings in "The Homosexual Villain." Although "the revolt against masculinity" frightened many men, it clearly represented a new respect for an extended and enriched value system. "These children of the future," Leslie Fiedler complained, "seemed to feel they must become not only more black than white, but more female than male." Was the end of civilization at hand? Indifferent to the long tradition of American mystical doctrines and idealistic philosophies that have often survived side by side with commercialism, technocracy, and rationalism, Norman Podhoretz thought so. Androgyny might change social priorities; belief in social consensus was not, after all, designed to overwhelm the difference between the sexes.[8]

In writing about children and nature and inner realities as well as of the mystery of existence, a number of women articulated broader visions of human possibility, as well as their own anger. Only if we ignore these women writers can we conclude with Morris Dickstein that 1950s writing reflects simply the quiet despair of the death camps and an overwhelming anxiety about the bomb.[9] Many women writing in the 1950s were preparing the way for change, not just proclaiming their alienation or affirming simplistic sentimental visions.

In other arts, women also flourished. Although she would not enjoy being categorized as woman, or placed in any one decade, Georgia O'Keeffe—an example of the difficulty of confining artistic expression to any ten-year period—continued to produce individual work of remarkable quality; so did Isabel Bishop. Identified with a new community of artists, Lee Krasner, Elaine de Kooning, Helen Frankenthaler, Grace Hartigan, and Joan Mitchell made important contributions to the abstract-expressionist movement while Louise Nevelson cultivated her individual style and Alice Neel developed as a realist. In 1953 I. Rice Pereira held a major retrospective show at the Whitney Museum; in 1959, Kaethe Kollwitz also presented a one-woman display of a lifetime's achievement. The 1950s were among the most productive years for Grandma Moses (see chapter 10). All sorts of "new old" women kept demonstrating that accomplishments could take place at any age. To define "women" as women of child-bearing age is another way to impoverish their intellectual heritage.

Distinguished photographers with well-defined identities from earlier decades continued to record the American scene: Dorothea Lange, Imogen Cunningham, and Berenice Abbott were photographing new aspects of the world around them. Eve Arnold documented the social fabric of the 1950s: McCarthy's hearings, religious revivals, proms, and lunch counter sit-ins. Margaret Bourke-White was still demonstrating that women could photograph *anything* men could. Nine million people would see the most popular photography show of the decade, naturally labeled *The Family of Man.* Designed with the advice of Dorothea Lange, to stress the importance of peace in a world that was splitting apart politically, the show included many examples of women's photographic skills, as well as many sympathetic illustrations of women involved in identical family rituals all over the world. By the 1970s, when *The Family of Women* was prepared, the "sentimental" values of the earlier show would be considered part of a new feminist ideology.[10]

And women contributed as much to American music. Although symphony orchestras rarely hired women—they did not then audition behind screens—attitudes were beginning to change. When Doriot Anthony Dwyer, undaunted descendant of Susan B. Anthony's brother, was appointed first flute in the Boston Symphony Orchestra in 1953, the news made the front pages. Positions in classical music, a male preserve, did not reflect the actual competitive talent of women. In 1954 the Boston Symphony also played *Psalm of Praise*, by the little-known contemporary composer Mabel Daniels. It was harder for women conductors: Antonia Brico spent most of the decade teaching. Talented conductors like Lorna Cooke DeVaron of the New England Conservatory, Iva Dee Hiatt of Smith College, and Margaret Hillis, director of the American Concert Chorus in New York, were permitted to excel as choral directors, fulfilling their abilities primarily behind the scenes. In 1955 Marian Anderson became the first black woman to sing at the Metropolitan Opera, leading a dazzling procession of black singers who would soon be known all over the world. And Beverly Sills began her long and brilliant career with the New York City Opera Company while Sarah Caldwell created the Opera Company of Boston. During the 1950s, too, Wanda Landowska and Sylvia Marlowe were helping to make the harpsichord as much a part of the American musical scene as the banjo. Folksingers like Suzanne Bloch and Odetta brought a great degree of sophistication to an ancient skill.

At a time when couples still danced cheek to cheek, teenage girls were guided toward marriage with the romantic lyrics played every afternoon on Dick Clark's "American Bandstand." Clean-cut, well-mannered Clark even insisted on a dress code for the middle-class teenagers who flocked to dance in front of his camera, and he carefully screened his music. But "American Bandstand" did not survive the intensities of rock 'n roll. Before the decade was over Elvis Presley—shown only from the waist up on the "Ed Sullivan Show" in 1957—turned the music world upside down. If Presley's 1955 hit "Baby Let's Play House" seemed to offer little change in attitude toward woman's role, there was nonetheless something liberating about his style. The integration of black and country elements in Presley's music, and its open sexuality, suggested a freedom from cultural expectations that had a loosening impact on the society as a whole. Some people were quick to see rock 'n roll as still another communist plot.[11]

Jazz musicians were as hostile to women instrumentalists as were classical players. During the 1950s artists like Ina Ray Hutton and Corky Hale began to work on TV; Vi Burnside, Tiny Davis, and Beryl Booker managed to play as a trio on 52d Street. Toshiko Akiyoshi, who made her debut in 1956 at the Newport Jazz Festival, also ended up working behind the scenes; but she became the highest-paid free-lance arranger in the country.[12]

Singers were in great demand. Billie Holiday, Ella Fitzgerald, Lena Horne, Sara Vaughan, and Pearl Bailey were not only singing in clubs during the 1950s but were also available to thousands of people on the newly invented LP record; so were musical-comedy stars like Shirley Jones, Gwen Verdon, Carol Channing, and Mary Martin. And Ethel Merman continued to belt out songs in three different Broadway productions.

Talented women appeared on every stage. The 1950s may well have been the golden age of the dance in America. Not only were great companies like the New York City Ballet thriving, but so also were a number of independent dance companies and distinguished choreographers. Martha Graham's troup continued to influence the style and training of all modern dancers as she traveled as far as Japan for the State Department to demonstrate the reality of American culture. During the 1950s, Agnes deMille, who had been staging musicals in every part of America, published two volumes of autobiography, describing her personal achievement in a society not traditionally sympathetic to dance.[13] Doris Humphrey, who directed her own company until she became crippled with arthritis, continued as artistic director for José Limon. Hanya Holm, Maria Tallchief, Tanaquil LeClerc, Pearl Lang, Ruth St. Denis, Iva Kitchell, and Pearl Primus also contributed to the vitality of American dance. Influenced by Thelma Hill, in 1958 Alvin Ailey created the American Dance Theatre, which would provide ongoing visibility for many talented black women as well.

When Carson McCuller's *Member of the Wedding* opened with Julie Harris and Ethel Waters in January 1950, it seemed to set the decade's tone for what women could do in the theater. But after Hellman's *Autumn Garden* and Hansberry's *Raisin in the Sun*, dramas concerned with the shaping of women's lives, there were few plays by women equal to the available wealth of talented actresses. Cloris Leachman, Ruth Ford, Viveca Lindfors, Jessica Tandy, Helen Hayes, Uta Hagen, Meg Mundy, Judith Anderson, Barbara Bel Geddes, Shirley Booth, Susan Strasberg, Kim Stanley, Ruth Draper, Ruth Gordon, Cornelia Otis Skinner, Ethel Barrymore, Martita Hunt, Lynn Fontaine, Eva Le Gallienne, and Josephine Hull were all appearing on the stage during the 1950s.

In spite of the blacklist, movies remained as productive of spirited female personalities as ever. Shirley MacLaine, Joanne Woodward, Audrey Hepburn, Eva Marie Saint, Ava Gardner, Marilyn Monroe,

Judy Holliday, Doris Day, Kim Novak, Grace Kelly, and Debbie Reynolds were all 1950s discoveries—innocent but bright. Jennifer Jones and Elizabeth Taylor seemed to improve as actresses during the decade. Older stars, like Katharine Hepburn, who appeared in *The African Queen* in 1951 and *Pat and Mike* in 1952, and Rosalind Russell, who made *Auntie Mame* in 1959, continued to act out roles of spunky eccentricity as well as to demonstrate in yet another sphere that growing old presented no obstacles to the spirited. Gloria Swanson stepped out of the past to give a stunning performance as a narcissistic aging star in *Sunset Boulevard* in 1951, while Jane Wyman created an "older woman" who was both sexually and spiritually attractive in *All That Heaven Allows* in 1956.

Although hard-working, optimistic Doris Day and sexy, vulnerable Marilyn Monroe comedies were tremendous box-office successes, it would be hard to insist that there was any one kind of woman idealized on the screen. Fifties films showed fewer career women than earlier decades, but they made more of women's ability to influence men for the better *(High Noon);* and they demonstrated a variety of direct but nonviolent ways women used to assert themselves *(The Quiet Man, Born Yesterday, On the Waterfront).*[14] Movies reflected the general ambivalence fifties women felt about professional lives. As Brandon French suggests, they often asked: "But what is the *human* advantage of an ambisexual power elite based on ruthless competition and exploitation?"[15] *Some Like It Hot*, one of the decade's funniest films, set women's creative values against a world of gangster men, as it also foreshadowed one message of the 1980s film *Tootsie:* only in women's high-heeled shoes can men sense what being a woman is really like. Androgyny appeared to touch every level of culture. If movie makers accepted women's inferiority, they nevertheless used highly individualized female personalities to dramatize woman's capacity to ameliorate corrupt institutions from the outside. And fifties films reinforced what Molly Haskell has brilliantly perceived as a myth of the freedom to "start over"—a woman's version of the American Dream.[16]

Television offered a brand-new field for women's imaginations. Nanette Fabray and Imogene Coca, Jayne and Audrey Meadows, Arlene Francis, and Dorothy Kilgallen instantly became national figures. Coca, called the finest comedienne in America in 1951, revealed an extraordinary talent for satire that included the images women were offered to define themselves; she made fun of fashion shows, torch singers, cocktail lounges, "all-girl" orchestras, and Hollywood versions of the femme fatale. Children's entertainers like Miss Frances of "Ding-Dong School"; Cora Baird, the puppeteer; and Fran Allison of "Kukla, Fran and Ollie," helped retain the idea that Nila Mack sustained on radio, that learning could be pleasure, during the same decade that was putting down progressive education. Former movie stars like Dinah Shore, Lucille Ball, and Eve Arden redefined themselves on TV.[17]

"I Love Lucy," a drama of the frustrations and fantasies of a housewife whose husband would not permit her to go out to work, was the most popular show of the time. The wild eccentricity that Lucy represented invariably proved more amusing than her husband's serious attempts to entertain. And the birth of Lucy's baby as part of her television role during a decade when CBS would not allow the word "pregnant" to be used on TV had an important impact on American society. The producers wanted Lucy to stand behind chairs so that the pregnancy would not show, but Lucy and Desi, television symbols of the myth of successful marriage between different cultures, insisted on making their baby part of the show. If Lucy Ricardo was doomed to domesticity, Lucille Ball was demonstrating that having a baby should not force any woman to give up her work. Over two million more people watched Lucy's television birth in 1953 than watched President Eisenhower's inauguration address the next day.[18]

Domestic comedies like "I Love Lucy" and "The Honeymooners," with Audrey Meadows and Jackie Gleason, may well have been the ultimate comment on too much "togetherness," but alternative lifestyles were hard to treat seriously. Eve Arden's "Our Miss Brooks," a series about a spinster high-school teacher, could not go so far as to suggest that teaching was a wholeheartedly fulfilling life. Women coped with their dilemmas by laughing at them, and by slowly realizing that these shows barely suggested their full potential. Mockeries of marriage usually transcended stereotypes by emphasizing female ingenuity, however, and they helped women to define themselves as a "minority." Humor had to be an important part of women's defenses in the 1950s, when men were rarely heroic, and opportunities for well-rewarded work scarce.

More useful in terms of establishing serious images for American women were the few intelligent talk shows. Pauline Frederick analyzed international problems; Virgilia Peterson reviewed books;

Martha Rountree made her news program available to members of Congress for discussion of important domestic matters. In a forum for high-school students, Dorothy Gordon demonstrated respect for the ideas of the young; and Ruth Hagy moderated a similar show for older students, "College Press Conference." Harriet Van Horne, Betsy Palmer, Betty Furness, and Maggi McNellis attempted to help more confined women expand their narrow domestic worlds. In Cleveland, fifty-five-year-old Dorothy Fuldheim began a controversial talk show that was going strong in the 1980s. During the 1950s the new medium, not yet defined by the rigidities of convention, permitted a good number of women—not all young and beautiful— to make themselves visible to the American public. But television did not begin to fulfill its educational potential. Too often it catered to advertisers' dreams of what the ideal woman consumer should be.

American women dazzled the world of sports during the 1950s. Andrea Mead Lawrence, a skier, was the first United States athlete to win two gold medals in the 1952 Olympic Competition; she picked herself up after falling in one race and went on to win. Tenley Albright was the first American to win the gold medal for figure skating in 1953, and Carol Heiss won in both 1956 and 1957. Pat McCormick, a diver, also won a gold medal in 1955. In tennis, the black pioneer Althea Gibson brought honors to America twice at Wimbledon, after becoming the first black to play in and win the United States Lawn Tennis championships in 1957 and 1958. Maureen "Little Mo" Connolly also proved herself a Wimbledon champion three times in the 1950s. And Babe Didrikson Zaharias continued to win trophies playing golf even after a cancer operation.[19] If the Second World War had not already persuaded American women that they were physically capable of doing just about anything, the record of women athletes in the 1950s would have been as convincing.

Religion has often been a source of community and personal strength for women immersed in child-rearing as well as for women living alone. But although the great religious fervor of the times put many women's names on membership rolls, it did little to provide them with positions of power or influence. Before the decade was over, however, a number of religious hierarchies began to include a few women at decision-making levels and even in some cases as ministers. As early as 1951, the year the first woman Methodist minister was ordained, women deacons were urged upon the Southern Presbyterians to increase the numbers combating communism with Christ. Mary Lyman, in 1950 ordained a Congregational minister at the age of sixty-two, became the first woman to hold a faculty chair at Union Theological Seminary. Before her retirement as Dean of Women Students in 1955, she played a vigorous advocacy role for other women in the ministry; and she reflected women's concerns for international accord in her work for the World Council of Churches, written up in 1956, as *Into All the World*. In 1957, New York City would boast its first woman Presbyterian minister, and also its first female Episcopalian vestry "person."

The most visible woman theologian of the decade, Georgia Harkness, taught at the Pacific School of Religion in California, suggesting the continental span of growing female influence on institutional religion. The three books Harkness published during the 1950s emphasized the idea that Christianity should have meaning for the people in the pews, a belief designed to make greater use of women's social gifts.[20]

Individual nonbelievers, however, were suspect because Communists were by definition "Godless." In 1956, Elinor Goulding Smith wrote a brave article for *Harper's* from the viewpoint of a beleaguered agnostic: "Won't Somebody Tolerate Me?" She championed a return to a period of respect for "one another's beliefs or disbeliefs." In West Virginia, the unconventional Dr. Louella Mundel was dismissed from her job at Fairmont State College, primarily "for being an Atheist who didn't believe in God." Although she won a suit against the tautologous libel, Mundell's persecution at the time drove her to the brink of suicide.[21]

In 1952, the same year Rachel Carson's *The Sea Around Us* led the best-seller list, the second book most Americans were reading was Catherine Marshall's tribute to her chaplain husband, *A Man Called Peter*.[22] By 1955, Marshall's book had sold almost 1.5 million copies. When it appeared as a movie, it was advertised as showing that religion could be "fun."

Some social realities remained less fun. The "other America," the world of the poor, although it received little attention from institutions during this decade, continued to be important in the religious imaginations of a few notable individuals. Dorothy Day's *Catholic Worker* mission to the poor, on the Bowery in New York, remained a haven for hopeless human beings who were all but invisible to most churches. Evicted in 1956 from the old building on Christie Street, where she housed and fed about three hundred people a day for over twenty-one years, Day counted on "miracles" to help her make necessary repairs, but failed to recognize one in the shape of W. H. Auden, who stepped out of a crowd with a check for her fine.[23]

Edith Lowry, a Protestant minister to migrant workers, was another such concerned Christian; in 1950 she took over the Home Missions for the National Council of Churches. Many unsung women volunteers worked beside these organizers. And although a few southern fundamentalists would cite the Bible to justify segregation, more often churches supported the great passive-resistance movement that originated in the South. Religious sanction enabled many apolitical women to feel involved in the movement toward integration, which became the important social achievement of the decade.

Dorothy Rogers Tilly, a leader in Methodist church work, stood out as a civil-rights reformer in the Fellowship of the Concerned, a network of volunteer women from twelve southern religious groups committed to the idea of "equal justice under law." Bombing threats from the Ku Klux Klan did not deter Tilly's involvement with the group, which gained more than 4,000 members during the decade. Virginia Foster Durr was another prominent woman, who worked with the Southern Conference for Human Welfare, the League of Women Voters, and the NAACP to bring about integrated schools and general human rights in Alabama. If their names and those of the women who worked with them are not well known, it is not because their work was insignificant or because their voluntarism was trivial.[24]

Although anthropologically women have been equated with nature and men with civilization, Mary Beard thought that sexual roles could often be defined the other way around. She saw women, the nurturers, the inspiration for creativity, steadily maintaining civilization in the face of male barbarism. Involvement in peace movements and pacifism, for example, continued to provide individual women with lives of value in the face of new technological barbarities. During the 1950s, Emily Greene Balch turned her attention to our relations with China; Nora Barney urged a cease-fire in Korea; and Mabel Vernon of the WILPF worked on Latin American peace agreements. Locked out of the military industrial power complex, such activists, conditioned to establishment hostility, continued to corroborate Beard's viewpoint by playing the most obvious civilized role—peace maker. "Women Strike for Peace" and SANE, The National Committee for a Sane Nuclear Policy, were both founded in the 1950s.[25]

And a great number of women, even some who worked full time, involved themselves in the specific needs of their own communities. How should we classify the range of social involvement they represent? Some eventually became professional politicians, some, social workers; and some, political activists. Rosa Parks, Autherine Lucy, and Daisy Bates, the most visible black women among the civil-rights protesters, would never have defined themselves as radicals; they wanted nothing more than to share the American Dream. How should we categorize the range and variety of Eleanor Roosevelt's interests? Often what seems most valuable about the women of the 1950s is the way they manage to escape conventional definitions, not only by being active at all ages but by redefining a role or profession in some more socially useful way—outside the system—to become, in Mary Beard's terms, a force rather than a statistic.

Among the women still on the scene in the 1950s not content to blame inequities in American life on communist conspiracy were inspirational types like Helen Hall, honored in 1959 after twenty-five years as director of the Henry Street Settlement House in New York City. On the original advisory council for the Social Security Act, Hall spoke of the satisfactions of a career that had made New York seem like a small town. Her focus had necessarily shifted from the nation to the neighborhood; during the 1950s she also extended her role to become an educator, struggling to interest the people on the Lower East Side in their new neighbor, the United Nations. Carrying on the tradition of Jane Addams, Hall connected an emphasis on education with a belief in a democracy committed to help people act as responsibly as possible. Mary Calderone, similarly, attempted to clarify the importance of education in sex for a nation growing less and less inhibited. And Margaret Sanger not only set up the International Planned Parenthood Association in 1952 but also pressured a philanthropic friend, MIT graduate Katherine McCormick, to subsidize research on the liberating new birth-control pill.[26]

Women who devoted their lives to helping others were frequently written up in the *New York Times* as good examples. Maryal Knox, a trained theoretical mathematician, would boast in 1952 that she had coped for fifty years with the nontheoretical problems of the East Harlem Neighborhood House. Instead of bemoaning the loss of her

mathematical career, she was distressed that the growing emphasis
on specialization would deny similar alternative work to people like
herself. Because she had no academic training in sociology or social
work, she protested that "no settlement would hire me today."[27] But
changing attitudes toward professionalism also opened up a few positions. Katherine Brownell Oettinger, in 1957 the first mother ever
to head the Children's Bureau, made the point that age was becoming an asset in social work.

Public utterances of women continued to emphasize caring roles.
Some who had been trained professionally often demonstrated a capacity to use their skills in a broader social context. Karen Horney,
for example, in 1958 opened a free or low-cost psychoanalytic center
for men, women, and children who could not afford private care.
Under Dr. Leona Baumgartner, Commissioner of Health for New
York, the city was judged "the healthiest in its history." Baumgartner
distributed the new polio vaccine without charge, and concerned
herself with the unpopular idea of quality daycare; she believed doctors should involve themselves in social struggles. Dr. Helen Wallace
created a child-care center in East Harlem in 1956 that concentrated
on preventive medicine. Eleanor Campbell, who entered medical
school when her daughter was seven years old—not an easy accomplishment in any decade—founded the Judson Health Center and
devoted her entire practice to medical social work. In the Far West
Ella Deloria, distinguished anthropologist and linguist, ran a mission
school for the Dakota Indians from 1955 to 1958. If these women
were driven to lives of social concern because they were denied more
conventional access to power and success, they nevertheless also
made people realize that such needs were as urgent and important as
was personal recognition.[29]

Pages might be filled with the names of women who contributed
time outside the home to improving society. The dean of the New
York School of Social Work remarked at one point during the 1950s
that if the volunteers were to go on strike, within six months our
country would degenerate into bureaucratic dictatorships.[30] If some
women remained Helen Hokinson cartoons, unaware of the role
they played in preventing any shift in social priorities, more began
to see their volunteer activities as lobbying for institutional change.
Women organized to "save the children" and prepared the way to
"ban the bomb." The gifted editor and writer Lenore Marshall managed in her spare time to become a founder of the National Commit-

tee for a Sane Nuclear Policy, an articulate group that continued to question American investments in nuclear war.

Under Eleanor Roosevelt's leadership women provided support for the newly formed United Nations organization and urged the study of international problems; the "teach-in," which would become a familiar means to organize sentiment in the 1960s, was well rooted in the open forums of the 1950s. When the Daughters of the American Revolution in 1959 attacked the United Nations for subverting our Constitution, Eleanor Roosevelt, with acid grace, noted that the DAR did wonderful work in preserving historic monuments—but, she concluded, they were out of touch with the world.[31]

Women's Club meetings announced with regularity in the *New York Times* included discussions of Managing Money, Fluoridation, Plastics for the Household, Strengthening Family Ties, Our Responsibility for a Peaceful World, Home Decoration, and Life in China. Women with leisure shattered into dilettantism by the sense of having too many choices did not clearly see their opportunities as unequal. The women organized in such groups as the General Federation of Women's Clubs and the League of Women Voters, as William O'Neill pointed out, gave their energies to altruism and benevolence to the point where almost everything they did had to be justified in such terms.[32] It may be healthy to report, however, that the National Federation of Business and Professional Women, a group committed to the support of the Equal Rights Amendment, was also growing during the decade; by 1956 it had 165,000 members.

Yet the League of Women Voters had the most impact on the political lives of middle-class women at the time. In the years between 1950 and 1958, membership in the League increased by 44 percent. Extending over forty-eight states in 1,050 local leagues to include some 128,000 members, the League offered an outlet for the energies of educated women all over the country who wanted to inject a dimension of humanitarian concern into active political life. Nonpartisan always, the League believed that political salvation lay "in our capacity to advance human life and thought."[33] But the women voters worked slowly. It was not until 1958, a whole decade after our government had been pursuing such practices with vigor, that the League recommended modification of loyalty-security programs to provide the greatest possible protection for the individual. To the feminists of the next decade, their caution appeared genteel. Yet the study groups they set up in the 1950s, committed to exploring water resources and foreign policy and conservation needs, were ahead of their time in awareness—if all too detached in applicability. During the 1950s, League women discussed how to get more women involved in political life, but they did not work to attract women who had not gone to college and they were themselves often hesitant to jump into the dirty waters of party compromise.

A 1973 feminist analysis of a 1957 speech by Mrs. John Lee, then President of the League of Women Voters, expresses disappointment in Mrs. Lee's pride in being "left out of the picture," in letting the male legislators believe that *they* had masterminded an important change that League members had pushed.[34] Yet it is important to realize that even during this "bleak" period the women satisfied to work behind the scenes were also learning to become more assertive, and that many were using League work as an apprenticeship for later visibility. Lucia Bequaert, a League member who became Executive Director of the Boston YWCA in the 1980s, wrote: "Although it may have been strategically unwise to have been identified with broad issues of moral and social reform, it was not a total liability. If an influential number of persons in a society come out for an ideology based on humanistic goals and the achievement of personal freedom, the society must somehow be affected." Finally, Bequaert insisted that "while one cannot measure the effect on society of changed individual attitudes, there is no doubt such personal changes remain just below the surface, fermenting and transforming, until a later opportunity for realization presents itself."[35]

In 1954 Eleanor Roosevelt and Lorena Hickok published a tribute to women in American politics, *Ladies of Courage*. Advertised with a "chapter which discusses why women should enter politics and offers concrete information on how to start," the book was meant to be a call to action.[36] Although both authors were committed Democrats, they fell in with the nonpartisan spirit they believed would appeal to more women. Margaret Chase Smith, Clare Boothe Luce, and Oveta Culp Hobby got as much attention as Anna Rosenberg, Truman's Assistant Secretary of Defense, or Perle Mesta and Eugenie Anderson, gifted Democratic diplomats, and Helen Gahagan Douglas, whose gallant Democratic political career had just foundered on anticommunist hysteria in California.

The New Deal optimism about women's political possibilities expressed in *Ladies of Courage* appeared as out of place in the 1950s as the "Ladies" of the title seemed in the decades that followed. Yet Roosevelt never made women's political involvement sound easy, nor did she ignore the problems of coping with children or feeling inadequately educated or poorly trained. Her own example continued to inspire younger women with the idea that their sensibilities were needed in political life.

Had Roosevelt and Hickok been writing about what was happening in women's education in the 1950s they might have similarly cited the number of successful women educators still on the scene. Of her remarkable teacher, Marie Souvestre, Eleanor Roosevelt had once written: "Whatever I have become since had its seeds in those three years of contact with a liberal mind and strong personality."[37] Although her own leisure class had frowned upon college for women, Eleanor Roosevelt understood how essential education was for strengthening female egos. The early years of the 1950s still offered many women access to the strength provided by close relationships and positions of power in all-girl schools where women took satisfaction in not being men. Before the decade was over, however, acceding to the idea that separate was not equal, we came to believe that coeducation was the only way to enhance women's sense of equality. By the beginning of the 1970s, male colleges, prep schools, selective public schools, professional schools, and seminaries all over the country would open their doors to women—and fewer women like Marie Souvestre would be hired to teach in more professionally oriented programs. Women had to explore different sources for self-esteem.

Adlai Stevenson's address to the graduating class of 1955 at Smith College linked the recurrent trend toward specialization with conformity and narrow-mindedness. In the day of the organization man, he begged the young women graduating not to define themselves by any profession but to see themselves first as individuals: "We will defeat totalitarian, authoritarian ideas only by better ideas; we will frustrate the evils of vocational specialization only by the virtues of intellectual generalization," he declared. Going on to decry "the hostility to eccentricity and controversy," embodied in the anti-communism of the time, he urged his female listeners to become "idiosyncratic" or "ornery" to combat the "tribal conformity" that represented the path of least resistance to life. If many graduates interpreted his 1955 speech as urging complete avoidance of the world, others were inspired to seek more original ways to enter it.[38]

Reading this much-attacked oration in later decades may make it easier to understand why so many educated women felt the immediate obstacle-laden pursuit of profession—"the evils of vocational specialization"—less interesting than trying to maintain the quality of life from their homes. They did not necessarily identify "civilization" with the professional-military-industrial power structure of the period; they backed away. When the *New York Times* reported that over 70 percent of Russia's doctors in 1956 were women, and that the Israelis were drafting women into their army, American women were not envious of the implicit equality. Trying to justify their lives as a pursuit of complexity, educated women did not realize that the role they were playing may have been as economically prescribed as the Sabras'. In January 1950 the Carnegie Corporation report asserted that the well-rounded individual would have a better appreciation of democratic values—a better capacity to think, and an increased understanding of world affairs. As late as 1958, even the Harvard Medical School (open to small numbers of women since 1945) advertised for applicants who had not majored in science.[39]

Although there were, indeed, larger numbers of women going to college in the 1950s, only 37 percent of those who entered stayed to graduate, and the percentage of women who went on for higher degrees was lower in the 1950s than in the 1920s and 1930s. Most women put other values before the pursuit of their own careers, as Betty Friedan herself had done, turning down the fellowship that would have given her a Ph.D. in clinical psychology. Yet as Friedan later noted, the 1957 questionnaire she circulated to her classmates revealed that Smith alumnae managed to create a great variety of fulfilling activities: "They set up cooperative nursery schools, teenage canteens and libraries; . . . they innovated new educational programs that finally became part of the curriculum. One was personally instrumental in getting 13,000 signatures for a popular referendum to get politics out of the school system . . . one got white children to attend a *de facto* segregated school in the North. One pushed an appropriation for mental health clinics through a state legislature. One set up museum art programs for school children, etc., etc., etc." Friedan's list was a living testimony to Mary Beard's vision of woman as civilizer. That such women all worked outside the conventional realm of success without compensation, in order to live on their own terms or take care of their own families, is worth emphasizing. Many other middle-class women, content with

part-time jobs, gave up chances for promotion, health benefits, retirement funds, and equitable pay in order to be able to raise their
children as well as to avoid the stresses of discriminatory competition. Yet although many women at this time were satisfied to sacrifice careers, they were almost all, as Betty Friedan concluded,
"unconsciously planning for freedom."[40]

An important new fact brought out during the 1950s was that the
average American woman had over forty years to live after her
youngest child went to school. We were just beginning to record lon-
gitudinal differences in women's development that would help educators realize that women needed educational opportunities *after* the
years of child-rearing as well as before.[41]

Although it would take more than another decade before many
college undergraduates would find even small numbers of "older"
women sharing their classes, in 1955 the New School for Social Research set up a Human Relations Workshop to help women who had
been homebound pursue broader goals. In 1959 the University of
Minnesota set up what amounted to a revolutionary program to encourage older women—*usually in their thirties*—to get degrees. Most
adult-education programs at that time gave no credit and led nowhere. In some fields where there were labor shortages, like nursing
and teaching, courses were also immediately tailored to meet wom-
en's (and society's) needs. Brooklyn College in 1956 opened a special
program for mothers to help alleviate the teacher shortage. The "special" concession was that classes were held during hours when the
thirty-one women involved could count on their children being in
school.[42] Another educational innovation designed for women with
liberal-arts backgrounds was the Master of Arts in Teaching degree.
Instead of stressing jargon-saturated "education" courses for badly
needed high-school teachers, the M.A.T. provided America quickly
with teachers who knew subject matter as well as teaching techniques. The number of women who might have gone on for
Ph.D.s—instead of taking this lesser degree—had they been similarly encouraged, remained society's loss, but the high schools profited from their presence. In Boston, the Women's Educational and
Industrial Union sponsored a program of shared jobs for elementary
school teachers so that young mothers could spend half-days at
home.

"Unless we get more women equal education, we can't get them
equal pay and opportunity," declared the president of the National

Federation of Business and Professional Women in 1952.[43] Yet, if the struggle to get more flexible conditions for women's education has been long and slow, the struggle for equal pay and equal opportunity has been even slower. Many women, even women with children, did not stop working after World War II. The war left them sure of skills they never suspected they had. Conditioned to play new roles as workers they did not want to return full time to the home; and a growing number of single women also had to support families. Although some, like Betty Friedan herself, were pressured into giving up good jobs to returning veterans, great numbers of married women stayed in the work force as clerical workers, and older women continued to take whatever work was available for them to do.

Office work represented a step toward independence for the women who would have been factory workers or house servants a generation before, but salary statistics for the 1950s represented little progress. During the early years of the decade, the Equal Rights Amendment was discussed regularly in Congress, yet the early feminists still on the scene, who thought the ERA would harm women by eliminating protective legislation, could not realize—from still another angle—that separate was not equal.[44] When Eleanor Roosevelt decided in 1953 to support the amendment a good number of feminist opponents began to reassess their stand, but there was no real organized pressure for action.

By 1950, the year the Women's Trade Union League dissolved, most of the issues that had engaged women labor leaders in the past had faded. In a 1953 article, "The State of the Unions," Mary Heaton Vorse, a prominent labor journalist, noted that American labor had "swung away from its own ideas of a class struggle almost without realizing it."[45] The dream of consensus also shaped a few women capitalists.

Although access to the world of American business was not easy without male connections, a few American women had also begun to excel as executives. Some shared their husbands' work. Blanche Knopf continued to help run the publishing concern that bore her husband's name; Lila Wallace also helped direct the *Reader's Digest;* Olive Ann Beech persuaded her husband to let women race their aircraft, winning an award in 1952 from the National Aeronautic Association. Advancement without connections appeared possible, too, in fields where women's attitudes and opinions had to be respected; a few women attained positions of power in communications. Ruth

Waldo, a pacifist who set up a trust fund for the American Friends' Service Committee in 1953, became the first woman vice president of the J. Walter Thompson Advertising Agency; Judith Waller was Public Service Director at NBC until she retired in 1957; Geraldine Zorbaugh was made a vice president at ABC in response to her creative contributions to television.[46]

But the most visible businesswomen were always those who turned women's traditional needs and talents into commercial dimensions. Madame Alexander employed over 15,000 people making dolls, the same talent that had catapulted Dorothy Shaver into the presidency of Lord and Taylor. After the war, Jennie Grossinger began to extend her maternal Jewish hospitality to everyone, as Margaret Rudkin similarly turned her family baking skills into an industry at Pepperidge Farm. In a period when women wanted to appear womanly, cosmetics and fashions also flourished; during the 1950s American designers, like American artists, became world leaders.[47]

Although many women still wore girdles, white gloves, and hats for dressy occasions, designers began to make more "casual" clothes and "separates"—all-purpose items that seemed to suit the many different roles women played both in and out of the home. Sweaters, skirts, and blouses began to replace more formal dresses. The production of women's skirts jumped from 24 million in 1947 to 75 million in 1953. Pants were also becoming a part of every suburban wife's wardrobe.[48]

Leafing through the *New York Times* of the 1950s, it is hard to find the names of women scientists. Theoretical scientists like Ethel Harvey, the cell biologist, or Maria Goeppert Mayer, the first woman to win the Nobel Prize for theoretical physics, or Cecilia Payne-Gaposchkin, the Harvard astronomer, or Rosalyn Yalow, later a Nobel Prize winner in nuclear medicine—all of whom managed both to work and to have families—were the exceptions. Their brilliance could not be denied; but they labored so hard at the two jobs they were doing they could hardly take time to publicize themselves. Betty Friedan's statement about growing up without ever having known any woman who "used her mind, played her own part in the world, and also loved, and had children" would have been applicable to most young women in the 1950s.[49]

Just as some women doctors visibly involved themselves in social issues, so did some professional scientists. Ann Haven Morgan inspired a number of fifties women to regard life in ecological terms;

her 1955 text, characteristically (for the era) titled *Animals and Man*, emphasized how important it was in teaching biology to stress the relationship of human beings to nature as a whole. After *The Sea Around Us* achieved worldwide distinction in the early 1950s, Rachel Carson saw herself in an advocacy role for nature and the public good against the pesticides industry. Her gift of clarity made her a formidable foe of special-interest groups because her personal vision was never just professional. When she finished *The Silent Spring*, she commented:"The beauty of the living world I was trying to save has always been uppermost in my mind."[50]

During the 1950s young women who wanted families were actively discouraged by institutional and attitudinal barriers from also playing professional roles or competing with men for better jobs. As technology made every world more systematic, few efforts were made even to disguise the discrimination against women. Yet many young women found ways to lead more socially involved lives, and many older women continued to enter the work force at lower levels. Any serious assessment of the decade must attempt to register the variety and unconventionality of the activities women found—besides motherhood—to define themselves as human beings. Women often enjoyed their babies; for a while many even appreciated the intimacy of "togetherness" and found a momentary outlet for managerial skills in directing a household. But, raised just as American men had been on the dream of personal fulfillment built into the American myth, a great number of women, healthy of body and vigorous in mind did not define themselves entirely by their gender roles. They counted on establishing new identities in those forty freshly discovered years after their children reached school age. They did not put away their books or withdraw from the serious problems of their communities. Many of the already educated middle-class women remained among the most literate members of American society and helped redefine important spheres of voluntary commitment. To judge these women by the same developmental yardstick we use for men is a mistake. In the process of naively waiting for American institutions to help them become complete human beings, however, some women were also left behind, trapped in suburbia like Evan Connell's pathetic Mrs. Bridge, the heroine of a 1958 novel who ends up locked in her own garage.[51]

To accept the truth that Betty Friedan probably would not have written *The Feminine Mystique* had she gone on for her doctorate in clinical psychology must cause us to wonder about human complexity. Historically Friedan's book became an important factor in changing the way most American women saw themselves—a modern version of Charlotte Perkins Gilman's 1898 *Women and Economics,* also a great popular success. That women must keep on responding to the same problems involving their either/or roles as mothers and workers at different times, in different imaginative ways, must become an accepted reality until institutions change. What we have to understand more adequately are the many ways women have of asserting their own values when they are not included in traditional power structures, and how they often attempt to change things when they are.

The 1950s became the decade when many women first confronted the reality that American society made no concessions to their problems as wives or mothers or divorcées or underpaid workers. The number of exceptional women out in the world, defined by their professions, served to remind the others at home of how frequently women's astonishing capabilities were thwarted by rigid institutional policies and inflexible attitudes. Seeing themselves as bearers of children who would live long, active lives, women began to understand that they had special needs, that society might do much more to make good use of their talents. To "underestimate" their power was to underestimate their capacity for change.

Adlai Stevenson, commencement speaker, Smith College, June 1955.
Courtesy of Smith College Archives.

Chapter Three

Education: Functionalism, Facts, and Democratic Ideals

"The woman's fundamental status is that of her husband's wife, the mother of his children," argued Talcott Parsons in 1949 in one of the clearest definitions of his distinguished sociological career.[1] Perhaps he wondered what so many Radcliffe students were doing in his classes; they certainly were not questioning his authority.

In a survey of her 1951 Radcliffe classmates written for the *Ladies' Home Journal* in 1980, Rona Jaffe, unmarried author of many bestsellers, discovered that a number of fellow students had learned Parsons's lesson well: "We married what we wanted to *be*," stated the wife of a college dean; "If we wanted to be a lawyer or a doctor we married one." Trying to find out what had become of her generation of college graduates, Jaffe discovered that a great many had expected to find their identities through their husbands—they had not been trained to develop separate selves. And many subsequently regarded their lives as failures. By 1980 Jaffe concluded, these women had nevertheless become "articulate, intelligent, caring, strong, resilient individualists." They had by mid-life transcended whatever anger they harbored at being in some sense betrayed by the men and institutions they loved and trusted. "We have gone beyond the rage and we *like* ourselves," Jaffe summarized: "The world changed, we changed with it and know we are still changing, that you never write The End to a life until it's over."[2]

Although it seems probable that Rona Jaffe's angriest classmates would not voice their opinions on a *Ladies' Home Journal* questionnaire, it is also true that by the 1980s, in a culture proud to demonstrate progress, many women had become optimistic about late life changes. (Erik Erikson's *Childhood and Society*, which first made people aware of developmental stages in men's lives in 1950, was in its forty-third printing by 1978.) What was true for men seemed true in different ways for women. Accepting the reality of a variety of changing possibilities at different stages of life, by 1980 we had begun to modify some of our educational institutions to fit complex human needs. Many older women whose earlier lives had been defined by the narrowness of the either/or training Betty Friedan deplored as essential to the "feminine mystique"[3] were back at school. Even a few elite professional programs had opened their doors to "continuing education"—linking a long-needed social responsiveness to the more exciting discovery that adult education frequently made money. But during the 1950s few institutions were interested in helping women become professionals.

Although university campuses had become accustomed to the presence of older married students because so many ex-soldiers had returned to school on the GI Bill, wives for the most part were working to help put husbands through college, not taking courses themselves. A few schools like Carleton College in Minnesota even continued to outlaw married students. The idea that marriage was not compatible with serious scholarship—usually not a realistic issue for men—played a background role during the 1950s in modifying women's ambitions. It became common for married women to drop out of school, as the 37 percent college completion figure demonstrates.[4]

Conservative women's colleges at the time were reluctant to make changes in institutional structure to accommodate the needs of somewhat older women with children who had not completed bachelors' degrees.[5] Bemoaning the failure of women to make better use of their intellectual capacities, such schools could not understand the necessity to adapt their programs to make it possible or easier for them to do so. They seemed to blame women for taking their gender roles as seriously as their education. One Wellesley drop-out, an honors student in her early thirties who found herself suddenly alone with four young children to raise and little money, was told that to come back she would have to take classes full time and also fulfill a gym requirement. A Radcliffe Phi Beta Kappa with three children who wanted to return to graduate work on a part-time basis was told that priority would be given to full-time, "serious" students. The idea that having children meant giving up any participatory intellectual life was reinforced by every institution—woman's fundamental status had to be that of "her husband's wife." When Betty Friedan urged a national education program for mothers, similar to the GI Bill, in the next decade, to compensate women who had stayed home with children she remarked that the only women she knew who were able both to take care of children and to continue professional lives had made strong early commitments.[6]

Rarer still were the older women with a clear sense of vocational mission like Gerda Lerner, who knew her own mind well enough to be able to shop around for a graduate school and found an exceptional chairman willing to tailor institutional requirements to fit the scholarly needs of an "eager, somewhat superannuated and certainly 'different' student."[7] By the time Lerner received her doctorate at the age of forty-six, she had plotted her research for the coming twenty years. Pioneering education in women's history, Gerda Lerner would make it easier for other women to confront the difficulties women have always faced. Like Mary Beard, however, she would also celebrate their strengths, helping us realize that "the true history of women is the history of their ongoing functioning in that male-defined world *on their own terms.*"[8] Although Lerner's personal achievement might not have been as easy to imitate outside New York City, her accomplishments, understood in terms of the intransigent educational attitudes she encountered at the time, remain inspirational. Like the "worthy" women she talked about in *The Majority Finds Its Place: Placing Women in History,* Lerner herself provided an important example by redefining her career in mid-life, then going on to achieve a high level of professional recognition. The Organization of American Historians elected her its president in 1981.

Sarah Lawrence College appreciated Lerner's skills at an earlier date when they hired her to set up one of the first distinguished pro-

grams in Women's Studies in America, not long after the experimental women's college had also set up its revolutionary program
encouraging older women to come back to school. Sarah Lawrence
had managed to get a small grant to help women with children work
for degrees or do graduate work on a part-time basis that would fit in
with their obligations as mothers. Esther Raushenbush at Sarah
Lawrence agreed with Virginia Senders, who was setting up a similar program at the University of Minnesota—as Virginia Bullard was
also doing at Northeastern University in Boston—that the overwhelming response to all these efforts at schools in the early 1960s
was the result of the intense hunger for education brought about by
the institutional indifference of the 1950s. When the Sarah Lawrence
grant was announced in the *New York Times*, the switchboards were
put out of commission with calls. "It was like bank night," the oper-
ator said—"as if they had to get in there right away, or they might
miss the chance."[9]

As almost every school in America became coeducational before
the 1960s ended—after the legal insistence that separateness and
equality were not the same—some feminists realized uneasily that
two of their prominent leaders, Gloria Steinem and Betty Friedan,
had gone to an all-women college, Smith, which continued to stress
its value as a place where women could attain leadership positions
and also encounter examples of their own sex in positions of power.
Sensitive educators began to understand that the training of women
might demand more complex awareness than mere exposure to facts
in any male-determined intellectual system, although such facts at
the best women's schools were never to be watered down. Eleanor
Roosevelt, we recall, had paid special homage to a woman teacher at
an all-girls finishing school.[10]

In 1951 Mary McCarthy published a tribute to the women professors who had educated her. "The Vassar Girl" was an appreciation
of "the idea of excellence, the zest for adventure, the fastidiousness
of mind and humanistic breadth of feeling that were so noticeable at
Vassar during the long reign of *emeritae*."[11] Under the guidance of
many unmarried women, McCarthy noted, Vassar had produced
Edna St. Vincent Millay, Constance Rourke, Muriel Rukeyser,
Eleanor Clark, Elizabeth Bishop, and even an ex-Communist spy,
Elizabeth Bentley. Mary McCarthy relished her associations with
these female professors, "fine women of the old liberal school" who

she believed were dying out in spite of Vassar's commitment to women teachers as a "discriminated against minority in the college teaching field." She wondered if the symbolic new faculty member, "a mother of four" who believes that the one-sided person is the enemy of society, would triumph. This new professor—who had rejected the either/or option—Mary McCarthy saw as "a pioneer, like the spinsters who preceded her, and an iconoclast like the suffragettes she spurns."[12] Sensitive to the growing limitations of the decade, McCarthy realized, however, that the teacher-mother, in spite of her value as a new role model, might be too "radical." The hypothetical vision she finally created of the 1950s Vassar graduate reminds us of Betty Friedan's sociological survey of Smith alumnae; McCarthy yearns for greater power for these women, yet remains respectful: "She is the woman who changed the local school situation from a political machine to an educational institution. She is the woman behind the League of Women Voters, Planned Parenthood, and yes, the 4-H Club. She won't very often be found sitting at the luncheon bridge table. She'll be found, actively, thoughtfully, even serenely, playing her role as an intelligent citizen."[13] The one lesson a girl could hardly avoid learning if she went to college between 1945 and 1960, Betty Friedan wrote, "was *not* to get interested, seriously interested, in anything besides getting married and having children."[14] But in fact Friedan's own book documented that these women gave a good bit of time to community interests—if not to their own careers. Nor was their voluntary activity mindlessly for the middle class.

Another burgeoning feminist, noticeably absent from Rona Jaffe's *Ladies' Home Journal* survey of her 1951 classmates, Adrienne Rich, also felt the importance of honoring the women teachers who helped her discover her abilities at an all-girls preparatory school. In "Taking Women Students Seriously," an essay in *On Lies, Secrets, and Silence*, Rich wrote:

These women cared a great deal about the life of the mind, and they gave a great deal of time and energy—beyond any limit of teaching hours—to those of us who showed special intellectual interest or ability. . . . Although we sometimes felt "pushed" by them, we held those women in a kind of respect which even then we dimly perceived was not generally accorded to women in the world at large. They were vital individuals, defined not by their rela-

tionships but by their personalities; and although under pressure of the culture we were all certain we wanted to get married, their lives did not appear
empty or dreary to us.[15]

At Radcliffe (called by its own name in the 1950s but not really
independent of Harvard), Rich concludes,

I never saw a single woman on a lecture platform, or in front of a class,
except when a woman graduate student gave a paper on a special topic. The
"great men" talked of other "great men," of the nature of man, the history of
mankind, the future of man; and never again was I to experience, from a
teacher, the kind of prodding, the insistence that my best could be even better, that I had known in high school. Women students were simply not taken
seriously.[16]

What we were learning in the 1950s, as Margaret Fuller and Charlotte Perkins Gilman had learned before, was that women's education often amounts to much more than the theories and facts they
record in their notebooks. Retreating from a decade of action during
which women had held every possible kind of job, it seemed odd to
confront parietal rules designed to protect the weak, and rows of
beds in the basements of classroom buildings for the use of the deli-
cate. A few middle-class women began to think about the nature of
their own educations—the source of their strengths, the reasons they
accomplished less, if in fact they did, and the way accomplishment
and achievement had been constantly defined by men. On the surface the 1950s seemed to suggest a decade of glorification of motherhood, but in fact mothering was so denigrated that women who gave
their serious energies to it for any period of time were considered
unfit to do anything else. The sanctification of the mother paralleled
the nineteenth-century celebration of the "lady," a substitution of
praise for the institutional modifications that would have allowed an
entire group of people to become more complete human beings.
While the nineteenth century thought women too weak physically
to be educated, the twentieth talked about their "natural superiority."[17] The *New York Times* in 1956 thought it newsworthy to write
about a mother and daughter competing for degrees at Rutgers. The
mother, while also taking care of her house and family, was "permitted" to take six courses to catch up. Another woman who commuted
from New Jersey to Brooklyn College three nights a week so she

would not have to leave her children alone during the day, the *Times* reported, was graduating Phi Beta Kappa, with plans to go to law school. That a few such women made the newspapers suggests the rarity of their achievement, but the *Times* reported also on the conferences and comments on women's education that emerged from a decade of introspection. Between the ads for white gloves, flowered hats, and girdles, and the pages of child-rearing advice and wedding announcements, appeared a decade-long sense of concern about what was happening to the talents of women.

Although many fifties educators, like Lynn White of Mills College in California, were as concerned with helping women become better wives and mothers—"sex-directed educators," Friedan calls them—as with helping them fulfill their intellectual potential, there can be little doubt that they were also genuinely concerned about what was happening to women's role. The educators who wanted "functional" rather than analytical education for women forced others to think more about modifying all institutions.

A careful reading of Lynn White's *Educating Our Daughters* (1950), the key theoretical document on women's education at the time, suggests that White's concerns were more complex than feminist critics were able to admit—that he belongs as much in the growing tradition of androgyny as in the sexist world that wanted to keep women locked in the home.[18] White did not hesitate to attack the eastern educational establishment for being "permeated not merely with indifference but with antagonism towards women." In order to "fulfill their responsibilities to the feminine part of the population," he insisted, those who form the policies of coeducational schools "must open their faculties to competent women according to their individual merits and abandon the present shameful discrimination against them."[19]

Aware that "our colleges have neglected the mature woman and her needs," White sometimes even appeared ahead of his time. He praised schools like Bennington and Sarah Lawrence for giving more attention to the arts, which he characterized as less "concerned with the laurel-crowned genius or the strong man" than the social sciences were. And he attacked Harvard for not having appointed a woman professor in the arts and sciences until 1948; Radcliffe he saw as a "piteous example of female docility" in its willingness to follow the Harvard curriculum. White wanted all educators to confront "the extraordinary degree they have occupied themselves with heroes and

hero worship."[20] His educational theories were meant to challenge
the male establishment as much as they were designed to define
woman's place.

Like Adlai Stevenson, White believed that women who did not
have to support themselves could use their educations outside the
traditional power structure to maintain nonconformist ideals. He
also speculated that liberal studies might ultimately be more *practical*
for women who could not predict the exigencies of their lives as
clearly as men could. Unfortunately, as Betty Friedan later pointed
out, such theories played into many women's traditional doubts
about themselves.

"What happens" Friedan would ask, when education itself "gives
new authority to the feminine 'shoulds'—which already have the authority of tradition, convention, prejudice, popular opinion—instead of giving women the power of critical thought, the
independence and autonomy to question blind authority, new or
old?"[21] The deeper implications for a democratic society seemed as
devastating as the totalitarian mentality of McCarthyism. Women
who were supposed to be raising their children to accept the responsibilities of free choice were offered almost no choice for themselves.

During the 1950s the American Council on Education sponsored
two conferences related to the education of women: in 1951, Women
in the Defense Decade; and in 1957, The Education of Women:
Signs for the Future. In 1953 the Council established the Commission on the Education of Women, which published an interim report
in 1955, *How Fare American Women?*, to publicize the attention being
given to women's education.[22] Few positive recommendations for
change emerged from the first meeting. The "defense decade" attempted to relate women to the Korean War as guardians of democratic values; "self-fulfillment" was not an issue. Concern was for the
"well-adjusted family" as an essential "safeguard to our way of life."
Moral values, admittedly weakening on many levels of American life
(as when have they not been?), were to be restored through close
parent-child ties. Even though defense needs might make some demands on women's time, our leaders were certain that "women's primary responsibility must continue to be the home, for in these days
of strain and insecurity the family unit must be improved and intensified." As an added aside, however, came the conclusion: "But at the
same time, the American woman must prepare herself to play her
role in public affairs."[23]

Millicent McIntosh, herself a superwoman who managed to raise five children while she was president of Barnard College, had, in 1950, joined Sarah Gibson Blanding of Vassar and Mildred Horton of Wellesley to "Caution That First Duty Is to Children"—as the *New York Times* headline put it. Although McIntosh stressed that women's first responsibility was to the children—that "home comes before all else"—she also told students at Sarah Lawrence that women make better mothers if they do not spend all their time on the physical care of their children.[24] In a society with almost no organized daycare and with fewer and fewer servants, women's ingenuity would be challenged. One harried mother in 1951 responded with her ironic vision of herself in a letter: "Yes, go swim. But don't go near the water. Take on yourself civic and economic responsibilities while you also wheel the baby, get Johnny a nourishing lunch while baking for John a bedeviled cake, study the Sunday school lesson, read up on foreign policy, meantime not forgetting the daily dusting and two dozen other small drudgeries and finally, firmly resist fragmentation."[25] She ended with a plea for better day nurseries, which had, of course, been available for workers during World War II but were dissolved almost at once by Congress afterwards, perhaps with the intention of keeping women out of men's jobs. The problem was neatly articulated by Florence Kluckhohn: "The American woman stands today confused by a culture that trains her to compete with men for a career, and then expects her to be content with being wife and mother."[26]

A course called "Modern Woman's Dilemma" offered by a man at the New School for Social Research approached the problem typically by stressing individual rather than social solutions. If every woman could define herself more precisely she could probably benefit from whatever resources society did offer. Such an approach mirrored the more common middle-class reliance on psychiatry as a tool to help women confront difficulties they ascribed to their own failings. That psychiatry, for the most part, championed conservative values was a lesson women had to keep learning. Ida Davidoff, who went on after her four children had left the nest to get a doctorate at the age of fifty-eight, was made to feel strangely deviant by a distinguished New York psychiatrist in the 1950s, for wanting to do more with her life.[27]

With some reluctance the New School played an exemplary role in New York City. Alice Cook's personal efforts led to the setting up of a human-resources workshop during the 1950s designed to help women assess their potentials at different stages of life. Many women enrolled. Members of the group recall Cook's struggles to get the New School to take older women seriously as daytime adult students, in spite of the school's longtime commitment to unconventional learning. It was Cook's singular dedication and, again, the money generated by the social response to her program, that finally persuaded the New School to keep the program going.[28]

A few women's colleges made valuable gestures toward keeping their own graduates intellectually alert. Barnard in 1952 invited alumnae to audit courses without charge; it stressed the fact that such courses were open to everyone who had attended Barnard, not just graduates. During the 1950s, too, Radcliffe began a series of stimulating "seminars" which were also open to the community. Significantly, neither program offered additional "credit," which might have contributed to women's vocational or professional potential.

In 1953 the Ellis L. Phillips Foundation in cooperation with the American Council on Education provided a $500,000 grant to ascertain "what education is relevant to making women effective as individuals, as members of a family, as gainfully employed workers and as participants in civic life." The studies were to include research on women's spiritual and moral values and on the constructive use of their leisure time. From these inquiries came suggestions again for more continuing education to fit in with women's child-rearing demands and for better counseling—institutional modifications that would benefit women of all classes.[29] When Mrs. Thomas Lamont that same year gave $3 million to seven women's colleges it was because she believed that the quality of teaching at women's schools, along with the high intellectual and moral standards such schools fostered, was inadequately appreciated. She believed that women's institutions made an important special contribution to the values of American life. Almost every mention of women's education during the 1950s connects it with the need for moral values, recalling the nineteenth-century belief that women could be purer and more dedicated to culture than men because they were not involved in the crude competition of the outside world. Middle-class women were still being educated primarily for the moral improvement of society, not for their own intellectual fulfillment except insofar as the two sometimes overlapped. They were not being trained to compete with men, but still to inhabit a different reality—"separate spheres."

As more and more women responding to the open ambivalence continued to drop out of school at higher levels, concern grew. Many colleges thought the answer was to offer more "functional" courses, to make the training of the mind more relevant to women's daily lives. Mills College included a course on "Voluntarism" in its catalog, as well as a "Marriage" major. Even the University of Chicago in 1954 devised a course called "Parenthood in a Free Nation," not only to interest women but also to explore how democratic values were entwined with personal development. By 1955 Millicent McIntosh had changed the emphasis in her complex vision of women's lives; the *Times* described her *first* concern as what was happening to women's minds. She begged the graduating class at Barnard not to allow their intellects to be washed away with the laundry.[30]

Noting that job discrimination against women often resulted from their own uncommitted attitudes, McIntosh suggested that graduates seek independence after school, not immediate marriage. But the *Times*, even then, intruded the impossible contradiction that, once married, women would have to remember that "a woman's first responsibility was to the happiness of her husband and children and to the completeness of her home." McIntosh finally recommended continued serious reading, cultivating a hobby, and "doing something regularly for someone else" as a woman's means to maintaining responsibility to her own intellectual growth, her college, and her community. Margaret Clapp of Wellesley similarly advised young women in 1959 to develop "abilities and interests which might be carried into marriage, set aside in the years of child-care and then renewed without undue difficulty."[31]

When Mabel Newcomer's devastating statistical account of what was happening, *A Century of Higher Education for Women*, appeared in 1959, many Americans expressed alarm. Although the proportion of women among college students in the United States had increased to 47 percent by 1920, in 1958 it was down to 35.2. Five women's colleges had closed down; twenty-one had become coeducational; two had become junior colleges. In 1956, three out of five women in co-educational colleges were taking secretarial, nursing, home economics, or education courses. Fewer than 10 percent of doctorates were granted to women, compared with one in six in 1920 and 13 percent in 1940. Not since before World War I, Newcomer reported, was the percentage of women receiving professional degrees so low.[32] The launching of the Russian *Sputnik* also brought a flurry of concern about the scarcity of women in science. In Russia, we discovered, 69 percent of the medical students and 39 percent of the engineers were women; some educators interpreted the fact that only 20 percent of all science and math majors were women as a loss of creative talent. Although it was possible to take comfort in the actual numbers of women in school rather than in dropping percentages, comparisons with men remained painful. Betty Friedan rightly protested that the United States was probably the only civilized nation where the proportion of women gaining higher education had decreased over the preceding twenty years. Comparing our record with that of France, Friedan pointed out that by the 1950s a larger percentage of French women were getting higher education and that the proportion of French women in the professions had more than doubled in fifty years. There were five times as many women doctors proportionally in France; our medical schools in the 1950s made no secret of having quotas of 5 percent for women admissions; law schools were even lower.[33]

The group of educators who gathered in 1957 to look at "Signs for the Future" anticipated the exposure of such knowledge without the exact figures. Education, Judge Mary Donlon noted, was behind the parade in making necessary changes—although by 1957 the tendency to punish bright women for getting married or pregnant by denying them further education was theoretically beginning to disappear. If some educators accepted the opinion that research on women was merely one aspect of research on man, there were others, including Dean Eunice Roberts of Indiana University, who insisted that the patterns of women's lives were conditioned by their biological roles. Noting that "the split career, the double career, the child-bearing period, and the possible lonesome mature years" frequently caused women problems different from men's in charting their educational plans, Roberts's observations had greater impact on the commission's final recommendations for change. It was agreed unanimously in 1957 that educational programs be adapted to the specific needs of women through more flexibility in admissions and scheduling procedures, use of educational television, adult education, refresher courses, and devices for enabling women to come back into the educational and career stream more easily.[34]

Pressing demands for nurses and elementary-school teachers brought immediate concessions in training for such conventional women's jobs, just as the need for workers during World War II generated funds for daycare. But, in fact, the educational establishment did not adapt quickly to women's needs—not even so much as to establish easy patterns for transfer of academic credits for women who dutifully followed their husbands' jobs. When the Educational Testing Service at Princeton produced college-level equivalency exams in the 1960s to enable older students to write off credits for acquired knowledge, such exams were often not accepted by schools that relied heavily on the Scholastic Aptitude Tests and achievement test scores produced by the same agency to evaluate the young.

In 1963, when the Commission on Education turned into the Kennedy Commission on the Status of Women, identical issues emerged. By 1963, however, the problems were more clearly identified so that educators could see how women of every class were segregated unfairly or denied access to male activities from kindergarten on. The theoretical speculations of the 1950s produced the more organized "consciousness raising" of the 1960s that enabled women to demand that their daughters' educations include shop and automobile mechanics and the right to play Little League baseball. Before the next decade was over, women would also demand schoolbooks with illustrations of working mothers and pictures of women as doctors as well as nurses, so that little girls could envision more extensive career alternatives for themselves. And the "new feminists" would ask teachers to include facts about the achievements of women in history and literature and art at every level of the curriculum, so that their children might take more pride in the female intellectual heritage that was rightfully theirs. Although fifties women were loath to diminish their own accomplishments behind the scenes, they came to regard themselves as educationally disadvantaged.[35]

The Kennedy Commission, chaired by Esther Peterson after Eleanor Roosevelt's death, felt secure in its mission to bring more women into every level of American economic life. It recognized that education and vocation are "inextricably combined," and understood and underlined the pervasive failure of the American educational establishment to adapt its resources to women's needs. Adult education had to be taken seriously: "So far," the group asserted, "neither in monetary allocations nor in quality of instruction have formal education institutions, foundations, or indeed the individuals concerned caused it to receive the attention it merits in a rapidly moving industrial society."[36] Too many adult-education courses re-

mained busy-work to keep middle-class women out of mischief or
ended up as means of adding superficial culture to their husbands'
work worlds; adult education programs at the time rarely offered any
credit or a sense of mastery in an intellectual field as reward for hard
work. Such courses met neither society's need for well-trained and
disciplined women nor the women's own needs for intellectual rigor.
Little concern existed for uncovering the many talented women—so
obvious in the early grades—who by high school had been buried by
cultural indifference or turned away from education by social prejudice. For working-class women and blacks who often had to work to
support their families, more flexible education was understood to be
essential to upward mobility, but opportunity for such education
was rare.

Mary Bunting, then president of Radcliffe, head of the subcommittee concerned with women's education, stressed the need for better counseling at every level as well as for more funding to help
women continue their educations. Ineffectual or, worse, deliberately
discouraging counselors were keeping women from developing their
abilities to get jobs related to their potentials; too often high-school
advisers funneled bright students into home economics and secretarial programs simply because they were girls. Bunting's group
stressed the dangers of gender counseling, which reinforced roles
held up to girls from infancy and "deflected talents into narrow channels."[37] Recognizing that talented women of *all* social classes needed
extra encouragement, the commission saw sensitive counseling as a
way to lift aspirations beyond "women's roles." Too often, the group
reported, "lack of parental stimulation conditioned grade-school
youngsters from low-income families to settle for less education than
their abilities warranted, and daughters of families able to pay for
higher education saw no reason for going as far as they could."[38]

Although the National Defense Education Act of 1958, which
poured money into American education to help us surpass the Russians in space research, provided funds to train 12,000 counselors for
secondary schools, the ratio by 1963 was still one counselor to 550
students, with shortages most apparent in low-income areas; few
counselors had any supervised experience with girls, and many
worked on "obsolete assumptions." Because eight out of ten women
would end up in the work force for at least a part of their lives, the
1963 commission recommended that more imaginative counseling be
available to women at every stage of life. Counseling was considered

necessary not only in schools but also in state and private employment agencies able to recommend training programs for new job opportunities because "in a democracy offering broad and ever-changing choices skilled counseling becomes an inseparable part of education."[39]

Although the figures suggest that the number of new advisers was too small to make much difference in the career choices of women in the 1960s, there can be little doubt that women profited in a general way from the stepped-up emphasis on education that *Sputnik* brought about. By the mid-1960s community colleges were being founded at the rate of one every two weeks. And more and more schools—if not the most elite—were allowing proficiency tests as a means to obtaining credit for knowledge acquired outside regular academic courses. Eventually we decided not to remain that rare civilized culture that educates its "strongest, ablest women to make a career out of their own children."[40]

Although in practice the 1950s produced little to encourage women's education, in theory the decade appears rich. In the anthropological thinking of Margaret Mead, which dominated the period from *Male and Female* in 1949, and *New Lives for Old* in 1956 to the biography of Ruth Benedict, *An Anthropologist at Work*, in 1959, we may find the most insightful thinking about women's education since Margaret Fuller's *Woman in the Nineteenth Century*. Criticized by feminists as different as Diana Trilling and Betty Friedan for her realistic insistence on the primacy of woman's child-bearing function, regarded suspiciously by her own profession for attempting to popularize her cultural commentary, Mead nevertheless remains a complex and eloquent social critic whose dimensions extend beyond any one decade's ideology. Like Fuller, her broad human concern about the nature of our civilization set her apart from the issue-oriented feminist thinkers of her lifetime, but the depth of her appreciation of women's dilemmas should not be minimized.[41]

That the sex-directed educators of the 1950s and the many women then glorying in motherhood made use of Margaret Mead's anthropological data suggests Mead's own refusal to deny the satisfactions of mothering. But she never justified a lifetime of child-rearing as a fulfilling choice for women in a sophisticated society. "As a civilization becomes more complex," she wrote in *Male and Female*, "human life is defined in individual terms as well as in the service of the race, and the great structures of law and government, religion and art and

science become something highly valued for themselves. Practiced
by men they become indications of masculine humanity, and men
take great pride in these achievements. To the extent that women are
barred from them," Mead concluded, "women become less than human." No one understood better than she that "social inventions"
were essential to encourage women's contributions to civilization and
simultaneously enhance their humanity.[42]

In 1957, Mead wrote an article in the *New York Times Magazine*
stressing the paradox of our ambivalent attitudes toward women.
Women were often educated like men, she noted, but then denied
the right to dedicate themselves to any task other than homemaking.
"They were expected to regard homemaking as the ultimate career
and the needs of a husband and a few children as sufficient for the
most gifted and ambitious among them"—a reverse situation, she remarked, from the Soviet Union's, where every woman's "right" to
work came first. Mead urged that we reinstitute a broader range of
human ideals, "without which any civilization perishes." When she
insisted that home and family were good but not "the end-all and be-
all" of every human being in the society she seemed to justify her
own life's choices: "There are gifted men and gifted women, adventurous men and adventurous women, people who never stop thinking about what they are doing, people who work eighteen hours a
day, people who have to travel into far places and risk not coming
back, people who will give and give of themselves in the public
good." She continued: "People, not just men." Wryly amused that
men expected their sisters and daughters to be well educated and use
their skills, but not their wives, she concluded optimistically that
when a society as self-conscious as ours realizes it has a problem, it
will seek remedies.[43]

Mead's contribution to the self-consciousness that made us see
how extensively women's education was based on a network of cultural attitudes—not just on the hours spent in school—cannot be
overestimated. That the next decade would seek more concrete remedies for women's educational dilemmas would be a testimony to
Mead's wisdom, not a rejection of her humanity.

When she published the biographical tribute to Ruth Benedict in
1959, Margaret Mead gave us a moving example of one woman's intellectual struggles. Benedict as Mead knew her was not simply a
high-powered Vassar-trained thinker; she was a woman who experienced the "restlessness and groping" inherent in all of us. Accepting

that she would have no children, Benedict redefined her life in her mid-thirties to become a woman of extraordinary intellectual achievement. In recounting the story of Ruth Benedict's self-conscious reliance on the study of "the restless and highly enslaved women of past generations"[44]—the women who helped her realize that the "new woman" was hardly new—Margaret Mead presented an ongoing requirement for the education of women. She made us understand how much women need historical connections with their own female past in order to justify their intellectual ambitions. Before going on to do original anthropological work, Ruth Benedict had even written a short biography of Mary Wollstonecraft which Mead included with her other writings.

"Out of much bewilderment of soul," Benedict observed, "steadfast aims may arise."[45] So out of a decade that did little to develop its best women's minds, a consciousness of private need and public waste developed which would forge more positive institutional policies to provide greater numbers of American women with professional skills.

Student at Radcliffe Program in Business Administration employed at
New York Life Insurance Company.
Courtesy of Radcliffe College Archives.

Chapter Four

Work: New Statistics and Old Discriminations

W hen Rosie the Riveter handed her goggles to the men who were returning from World War II, she did not rush to put on an apron. It is a myth that most women who worked during the war were glad to return to domestic life; in fact, although some women returned momentarily to their homes after the war out of deference to returning heroes, they did not remain in the kitchen long. And many other women followed them back out into the work force. The "most striking feature of the 1950s," asserted William Chafe in his survey of the American woman between 1920 and 1970, "is the degree to which women continued to enter the job market and expand their sphere."[1]

The National Manpower Commission set up at Columbia University in 1957, under a grant from the Ford Foundation to explore important "manpower" needs in times of emergency and to improve the development of the country's "manpower" resources, was astonished to discover how much womanpower still played a role in American life. Committed to exploring "the training, skills, capacities, competence, and creativeness of the American people—that is, with the *quality* of our manpower resources," the commission could not ignore the continuing presence of women in the labor force. In-

FIGURE 1

Birth and Death Rates per 1,000 Population

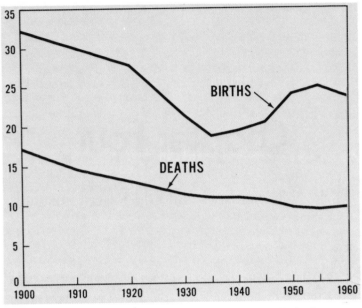

Reprinted from American Women *(Washington, D. C.: U. S. Government Printing Office, 1963).*

deed when the conclusions of this study, titled *Womanpower,* were published as a book in 1957, the results so surprised people that another conference was immediately scheduled to assess the startling news that not only were great numbers of married women working outside the home, but so also were many mothers—even, by then, mothers with preschool-age children.[2]

In 1957 a second conference of over eighty participants from government, industry, labor, education, social welfare, childcare, civic organizations, and churches was convened to look at *Work in the Lives of Married Women,* as their findings were labeled in 1958, describing a new pattern in American life.[3] How did the "virtual revolution" in women's employment outside the home find articulation in these conferences? What were the implicit conclusions related to women's working and to the "quality" of American life? Readers of the reports at a later period will be arrested by the tone of reluctant surprise

FIGURE 2

Percentage of Women in the Work Force

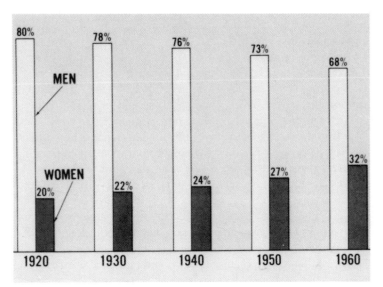

Reprinted from American Women *(Washington, D. C.: U. S. Government Printing Office, 1963).*

involved in accepting the statistics from the labor bureau and the bureau of the census. Whether or not married women should work outside the home was no longer a debatable issue—it was a fact of American life. The word "revolution" appears over and over in both texts, expressive of how radical what was being reported seemed—how jarring to the tranquil myth of domestic fulfillment. The kinds of jobs women held were generally not analyzed, however, and little attention was given to their salaries.

When Robert Smuts wrote his social history *Women and Work in America* in 1958, as a reaction to and elaboration of the womanpower report, he clarified the reality that women had always worked with many historical illustrations. Smuts stressed women's share in "the ceaseless striving to improve one's position that has always been the special distinction of American life."[4] By 1958, he noted, society had so accepted women in the work force that, far from being driven out in the short period of recession in 1957 after the Korean War, the number of women workers actually increased. Women who did not have to work were beginning to see themselves not as neglecting their families by working outside the home, but as helping them by raising their standard of living. Consumerism dedicated to the homemaker, ironically, often drove women out of the home in search of more money to buy new things.

Although sooner or later society might have recognized, as Esther Lloyd-Jones, head of guidance at Columbia Teachers College pointed out, that there was a vast new supply of talent available because women were having children earlier and living eleven years longer than they would have done fifty years before, it took World War II to demonstrate the range of their competencies. Lloyd-Jones stressed in 1957 the need the Kennedy commission would bring up again six years later, to *make women aware* that most would be working outside their homes for a total of about twenty-five years. Emphasizing that we were living "in a world that fairly explodes with change," Lloyd-Jones may have been the first to urge the need for more sophisticated counseling for girls, along with the need to clarify the connection between education and work. Educators, she insisted, had failed to recognize their opportunities and obligations in ignoring the average "older" woman of thirty-two who, seeing her last child enter first grade, confronted another four decades of living "without clear understanding of its patterns and possibilities."[5]

Since the number of women over thirty-five in the work force had jumped from 8.5 million in 1947, to almost 13 million in 1956, Lloyd-Jones insisted it was essential to provide them with more training, planning, and support and more "help from counseling agencies and educational institutions." She scored the ignorance of people, interviewed on the streets by pollsters, who wanted working wives back in the home.[6] These interviews, Erwin Canham, editor of the *Christian Science Monitor* (himself the son of a working mother) noted, still saw working women neglecting their children, lowering men's wages, and taking jobs from single women. To Canham, they revealed the continuing misunderstanding of the contemporary role and significance of women in employment. Such prejudices offered, he insisted, "just a small indication of the problem which faces all of us in making sure public opinion accurately appreciates and evaluates what is occurring."[7] If all working women returned to the home, the American economy would cease to function.

Making public opinion—labor and capital, law maker and executive—accept the fact that for the first time in the history of the United States there was a "substantial group of women for whom paid employment constituted far more than an experience in youth or a necessity imposed by misfortune"[8] became the mission of both human resources conferences in the 1950s. If historians of women often end up acknowledging that mythology becomes more important than fact, they nevertheless must know what the facts are. William Chafe summarizes them neatly: "In 1960 twice as many women were at work as in 1940, and 40 percent of all women over sixteen held a job. Female employment was increasing at a rate four times faster than that of men." Chafe goes on to clarify other important changes: "The median age of women workers had risen to forty-one, and the proportion of wives at work had doubled from 15 percent in 1940 to 30 percent in 1960." What seemed most astonishing was that, although the number of single women in the labor force declined over a twenty-year span, the number of mothers at work leaped 400 percent—from 1.5 million to 6.6 million—and 39 percent of women with children ages six to seventeen had jobs. By 1960 both husband and wife worked in over 10 million homes (an increase of 333 percent over 1940), and "mothers of children under eighteen comprised almost a third of all women workers."[9]

Although a great number of these were part-time workers, suggesting that the home remained first in women's priorities, the home was clearly not their only concern. Statistics clarified that many middle-class wives were entering the work force along with the women who needed the money for survival. By 1962, "over 53 percent of female college graduates held jobs, in contrast to 36.2 percent of those with only a high school diploma."[10] The quest for quality that the Human Resources Council was exploring demanded more of everything—not just goods, but education and culture as well.

Theory

The two short volumes *Womanpower* (1957) and *Work in the Lives of Married Women* (1958), published by the National Manpower Commission, not only documented the reality of women working but also dispelled many myths about their work and clarified areas for continued study and change. In 1957 the "revolutionary" womanpower conference tried to establish the relationship between women's education and the work in which they were involved. Although educational statistics grimly showed a drop in women in professional training, the report took satisfaction that the numbers of American women getting degrees compared favorably with the total college and university enrollments of Great Britain. In 1950, in spite of the great influx of GI Bill veterans, 43 percent of the over five million college graduates age twenty-five or over were women. Because the Human Resources Council was concerned with the development of intellect, however, there was genuine concern that these women were still seeking training in only the most conventional fields; "teaching, nursing, and library work" accounted for 70 percent of all women in the professions. That few women were studying science or going on to get Ph.D.s in any fields except "Education" was a fact. Formal education, the commission acknowledged, was "the major instrument through which potential ability is developed, and from this point of view the under-education of those capable of advanced schooling is a measure of wasted ability and talent."[11] Women, it had to be spelled out, were often examples of such waste because their motivation was not developed.

In 1957 the commission easily demonstrated that 95 percent of all doctors, lawyers, architects, and natural scientists were men. Only in editing and reporting had there been any gain at all in the numbers of women in more lucrative positions—often because they worked specifically on projects concerning women. By 1955 women were actually employed in every one of the 446 occupations listed in the 1950 census; but the percentage in high level positions remained small. What was happening was that women were replacing men in less desirable jobs or they were filling new jobs in offices designed with "women's skills" in mind.[12]

Women were said to be "tolerant of routine," "meticulous," and "dexterous." There was often reason to believe, the summary on "Trends" concluded, that "many employers found it pleasant to have their offices graced by young women." And it was hard to deny that clerical work, if less financially rewarding in the 1950s, was considerably "more respectable" than the factory jobs that had been available during the war to many of the new secretaries.[13] For the great numbers of noncommitted part-time workers who did not want responsibility or prestige because they put their families before professional or personal advancement, clerical work was deemed ideal.

Another myth destroyed by the war concerned the unreliability of female workers. Except for the longer or shorter periods when their children were very young, most women did not drop out of the labor market. They became an important group of loyal and conscientious producers. Older women, who demonstrated less absenteeism than men, continued to pour into the work force. Between 1940 and 1956 the percentage of employed women between forty-five and fifty-four years old nearly doubled; the same was astonishingly true for women between fifty-five and sixty-five. "The most spectacular development of recent years," declared the report on womanpower, was the rise in employment of women over thirty.[14] Yet the commission also recorded the bias against older women as opposed to older men in managerial positions; seniority was invariably the reward of long-term presence on the job—not of capability. And women continued to earn about a third less than men for doing the same work.

In jobs where women had demonstrated their physical capabilities, the commission noted, inequities were common. Typical was the Navy Yard that hired women as "mechanic learners" at 54¢ an hour while men classified as "laborers" got 75¢ for doing essentially the same job. The report urged the abandonment of sex-label categorization of work, which continued to result in damage to capable women; it stated clearly that "business and industry are still a long way from thinking of ability to perform as the sole criterion for job assignment."[15] Cultural prejudices had to be challenged over and over, the womanpower report continued; we needed to examine all policies of training and promoting women workers. Citing Anna M. Baetjer's *Women in Industry: Their Health and Efficiency* (1946), the commission asserted that motivational differences were the most important factor in determining what work women did—that the ability to perform any job was related to general intelligence not to sex. It should be obvious to everyone that "the proportion of those capable of high accomplishment is no smaller among women than among men."[16]

Labor union support for women was weak. More often during the 1950s, as picketing bartenders demonstrated in New York, women were seen as a threat to men's jobs. Of the more than twenty-four million women in the work force by 1960, only a little more than three million were union members.[17] When the AFL and CIO merged in 1955, they made no show of interest in women's problems. There had been no woman on their executive council since 1881.[18]

Thanks to the equality in federal Civil Service regulations, which had also instituted an equal-pay for equal-work provision in the 1920s, a small number of women had been able to rise to supervisory positions and some also had been encouraged to get technical educations during World War II. The War Manpower Commission had offered training to women in engineering, science, and management with the help of special shifts geared to women's need to be at home part of the day; consequently, a few women remained in positions of relative power after the war.

Three out of four women in the work force, polled in 1945, had intended to stay on. At the time organized labor did not drive them out because they were discovering that the myth that working women would lower wages was also untrue. Instead of lowering the wage scale, as had been presumed, women's presence in the labor force often provided an excuse to press for more humane benefits for all workers. That women had refused to work longer than a fifty-hour week during World War II in order to take care of families was held against them at the time, but considered useful as a bargaining argument in establishing the forty-hour week as a working norm. Had there not been so many returning veterans to accommodate and so many women able to enter the work force it is conceivable that patterns of discrimination during the 1950s might have been less pronounced.[19]

Perhaps the greatest shift in attitude that grew out of the war was the way women began to see themselves. Many married workers realized that they must be quite capable to hold down two jobs at once. Being paid for what they were doing—even if the pay was less than men were taking home, in a society dedicated to the cash nexus—could only enhance self-esteem. Self-assurance built up on the job managed often to overcome nagging doubts about whether their children would suffer. The paychecks women took home not only gave them an immediate sense of security but also helped sustain a sense of independence in a legal establishment that in some places still saw women archaically as their husbands' property. The paychecks that bought music lessons and summer camps for children helped many women feel that their children were better off than if they had remained at home.

When the commission dedicated to exploring "Work in the Lives of Married Women" published its findings on the children of working mothers, it was enormously cautious, but the facts it presented would not persuade anyone that women belonged back in the home. Indeed, there was some evidence that children of working mothers—if their mothers wanted to work—were actually happier and more responsible than those whose mothers stayed at home. Much, needless to say, seemed to depend on the commitment and attitude of the mothers as well as on the kind of childcare available in their absence. When Erwin Canham daringly speculated, "I think the day may well come when we will say the way to cope with juvenile delinquency as the result of bad family conditions is for the wife to go to work,"[20] he was reflecting a highly personal reaction to Eleanor and Sheldon Glueck's voluminous legal studies of juvenile delinquents. "Delinquency" was a great fear at the time.[21] One of the surprising new facts the study on working mothers brought out was that "many mothers are better mothers because they do work."[22]

Frances Lomas Feldman, a professor of social work at the University of Southern California, testified that "some women can be maternal only within certain time limits. Beyond this limit they become exhausted, irritable, even hostile and antagonistic. . . . Women like this often find in at least part-time work release from tension so that their maternal energy is renewed and the atmosphere in the home is calmer and consequently less anxiety-producing."[23]

Katherine Oettinger, Chief of the Children's Bureau, expressed belief "in the indispensability of adequate childcare and supervision for children whose mothers *are* working," noting at the same time how hard such adequate care was to find. Accepting realistically that we could not expect to "reverse a revolution," Oettinger expressed the extensive qualifications about women working that most members of the commission felt. What effects a working mother would have on her child would "depend," Oettinger insisted, on a number of factors: the kind of mother, the kind of child, the kind of family; why the mother works, how much she works, what she does; what her work does to or for her; how old her children are; what provisions she makes for them; and how they perceive their mother working. Work, in itself, did not make any difference, especially if the marriage partnership was strengthened, not weakened, by the mother's absence. If *most* mothers worked, Oettinger concluded, the child's sense of individual rejection would also be slight. But these concerns were invariably addressed as personal or individual matters, not as social issues that might involve broader government or industrial action.[24]

Eleanor Maccoby, then of Harvard's Department of Social Relations, agreed on the complexity of the issue: "A mother's working is only one of many factors bearing upon a child's development."[25] If the mother remained at home, but kept no track of her child or his actions, Maccoby asserted, he would be "far more likely to become delinquent." *The Achievement Motive*, published in 1953, suggested that the independence of children nurtured in families where mothers worked outside the home was a key to American success.[26] Yet there were no specific recommendations about public facilities as a way to enrich children's lives, in spite of references to the success of childcare arrangements in more socialized countries like Israel and England. "Informed observers" expressed concern at the "inadequate care many American children received from 8 A.M. to 6 P.M."[27] Most mothers, they noted, relied primarily on relatives or others living in their households to care for their children while they worked. At a time when social mobility was rapidly separating most families, there seemed to be good reason to worry about the welfare of the children of working mothers and the haphazard nature of American childcare. Public opinion, often more afraid of ideological indoctrination than concerned for the physical well-being or intellectual development of children, was never receptive to helping working mothers of very young children. The mothers themselves preferred to stay at home with infants.

During World War II, the Womanpower Commission noted, more than half the mothers with very young babies refused to take jobs with free daycare.[28] Although, paradoxically, the Children's Bureau and some labor unions were urging better maternity benefits and longer maternity leaves, they did not extend their concern for the mother's job to cover the needs of her children when she returned to work. The conclusion of *Womanpower* was that "Americans have had and continue to have severe reservations about married women with small children working outside the home."[29] It would be *Work in the Lives of Married Women* that articulated more precisely the need for more extensive childcare.

In the later report, the Chicago school system was singled out for praise for having established after-school and evening programs that enabled regular teachers to earn more money at the same time that children gained enrichment. Working for better standards and practices in daycare centers was described as a goal of the Children's Bureau, which advocated more effective licensing and supervision, better-trained staffs, smaller groups of children, and counseling services for mothers—along with public recognition that such facilities should be community based to avoid long travel demands on the children.[30] But even in a period of relative affluence it was apparent that such concerns were more theoretical than real. Although both reports asserted that no study had ever established a causal relationship between maternal employment and juvenile delinquency or the maladjustment of children, superstitions die slowly. The public was not ready to fund the excellent daycare that might have encouraged even more women to return to work. For the mothers who had no choice about working, the social cost of inadequate childcare was yet to be measured.

In 1953, when the distinctions between "health" and "welfare" and "education" were finally labeled arbitrary and a new government department was set up to oversee these areas, which had so much impact on women's lives, many Americans believed we were making progress. But one conference member reluctantly concluded that "the society as a whole does not yet care enough about its children"; and another remarked that in our desire to take advantage of the benefits of the revolution in women's work, "the society at large might not be sufficiently sensitive to the accompanying problems of child care and development."[31]

Monetary allowances (Aid to Dependent Children) had by 1958 been granted to single heads of households through amendments to the Social Security Act, so that theoretically mothers would not have to leave their children, but the amounts were often so inadequate that many urban mothers had to work anyway.[32] Legislation designed to regulate and control the fields and conditions of work for women was equally unrealistic. How were people looking at the Equal Rights Amendment in the 1950s?

With so many women in the work force it was natural that the question of equal pay for equal work should surface and that the idea of equality of opportunity behind the Equal Rights Amendment— up for ratification since the 1920s—should be reexamined. Both Democrats and Republicans endorsed the idea of equal pay on the party platforms of 1952 and 1956. In 1956, in his State of the Union speech, Eisenhower declared that the principle of equal pay for equal work without discrimination "because of sex" was a matter of "simple justice." Yet legislating for such simple justice and enforcing such legislation were acknowledged to be more complex issues. Even after the Equal Pay Act of 1963, and the antidiscrimination clause in Title VII of the 1964 Civil Rights Act, women found enforcing equality—with class action suits—a difficult matter.[33]

At the beginning of the 1950s most of the earlier feminist reformers remained opposed to an Equal Rights Amendment because it would wipe out the protective legislation for women—including maternity benefits, better hours, and lighter jobs—that the old-time reformers had struggled to get on the books. United against the Equal Rights Amendment in 1952 were the Women's Bureau of the Department of Labor, the National Consumers League, the League of Women Voters, the YWCA, the American Association of University Women, and the women's representatives of the AFL and the CIO;[34] at the time of the merger in 1955 there was no mention of ERA. Long-time support by Eleanor Roosevelt reinforced their earlier stand. The Equal Rights Bill presented to Congress in 1950 and again in 1953 contained a proviso that it would not "impair any rights, benefits, or exemptions now or hereafter conferred by law on the female sex"[35] (the Hayden rider), meant to placate the reform feminists; the proponents of equal rights, however, felt that such a proviso destroyed its purpose. As always, the problem was how to ensure equity. When individual groups of workers, such as the American Society of Women Accountants, began protests against sex specifications for job definitions, and the United Auto Workers noted that women were barred from overtime work, more people began to realize how "deferential" treatment for women could be used to keep them in lower positions or limit their opportunities altogether.[36] Newspaper want-ads continued to categorize jobs by sex. Even in professional fields like college teaching, surveyed in 1958 by Theodore Caplow and Reece McGee and analyzed in *The Academic Marketplace*, women were thought to be entirely outside "the prestige system"[37] Before the decade was over, however, the notion that separate was not equal would also change many women's attitudes toward work. The conflict between "reformers" and "feminists," which had seemed clear in the 1920s, was less sure in the age of consensus. Redefinition of equality—an outgrowth of World War II experience—demanded surer access to the opportunities open to men. As early as 1953, turning away from many of her oldest friends like Frances Perkins and Molly Dewson, Eleanor Roosevelt publicly allied herself with the "selfish" interests of the National Federation of Business and Professional Women by shifting her original stand on the Equal Rights Amendment to favor complete equality.[38]

The congressional sponsor of the ERA in 1953, Katherine St. George of New York, wanted the bill to be put on the first docket before the 83rd Congress. Although the *New York Times* acknowledged that Mrs. Roosevelt's disinterested shift in sponsorship had caused many women's groups to reconsider their attitudes toward the ERA, they put St. George's story on the woman's page in the middle of the wedding and engagement announcements.

The *New York Times's* references to women working during the 1950s reflected all the issues brought out in the Columbia conferences—the welcome unconscious consciousness-raising that honest journalism can bring about. There was no editorializing about women. The *Times* reports were representative of the problematic nature of American attitudes toward women's work. Unaware of any ambivalence—the *Times* staff, after all, boasted a number of distinguished women journalists—the newspaper nonetheless sent out mixed messages. It would often praise women's capabilities at the same time that it suggested that fulfillment of such talents might be in conflict with women's main role as the nurturer of values. Self-fulfillment and selfishness might easily be identical. Distinguished women like Olive Remington Goldman, UN representative, and Mary Roberts Rinehart, writer, were carefully described as mothers first.[39]

In January 1956 Reka Hoff, a lawyer, responded to an earlier attack by Sloan Wilson on "The Woman in the Gray Flannel Suit." Career women, she angrily asserted, were forced to keep justifying themselves: "If unmarried their career is designated a 'substitute' for marriage; if married, their career is designated a 'substitute' for motherhood; if a mother, their career brands them as selfish and neglectful."[40] Hoff insisted that although she was a member of a minority group, she was not the "neurotic" and "compulsive half-woman" Sloan Wilson had written about.

Bernice Fitzgibbon, head of her own advertising agency, pointed out in an incisive interview that people never objected to women doing dirty-work: what they objected to was giving women jobs that were equal to men's. The *Times* balanced such radical statements with articles on how a wife should care for her husband's cigars, and quotations from a 1956 YWCA pamphlet defining woman's basic role as "bringing strength, security and serenity to those about her," and helping develop "these same qualities in the life of the community."[41]

Practice

At a period when the Harvard Business School refused to admit women into its two-year training program, believing that the two-year investment in time would be "a risky investment" in people whose years on the track to corporate success might be limited by child-bearing, the *Times* also managed to pay tribute to a number of successful businesswomen. Such women usually survived by entering fields of little interest to men; often they did not choose to marry.

One of the most satisfying successes of the decade was the establishment of the Caedmon Record Company by Barbara Cohen and Marianne Roney to make poetry available on the new LP records; they sold over 100,000 copies of Dylan Thomas's readings. Often women exploited traditional talents that fit in with new needs. Melanie Kahane's industrial designs, for example, were in great demand as the suburban housing boom continued.[42]

Dorothy Shaver, who began her career as a retailer selling handmade dolls, was frequently in the news. Made president of Lord and Taylor in 1945 at a salary of $110,000, the largest on record for any woman in the country (*Life* magazine pointed out that it was a quarter of what men in similar positions got), Shaver received a number of awards for her support of American designers. In a pioneering, perhaps maternal, gesture, Shaver called attention to many original American women talents; Claire McCardell, Carolyn Schnurer, Lilly Daché, Anne Fogarty, Mollie Parnis, and Pauline Trigere flourished under her sponsorship. Never married, Shaver used her personal fortune to offer distinguished service awards in medicine, the arts, housing, education, and international relations. Over a thousand people attended her 1959 funeral.[43]

In 1958 in Philadelphia, Mildred Custin was also elected to the presidency of Bonwit Teller. Such positions of power in merchandising or management in the clothing industry, which was traditionally part of women's sphere, were not, as one would suppose, common. Lillian Hornbein, head of another career agency, remarked that same year that although 90 percent of all shoppers were women, and 80 percent of all clothing workers were still women, she had trouble placing women as retail executives. Of the six women store presidents in America, Hornbein noted, three had inherited their own stores. Hornbein openly criticized the superstitions about women's mid-life instability, along with apprehensions about family reactions to long hours or moving, or concern over the stress of business pressures; World War II had demonstrated the fallacy of such fears.[44]

Edna Woolman Chase, editor of *Vogue* and also the mother of successful writer Ilka Chase, published her autobiography in 1954 at the age of seventy-seven. "Under her direction," wrote Elizabeth Fox-Genovese, "the magazine gained a reputation for high editorial and graphic quality and assumed an important role in the world of international fashion."[45] Other fashion-related fields also tolerated women executives. Hazel Bishop, Helena Rubinstein, Elizabeth Arden, Frances Denny, Estee Lauder, and Germaine Monteil all profited from a decade that urged women to be as feminine as possible. The age of "togetherness" demanded that women devote more energy to staying attractive—ostensibly for their husbands—than to developing their minds.

The 1950s' emphasis on women's separate spheres kept being underlined by the *Ladies' Home Journal* slogan: "Never Underestimate the Power of a Woman." Although the power such magazines dealt with might be regarded as women's compensation in the home for not having power to make decisions in the world, it seemed *real* on its own terms. Many of the women who read the *Ladies' Home Journal* were content, as women have often been, to put their energies into smaller worlds. But it is hard to believe that most women, as the *Journal* suggested in one such ad, would have felt sorry for Beethoven because he could not give birth to a baby. *McCall's* magazine attracted advertisers in 1958 by urging them to look "inward and homeward." The editors stressed the belief that "there, in the heart and at the hearth, lies our abiding fund of strength."[46] The women who worked only in their own homes rarely stopped to wonder about who was profiting from their domesticity. That their work— cooking, cleaning, and taking care of children—was as real as the work listed by the Bureau of Labor Statistics must be insisted upon in any discussion of the decade's labor. During the 1950s there was no talk about paying housewives. Popular magazines reflected social change as well. Before the decade was over, *The Woman's Home Com-*

panion would be out of business, while new magazines like *Glamour*, *Charm*, and *Mademoiselle*, catering to women working outside the home, gained in circulation.[47]

A few women managed to project their domestic talents into amazing fortunes. Margaret Rudkin of Pepperidge Farm turned her own hearth into a million dollar business. Out of concern for an ailing child, Rudkin developed an interest in "proper food for children", which she extended across the nation during the 1950s. Forty years old when she turned her own baking into a commercial enterprise, Rudkin sold the bread company to Campbell's soup in 1960 when it was averaging $32 million in annual sales. The quality of Rudkin's baked goods, remarkable for mass production, remained important to her, and she saw to it that the salaries of her employees were better than average.[48]

Another successful cook, Irma S. Rombauer, in 1952 revised her classic *Joy of Cooking*, a book also designed for her own family, which turned everyday culinary skill into a great fortune. Most American women, however, neither spent many hours in the kitchen nor found riches in domestic chores; few could turn daily responsibilities into profit. The Women's Bureau reported in 1953 that the average working woman's income remained less than half of that received by men.[49]

In 1952, in fact, the *New York Times* also described three hundred women who were lining up for charwomen jobs because such work demanded no skills and could be done part time; $40 a week was considered good pay then for work that was also attractive because it could be done at night, when husbands were available to stay home with the children.[50]

A number of *Times* articles about older women, not competing with men and no longer responsible for the values of children, seemed designed to allay apprehension about women working. Heroic tales about a brave seamstress, Rosa Parks, and an outspoken journalist, Eleanor Roosevelt, alternated with occasional anecdotes about bank-robbing grandmothers and seventy-four-year-old firewomen, to destroy a number of stereotypes about aging. The rocking chair during the 1950s became the symbol of the nursing mother, not of the old lady.

In a culture identified with youth, tributes to age appeared with surprising frequency; perhaps older women were also considered less threatening because they had outlived the violent decades of political radicalism and were less sexually distracting. But they did not stop working. The *Times* wrote up the activities of Isabel Bryan Marks, publisher of the *Villager*, who had turned Greenwich Village into her intimate neighborhood and was still going strong at eighty-two. Alice Austen, a gifted photographer who had retired to the "poorhouse" at seventy-five, was "rediscovered" and honored on her eighty-fifth birthday in 1952. In White Plains, the *New York Times* discovered an eighty-year-old woman sheriff, a mother of six, who was far from being ready to retire. A 1956 obituary for Ida Fischer, an artist whose mosaics had been collected by a number of distinguished museums, stressed that she had not begun to paint until the age of fifty after being inspired by Grandma Moses.[51] The most prominent older superwoman of the postwar period, Lillian Gilbreth, continued to lecture into her eighties as a consultant engineer. In 1954 Gilbreth published *Management in the Home*, a scientific response to her son's appreciative book on her efficient methods for rearing her own twelve children, *Cheaper by the Dozen*.[52] Although it was accorded little institutional attention, the forty-year gift of life to women beyond the years of childrearing engraved itself firmly upon the consciousness of the 1950s.

What the average woman might have picked up during this decade in spite of all commercial efforts to glamorize domesticity was reinforcement for the belief gained during the war that women could do all sorts of jobs at any age *if* they were given the opportunity. The most unconsciously feminist song of the decade was "Anything you can do, I can do better," from *Annie Get Your Gun*. It was in the 1950s that women doctors were first commissioned in the army and women paratroopers first jumped from navy planes. In New York banking, the first woman savings-and-loan president was elected; in Saint Louis, the first women were allowed to trade on the floor of the Merchants Exchange. In 1952 Mary McCusker became the first woman elected to the American Institute of Banking, and, after twenty years at Harvard, in 1956 Cecilia Payne-Gaposchkin was made a full professor of astronomy. The Second World War had established women's capabilities once and for all.

Along with the reality of more married women in the labor force came the slower acceptance of greater domesticity for the American male. One group of visiting Russian scientists in the 1950s were eager to describe American middle-class men washing dishes. A child-rearing article in 1958 noted that modern women had a harder time than the wives of nineteenth-century whalers because after husbands had started playing a larger role in the home, business trips caused more resentment. Margaret Mead described the "new" middle-class family as a "cooperative, too self-centered unit where the father was as much a part of the home as the mother."[53] Such intensive "togetherness"—later also held responsible for the rising divorce rate—was less obvious in the more extended working-class family where the division of work, as Mirra Komarovsky described it in *Blue Collar Marriage*, remained more certain.[54] But not for long. The husbands of the "beauticians, sales clerks, seamstresses, cashiers, waitresses, typists, secretaries, and factory workers" Lillian Rubin would interview in the early 1970s made a point of helping their wives with their work. The growing androgyny would have a significant impact on the world of work, even though, as Rubin finally observed: "There is more talk than action when it comes to the allocation and distribution of household and child-rearing tasks."[55]

During the 1950s there was more talk than action concerning every aspect of women's lives. That the talk often represented the highest kind of idealism may be inferred from the conclusions of the Columbia Conference about work, published in 1958 as *Human Resources: The Wealth of a Nation*. Designed originally to find out why two million men were declared unfit to be drafted during World War II, the conferences, as Eli Ginzberg reported them, understood that "the actions which a society takes to nurture, develop, and utilize its human potential will largely determine its health and welfare."[56]

Taking special note of the discrimination against women, Ginzberg reminded American employers that women possessed half of America's best brains. He scored the "widespread practice of subtly differentiating jobs held by men and women in order to justify what amounts to a substantially higher wage for men." He pointed out that women do not have "easy entrée to the wide variety of training programs that are available in most large corporations even after they have proved by a good work record that they are seriously interested in their jobs." The differences in turnover, he underlined, were not nearly sufficient to justify industry's training men and failing to train women.[57]

Stressing that the right to work was a moral as well as an economic imperative, Ginzberg criticized traditional institutional policies that operated to "waste" human potential. He pointed out the shameful reality that many young women of high ability did not pursue an academic course in high school, that others did not go on to college, and that even fewer went on to graduate work. Acknowledging the cultural complexity behind such decisions he joined the partisans for better guidance counseling and more scholarship aid to encourage young women of high potential. The pattern of women's education, he also understood, would have to be more flexible: "By the time a woman is in her late twenties or early thirties all her children are likely to be in school. At this point, many women begin to have free time. They then need basic and refresher courses appropriate to their age and maturity." Employers, Ginzberg insisted, must also be willing to train older women—"those over forty, who now comprise half of the female labor force." They must try to make adjustments in "hours, vacation schedules, or other conditions of work which would enable more women workers to dovetail their responsibilities in and out of the home." Conceding that such adjustments might raise costs, Ginzberg concluded that "any reasonable investment that society and business make in [women's] education, training and work is likely to pay for *itself* many times over."[58]

In the value-conscious world of the 1950s, Ginzberg had to insist that the expansion of opportunities for women would not denigrate the importance of the home or exalt the possession of wealth, but would simply present women with more options. Implicit in the offer of opportunity was the liberal democratic faith that the individual would "choose intelligently." What we needed most in the labor force, Eli Ginzberg believed, was good judgment—"experience rather than energy."

At the opening of an age of high technology threatened by the presence of world socialism, Eli Ginzberg asserted his own moving faith in the humanistic values he wanted to find in American work:

Only men and women can develop the ideas that serve as the foundations for scientific and technological progress; only men and women—even in an age of giant computers—can manage organizations; only men and women can operate and repair the new automatic machines which produce the goods we desire; only men and women can provide services to the young and old, to the sick and well, to those seeking education or recreation. Only men and women, not financial grants or ballistic missiles, determine the strength of a government.[59]

Betty Friedan would later criticize the Human Resources Commission, which sponsored this document, for discovering women's needs only in relation to men's failures. She might have been equally concerned about the relative failure of the commission's own eloquence to bring about any immediate improvements. There can be little doubt that having such an idealized record of the need for change ultimately may have had an impact on the future of women's work, but the concessions of American labor—at every level—to women's needs as mothers remained modest. Many bright young women simply stopped having babies.

Eleanor Roosevelt holding the Declaration of Human Rights.
Courtesy of the United Nations.

Chapter Five

Political Women: Party Connections and Outside Power

How much do statistics ever tell about the nature of participation in American democracy? In every decade the percentage of eligible voters who actually vote is an embarrassment to those committed to participatory government. Yet, in the 1950s, for the first time in the thirty years since women won the vote, they were credited with working together to put a president—Dwight David Eisenhower—in the White House. Ike's Republican victory and the subsequent dissolution of the Democratic Women's Division, which had provided so many jobs for women during the 1930s, appeared punitively connected in spite of assertions by Democratic party officials that women were better off integrated. Whether the Republican women were adequately rewarded with policymaking positions for their efforts to put in the new administration also seems questionable. There was no official commitment to women as a group—only an ongoing use of a few exceptional talents. Women did not recognize their power as a political force; they continued to work behind the scenes as concerned individuals.[1]

At the beginning of the 1950s there were still some strong older women in positions of influence who had helped shape the social policies of the New Deal. Jane Hoey, who had been responsible for welfare provisions (the Bureau of Public Assistance) for seventeen years under the Social Security Act, was almost immediately dismissed by Oveta Culp Hobby, Eisenhower's choice to head the Department of Health, Education and Welfare. Hoey had no trouble finding a job in the private sector with the National TB Association, but she protested her abrupt dismissal and the values that seemed connected with it. In 1955 she returned to public service on the United Nations Social and Economic Commission. Marion Glass Banister was still Assistant Treasurer of the United States in 1951; Nellie Tayloe Ross was Director of the Mint until 1952; and Clara Beyer remained Associate Director of the Division of Labor Standards until 1957; Anna Rosenberg who had been made Assistant Secretary of Defense by Harry Truman in 1950, the highest military rank ever attained by a woman, was also asked to resign. Frances Perkins, our first woman cabinet member, gave up her civil-service work altogether in 1953 to teach at Cornell.[2]

These women had all emerged publicly at a period in need of their talents and experience with social reform. But, as Susan Ware noted in her book on New Deal women, they had trained no cohorts to replace themselves, nor had they educated other women to protest the loss of many women's government jobs. They all saw themselves as gifted individuals who would help women simply by demonstrating their competence to hold high-level positions; they did little as a group to expand opportunities for women in government service. Mollie Dewson, age fifty-nine when she took over the Women's Division of the Democratic party, had worked steadily during the New Deal for patronage and committee representation for women. When she gave her papers to the Schlesinger Library in 1952, it was with the hope that younger women might "contemplate women's slow emergence from family and domestic affairs alone to public concerns."[3] Dewson might have added how valuable it had been also to have the support of a strong president's wife behind her pushing the use of female talent in government. The power of Eleanor Roosevelt in getting policymaking jobs for women during the 1930s should never be underestimated.

The New Deal "ladies" had indeed made it obvious that women were capable of political performance at high levels. In 1952 both parties placed women in nomination for the job of vice president of the United States. The Republicans chose Senator Margaret Chase Smith from Maine, whose impeccable character had made her many friends in both parties. As early as 1950, Smith had challenged Joseph McCarthy for libeling outsiders from the floor of the Senate and hiding behind the cloak of congressional immunity. Without mentioning his name she urged a declaration of conscience against "fear, ignorance, bigotry and smear."[4] The Democrats at the same time nominated India Edwards, who was then director of their women's division. Edwards, not usually reticent, had declined to take over the more powerful decision-making role of National Chairman in 1951, claiming that it would take too much of her time. When the women's division was dissolved, or "integrated," she perceived clearly the loss to American women but was by then powerless. The Republicans also dismantled their women's division in 1953 without even consulting their hard-working leader, Bertha Adkins, who had done so much to elect Ike. Realizing that this kind of "integration" represented a loss in the number of visible women who could be pushed into patronage jobs, Adkins tried to stress the idea that women approached political problems with a different point of view. Even Oveta Culp Hobby, as head of the Women's Army Corps, had managed to get pregnant women "released" instead of "discharged," a distinction that protected their future careers. That working women also produced children was not, then, a generally accepted political reality. Adkins managed to promote only a few exceptional women into public service.

Yet Eisenhower provided twenty-six high-level positions for women in his government besides Oveta Culp Hobby's in the Cabinet. Clare Boothe Luce and Frances Willis became ambassadors; Frances Bolton, delegate to the United Nations Assembly; Mary Pillsbury Lord, American member of the UN Human Rights Commission; and Ivy Baker Priest, a talented Mormon whose husband took over the management of their home, became Treasurer of the United States. Katherine Howard, Republican National Committee Woman in 1952, became Assistant Administrator of Civil Defense under Eisenhower; and Jane Morrow Spaulding, a West Virginia black civic leader, was made Assistant Secretary of HEW to work with Hobby.[5]

In office Oveta Culp Hobby, our second woman cabinet member, did little to justify Adkins's belief in the value of a woman's point of view. In fact she turned her power toward eliminating the role of government in social reforms. She had no commitment to any improvement programs to help the weak, perhaps, as Eleanor Roosevelt and Lorena Hickok generously implied, because she was so committed to the Republican laissez-faire ideal. Her handling of the distribution of polio vaccine, insisting on fees, outraged many who saw it denying the poor. When she returned to the private sector as a publisher in 1955, she catered to the advertisers: "She has not built a great newspaper or a great TV station," a fellow Texan wrote, "merely decent and profitable ones." The same kind of comment would apply to her government work.[6]

Newspapers during the decade often chided women to participate more in political activities as they also reported on the grim lives of "latchkey" children (whose mothers were absent when they returned from school) and the importance of a full family life. In 1952, at the meetings of the Home Economics Association, women's reluctance to play a greater role in politics because of the corruption of the political world was compared to the laziness of housewives closing doors on dirty rooms. Over and over it was made clear: women should send out good influences from the family; they were urged to communicate the domestic experience of living in the free society that men were defending ideologically. But they were to play this political role without actually leaving their homes.

The difficulty of being simultaneously domestic and political was not clarified. No one thought to point out the ages of the New Deal women—most were in their early fifties when they assumed positions of power—in clear contrast to the great number of child-enveloped women who dominated the scene in the 1950s. A number of political women like Shirley Chisholm, at the time literally surrounded by toddlers in her nursery school, would go on to redefine life at another stage, exemplifying the new developmental pattern. Chisholm, in fact, would even engage in a third occupation—college teaching—after leaving politics.[7] Yet many young women coping with small children managed to find time for voluntary political activities.

In the early 1950s—in the midst of recipes for quick chocolate cake, patterns for children's dresses, love stories that ended as celebrations of domesticity, year-long budgets, and speculations on how an impossible marriage should be saved—the Ladies' Home Journal made an effort to interest women in politics with a "new nonpartisan crusade" for working democracy at the local level. A full page New York Times ad urged Journal readers to send away for a how-to-do-it leaflet to help begin their involvement in "practical political activity."

Avoiding the anti-Communist hysteria rampant on the national scene and the widely publicized political corruption, the *Journal* emphasized traditional community involvement for women. "There is no way by which national politics can be more intelligent, more ethical, more courageous than the local groups in which it has its roots," the editors insisted; "you can do something about it."[8] A good number of women followed this advice at the time and publicized their activities. In 1953, Carmen Frederikson described the impact of women on an agricultural experiment station in Logan, Utah; the *National Civic Review* in 1953 published "Cincinnati Women Ring Doorbells—or How One Woman Got into Local Politics"; *America* magazine told how "Women Run the Rascals Out of Gary" (May 1950). Even the *New York Times Magazine*, in 1956, published a speculative article on having a woman president. If there were few visible women on the national scene, many more were having an impact on local problems where—as Maurine Neuberger, a 1952 congresswoman from Oregon, pointed out—they could influence thinking on education, health, traffic safety, and children.[9]

"If the party backs a woman you can be pretty sure they do it because they think it's a lost cause," India Edwards remarked. Loyal Democrats Lorena Hickok and Eleanor Roosevelt also acknowledged how hard it was for a woman to be put into nomination for positions of power. Men say that party politics are too tough, they wrote in *Ladies of Courage* in 1954: "Rarely do they admit that it is next to impossible for a woman to get the nomination in a district where her party can win."[10] The women who ran as independents— outside the two-party system—and won deserved special praise.

Although they took no specific stand on whether women could be good mothers while running for office, Roosevelt and Hickok's 1954 polemic contained a few examples of the remarkable women who managed to do both, such as Mayor Dorothy Davis of Washington, Virginia, whose daughter boasted that her mother did everything other mothers did and was mayor besides. "If the old-fashioned idea that a woman's place is in the home is correct," Mayor Davis declared, "then it's my contention that home must extend beyond the front gate."[11] Her administration produced an all-female city council in 1952. Roosevelt and Hickok also pointed to the number of active older women, like New Jersey representative Frances Bolton, who ran for Congress at age fifty-five and served in the House for twenty-eight years. Bolton argued that motherhood was an asset to a political career: "I believe that with certain limitations," she said, "women can do anything that men can. . . . Their intuition, their deep understanding of children and the family have an increasingly vital function in a world which today is studying the art of harmonious human relations."[12] Although Mabel Byrne, a successful precinct worker for thirty-five years, was reluctant to run for the legislature because she felt she could not spend so much time away from her daughters, one of these daughters later chose a different path; in the 1950s she would be the first woman to work full time on the Court of Special Sessions in two hundred years.

Roosevelt and Hickok, in describing the experience of Mary Norton, another woman who had entered politics in her forties, stressed the fact that she was no different from thousands of other women who might do an equally good job in Congress. Before her marriage Norton had been a secretary. These "Ladies of Courage" were uniformly examples of how women could translate their traditional concerns for social reforms into political reality.

All over America women played modest, but important, roles in grass-roots politics. In North Dakota, Brynhild Haugland had a hand in every law passed over a period of fifteen years to help meet farmers' problems and improve living conditions. Female talent was clearly available if men were willing to look for it—as the competent Eugenie Anderson also demonstrated as ambassador to Denmark. The first woman to sign a treaty with a foreign nation, Anderson became an example of feminine caring when she mastered Danish and entered into community life abroad. Like Perle Mesta, she also gave much attention to the youth of the country where she was stationed. Mesta set up a series of exchange scholarships in 1953, for Luxembourg students to use in the United States. Never hesitant to label herself a feminist, Mesta protested regularly about the scarcity of government appointments for women.[13]

More typical of the domestic women of the decade was Alice Leopold, who became secretary of state in Connecticut in 1953 and would go on to be director of the Women's Bureau. Leopold had spent most of her life involved in volunteer activities; she had been president of the League of Women Voters as well as director of a visiting nurses' program. In 1953, when elected to a position of power, she knew how to get an equal-pay-for-women bill through the state assembly because of her experience as a volunteer. Of course she made compromises, she told her friends, as one has to in every undertaking, but not at the sacrifice of integrity. In 1954 Leopold organized a conference of women's organizations to discuss the Equal Rights Amendment. At that time equity seemed more important; many women thought they did not want equality.[14]

Because they defined women's role as fighting for causes, Roosevelt and Hickok thought it natural for many political women, such as Alice Leopold, to find encouragement and training in volunteer work. Although by 1954 Eleanor Roosevelt thought the League of Women Voters had an "ivory tower" attitude, she herself had participated in its early programs and she continued to volunteer her services to a number of different causes. Many women deprived of male networks and organizational opportunities found voluntary associations the best source of training for active political life. Both Maurine Neuberger and Eugenie Anderson had been members of the League, as had Representative Edith Green of Oregon and Olive Remington Goldman of the United Nations Commission on the Status of Women. Ella Grasso of Connecticut, one of the rare Democratic candidates to win office at the time of Eisenhower's 1952 landslide, felt her work with the League carried over into the political structure. She eliminated over 500 patronage judgeships after being elected secretary of state. In a book on political women, Peggy Lamson quotes one pol saying of Grasso: "She shrill-voiced it to us continually."[15] Even before being elected governor, Grasso saw herself as a "state conscience." Other kinds of volunteer work also proved useful to professional politicians: Millicent Fenwick worked as a volunteer for the NAACP in New Jersey, for a prison reform group, and for the county Legal Aid Society before winning her first election to the board of education in the 1950s. Going on to be elected as a Republican member of Congress in 1974, at the age of sixty-four, and re-elected three times, Fenwick's career remains an example not only of women's capacity to go on living many lives, but also of the complexity of their moral commitment.[16]

Although in 1939 Eleanor Roosevelt thought women's suffrage had made "no really great changes in government," by 1955, when she was interviewed by Malcolm Muggeridge for the BBC, she had come to believe that the women's vote had made a difference in the interests of men. There were, she insisted, "far fewer men who were concerned about social reforms" before women got the vote.[17] Improved working conditions and benefits to children, Roosevelt believed, resulted from women's political potential. If the number of women politicians remained small, the number of women involved in different kinds of pressure groups outside the political system remained steady. Unpopular causes such as the Peace Movement also often provided focus for the energies of strong women. Florence Luscomb, Progressive party candidate for governor in Massachusetts in 1952, and Jeanette Rankin, who had been the only member of Congress to oppose our entry into both world wars, remained articulate pacifists throughout the Korean conflict. Vera Micheles Dean, author of *Foreign Policy without Fear* (1953), used an outsider's influence, as an executive of the Foreign Policy Association, to help diminish the narrowmindedness of official diplomacy.[18]

Civil rights, the most creative domestic issue of the decade, became a personal triumph for a number of heroic black women. And a number of brave white women also gave their energies to helping blacks obtain their constitutional rights. In 1954, Minnie Fisher Cunningham offered to mortgage her farm to keep the *Texas Observer* liberal; Virginia Foster Durr and Dorothy Rogers Tilly worked with organized groups of southern white women to help people accept the necessity for change. A number of women teachers got together under the direction of Warine Walker to urge their profession to work actively toward solving the problems involved in the integration of southern schools.[19]

Some women with political appointments used their professional status for causes that were unpopular. Miriam Van Waters, head of the Framingham, Massachusetts Reformatory, spoke out against capital punishment and for more extensive reform programs for juvenile offenders; Sarah T. Hughes, a district judge in Dallas, supported the ERA and also more funding for the Women's Bureau. Reva Beck Busone, a municipal judge in Utah, organized a rigorous campaign against alcohol that considerably lowered traffic deaths.

Other public-interest issues continued to find women pushing for what they saw as the quality of American life. In 1959 Persia Campbell was elected to the board of directors of the Consumers Union. In 1953 Freda Hennock—against much opposition—got the first educational TV station built in Houston, Texas; Hennock would also later become the first woman appointed to the Federal Communications Commission. At a time when horror comics were regarded as destructive to the imaginations of American children, two mothers, Mrs. Guy Trulock and Mrs. Theodore Chapman, devised ingenious ways to get children to swap comics for more serious books and pressured producers to use self-discipline in the comic-book industry. By the 1980s, the Illinois Citizens for Handgun Control founded by a 1958 graduate of Vassar, Patricia Koldyke with three friends, had over 25,000 supporters and a full-time staff working with 400 volunteers.[20]

During the 1950s antiwar activists like Lenore Marshall, worked in their spare time to help make other Americans aware of the dangers of nuclear stockpiling. The National Committee for a Sane Nuclear Policy, the Ban the Bomb movement and the Women Strike for Peace, were well organized before the decade was over. Individuals believed that personal protests could make a difference. Daisy Harriman, for example—at the age of eighty-four—led a march through the city of Washington in 1955, to protest the disenfranchisement of the District of Columbia.

The Modern Period, volume 4 of *Notable American Women* is a testimony to the many ways women manage to be political without being connected to the party system. Headings in the classified index—"Labor," "Housing Reform," "Peace," "Philanthropy," "Public Health," "Civil Rights," "Civil Liberties," "Social Reform," "Social Welfare," and "Consumer Affairs"—tell as much—if not more—about the way women define themselves politically as the category "Government and Politics" does. If women's impact as a "gender group" during the 1950s remains undistinguished, the impact they had as concerned individuals touched important areas of American life; they were frequently able to work to bring about a number of improvements for society, if not for themselves.

Part-time involvement in local activities or community needs was a respectable way for many young women in the 1950s to feel part of society and to educate themselves in issues of importance. Much younger than the women who had positions of power in the New Deal, fifties women still had many domestic responsibilities, and they had no encouragement from the community to compete with men for jobs with status. The daycare provided during World War II was hardly remembered. Middle-class women volunteered their spare time in all the categories listed in *Notable American Women*, and rarely felt their lives to be trivial. Voluntary associations, as Tocqueville remarked in his travels in the 1830s, have always played an important role in shaping the quality of American life: "A people among whom individuals lost the power of achieving great things single-handed, without acquiring the means of producing them by united exertion would soon lapse into barbarism."²¹ The habit of forming associations in a democratic society seemed essential to maintaining civilization.

Although the League of Women Voters, the nonpartisan group that attracted the greatest number of middle-class, college-educated women at the time, appeared nonassertive and slow to take moral stands on urgent issues to the feminists that followed, it played a valuable role in the 1950s in protecting both individualism and pluralism in American life by avoiding the single-issue commitment that would characterize more radical groups in other decades. The League's yearly planned programs of study throughout the 1950s epitomized the rational decency of the liberal imagination; if these women were ineffective, or detached, they nevertheless managed to call attention to a number of important issues in need of greater understanding.

In the late 1940s League members sponsored research into "The Preservation of Civil Liberties and Protection of Minority Rights against Discrimination"; in 1954–55, "Development of Understanding of the Relationship between Individual Liberty and the Public Interest" and a review of "The Bill of Rights and Individual Liberty Today." By 1956, two years after McCarthy's censure by Congress, they were evaluating "federal loyalty-security programs, with recognition of the need for safeguarding national security and protecting individual liberties." By 1958 they recommended "modification of federal loyalty-security programs . . . and commonsensical judgments to provide the greatest possible protection for the individual."²²

If League members did not see the political and economic position of women with any greater sense of urgency, it may have been because few League members had ever worked full time. Yet they were ahead of most Americans in recognizing the need for greater planning for natural resources and they consistently supported consumer-protection laws and more extensive civil-service legislation to improve government efficiency.

During the 1950s the League of Women Voters worked also to make Americans aware of our new international role. They supported aid for European recovery and more technical assistance for agricultural countries, and they "reluctantly" supported NATO and opposed the Bricker Amendment, designed to limit the president's treaty-making powers. From 1958 to 1960 their programs focused on

"The Evaluation of United States Foreign Policy, with Continued Support of the United Nations, World Trade and Economic Development and Collective Security."[23] They sponsored modified teach-ins during the Suez and Hungarian crises, and they worked steadily to involve more people in participatory government at a local level. It was natural that a number of women should have found League work good training for political careers or for full-time involvement in the social reforms that grew out of such studies.

Speaking of her mother, Mary Ingraham's, work as a volunteer at the Brooklyn YWCA, the entirely professional Mary Bunting (Yale Ph.D., Rutgers professor, president of Radcliffe) remarked: "Volunteering undoubtedly gave my mother fully as much leverage and satisfaction over a longer period of years as any paid position or political career could have provided, and it did so on her terms, terms that permitted her to schedule her time away from home flexibly, according to her needs and those of her family."[24] This volunteering also later turned into full-time work when Ingraham was made president of the National Board of the YWCA.

The range of volunteer social involvement was often more complex than subsequent activists realized. Herta Loeser, Boston director of a clearing house for volunteers, later observed that many of the volunteer jobs of the 1950s might be accurately compared with the advocacy groups of the 1960s because both worked *against* the profit-motive, which often compromised professionals.[25] By the 1970s, even Betty Friedan praised the committed woman volunteer for having "the most mature and strongest self of all." These women, Friedan recognized, had had to "structure a growth pattern" for themselves without any institutional support or guidelines.[26]

But a realistic problem with voluntarism was that it provided worthwhile activity only for middle-class women with spare time who did not have to earn money. That volunteers worked on their own terms did little to make flex-time, maternity leaves, and equitable pay available for the majority of working women who were also heads of households. Only organization could achieve similar freedom of choice for working mothers to "make their own terms." Middle-class volunteers frequently kept women's status low by giving time and talent that should have been paid for; they weakened the argument for more highly paid shared or part-time jobs, which would have allowed more working mothers (and fathers) to be home, and they interfered with public budgets for social-service work and

the arts by giving so much for nothing. Yet there can be little doubt
that their contributions during the 1950s also increased public
awareness and contributed to pressure for more ethical politics. The
work they did represented a clear commitment to noncommercial
values.

Eleanor Roosevelt, who had worked as a volunteer for the League
of Women Voters, the Consumers' League, the Women's Trade
Union League, and the Democratic National Committee, took a
stand against voluntarism when she realized that it might lower the
wages of working women. Although she gave away most of the
money she earned by writing and lecturing, Roosevelt made a point
of not refusing wages. In 1955, a time somewhat similar to the 1930s
because women were being urged to leave the labor force—not because there was a job shortage but because returning veterans received preference—Eleanor Roosevelt wrote an article for *Charm*
magazine called "What Are the Motives for a Woman Working
When She Does Not Have to for Income?"[27] Yet she too was driven
back into volunteer work when Eisenhower took away her job at the
United Nations. Committed to the importance of the UN during a
decade overshadowed by fear of communism, Roosevelt volunteered
her time to the American Association for the United Nations
(AAUN) in order to help organize local chapters in support of the
UN. Although her *Charm* article recalled how much her own self-
esteem had risen the first time someone offered her money to do a
job, she had to acknowledge also that few Americans cared enough
about the UN then to pay for the work she was doing as a volunteer.
She was always sensitive, however, to the impact of voluntary work
on the wage scale: "You must ask for what you had earned and ask
for a full price, since it was not fair to enter into competition in a way
which might lower the price standard for other people who had to
earn a living."[28]

While barnstorming the nation for the AAUN, Roosevelt kept up
her journalism: "Achievement in the marketplace . . . in our particular civilization, is almost essential to self-respect," she wrote. She
scandalized some admirers during the decade by appearing on a TV
commercial to advertise margarine, a practical way, she thought, to
remind watchers of the number of hungry children who would
profit from the TV fee she turned over to them. In 1954 her taxable
income was actually about $90,000.[29]

Yet she was also grateful for the volunteer's freedom to emphasize the values she *wanted* to work for. Eleanor Roosevelt expressed some relief that she had lost her job at the United Nations, for she was freed to speak out against the shift in policy that John Foster Dulles represented: the United States was no longer supporting the completion of the Human Rights covenants that were so important to her. After Eleanor Roosevelt left the UN in 1953, America did not even push for ratification of the completed Genocide Convention. To Pauline Lord, her Republican successor as UN ambassador, Eleanor Roosevelt wrote a note of sympathy. Human rights came first in her system of values; as an outsider volunteering time, Roosevelt felt freer to play the role Tamara Hareven defined for her as "America's conscience."[30]

Eleanor Roosevelt refused to be nominated for the Senate after her husband's death, and even refused to be on the Democratic National Committee after Stevenson's defeats in 1952 and 1956 because she felt her influence could be greater without clear-cut party connections. There can be little doubt, however, that she remains the greatest American political figure of the period immediately following World War II. To Joseph Alsop, she was "our last great man": Adlai Stevenson, for whom she campaigned vigorously at every political level, asked rhetorically at her memorial service: "What other single human being has touched and transformed the existence of so many?" At her 1962 funeral, attended by three Presidents of the United States, one of her loyal friends challenged Dwight Eisenhower for not making use of her diplomatic skills: "I made use of her," Harry Truman spoke out; "I told her she was First Lady of the World."[31]

The power Truman had given her as ambassador to the United Nations—the power to influence policy and make decisions—was what she continued to ask for women. Indeed, her final speech in 1952 to the Human Rights Commission of the United Nations was about the political rights of women. In a 1956 article in the *London Times* she described the importance of Truman's having asked her to be a United States delegate to the organizing committee of the United Nations. Truman's confidence in her astute political sense enabled her finally to step out of FDR's shadow.

Eleanor Roosevelt knew full well that Secretary of State Dulles

and Senator Vandenberg did all they could to keep her off the
United States delegation—they did not even invite her to the committee meeting, at which she was assigned to Section 3: Humanitarian and Cultural Rights—with the idea that there she would do least
harm. "I felt an outsider," she commented. After her later triumphant debate with Andrei Vishinski on the need to respect self-determination in the placement of refugees, the Republicans treated her
with more respect. "I knew that if I failed," she wrote, "it would not
be my failure alone but would be a failure for all women and there
would be very few women on our delegation in the future." Proving
herself on her own terms, as the New Deal women whose talents
she pushed in the 1930s had done, her tormented self-esteem continued to grow: "I felt that I had established a place for women and
somehow it gave me the confidence I so sorely needed."[32] Always
minimizing her personal achievements, Eleanor Roosevelt suggested
that what she had done could be done by any woman, with "hard
work" and conscientious preparation.

The self-reliance Roosevelt carried with her into the 1950s enabled her to speak out against injustices at home and to underline the
human goals she thought important. Afraid to summon her before
his Senate investigating committee, Joseph McCarthy felt her con-
tempt more than once. In "My Day" Eleanor Roosevelt used her
own international perspective to help Americans see how our country looked to outsiders; she reported Yugoslav speculation that we
were losing our freedom, for example, and she let Eisenhower know
how she felt about allowing McCarthy to slander General Marshall,
whose economic plan for Europe did much to prevent a Communist
takeover. When Ike failed at first to play a strong role in the Little
Rock integration crisis, she called him "a meek little rabbit." Richard
Nixon she publicly denounced on a TV show, "Meet the Press," for
accusing Helen Gahagan Douglas of being a Communist: "I have no
respect for the kind of character that takes advantage and does something they know is not true."[33]

Eleanor Roosevelt saw the new anxiety about communism in
terms of the old idea of "nothing to fear but fear." Her 1952 address
to the Democratic National Convention warned against the short-
sighted and selfish attempt to "distort the vision of the American
people." That America had become a world power and had to use its
own pluralism to strengthen its international role was a theme her
speeches and columns developed during the decade. She called New

York City in 1959 "the greatest community of human endeavor on earth"; and she worked—again as a volunteer—to bring about more integrated housing there. She took a position in favor of ending nuclear tests and she came out against capital punishment. A number of American Indian tribes used her column as a means to express grievances, which she thought entirely justified. "We took their land and entered into treaties," she wrote in 1959. "We have not given them either adequate medical care or education." Another time she used her feelings about Native Americans to suggest her international sense: "A great nation must respect small nations."[34]

"We must learn to live together or we will die together," Roosevelt wrote more than once, trying to plead for more sophisticated diplomacy on the part of the United States. Many of her admirers thought her too naive. She protested the loss to the country of the services of J. Robert Oppenheimer: "He was never accused of anything except of having felt, as most scientists do, that questions of science should be shared. . . ." The House Un-American Activities Committee was invariably seen by her as more un-American than the people it investigated.[35]

In her travels to Japan, the Middle East, Russia, and Europe during the 1950s, Eleanor Roosevelt took the point of view that she was articulating the concerns of most American women. In her "My Day" columns, the issue she devotes the most attention to is education; child welfare also appears an ongoing concern. In Israel—where she reported with pride that every woman worked outside the home—and in Tokyo, Roosevelt addressed the changing status of women. She was pleased that Israeli women played a strong political role and distressed that the elegant obis worn by Japanese royalty exacted a high price in the eyesight of the women who embroidered them. She wondered in her column why American tariff laws could not be modified to exempt handmade materials so that the Donegal weavers might survive. Otherwise, she feared, "women and children will be hungry."[36]

Internationally she managed to conciliate many people with warring ideas by diplomatically insisting that she was not an official statesman or a clever politician, as her husband had been. (Intimate friends, as Joseph Lash demonstrates, knew better.) Her sensitivity to a vast range of human feelings may well have made her, as one statesman asserted, the only human being alive able to deal with the range of hostile feelings involved in the shaping of the Human

Rights Declaration. The crassness she cited, of John Foster Dulles's asking the Israelis if the Bible they had given him contained the New Testament, after his presentation of guns to the Egyptians, must have struck many as the kind of indifference Eleanor Roosevelt took pains to avoid.[37]

While working at the United Nations Roosevelt pressed the issue of the need for more women's involvement in the organization itself, as well as for greater concern for the rights of women all over the world—without separating them into an inferior category. Emily Williams, an oral historian interviewing Marietta Tree, one of Roosevelt's successors at the UN, would ask why Eleanor Roosevelt was not invoked by the 1960s women's movement. "It is odd," Tree replied. "She was a liberated woman from the beginning."[38] What Eleanor Roosevelt considered her own faulty education—her failure to go to college—had made her especially aware of women's needs. But she also recognized the range of women's executive competence without specific training. When a Democratic president again took office in 1960, one of her first gestures was to present him with a list of competent women capable of filling many more offices than the new administration was willing to hand out. Kennedy appropriately rewarded Eleanor Roosevelt for a lifetime of political service by asking her to head the new committee to explore the role of "Women in American Life."[39]

Roosevelt was a complex feminist, a nineteenth-century type in her continuing self-effacement, which many might have accepted as truth. She was also deeply and openly devoted to a number of men: Franklin Roosevelt, Louis Howe, Joseph Lash, Adlai Stevenson, and David Gurewitsch, as well as to a few sustaining women, including Anna Rosenberg, Lorena Hickok, and Malvina Thompson. Unabashedly feminine in her continuing delight in children, flowers, and small animals, she sometimes even wrote about the state of her hairdo or not having time to buy new clothes. And she avoided commitment to narrow professionalism as the means to women's advancement, a trait that would make her suspect to feminists who believe women should be given men's opportunities for power. Few other women could achieve the influence Eleanor Roosevelt derived from association. She clearly relished a woman's freedom as an outsider, to criticize flaws in all the institutions she knew so well from the inside.

During the 1950s she was viciously attacked in letters for having been a gadabout mother, unfit to cast judgment on a patriotic American like Joseph McCarthy. But stories of grandchildren and daughters-in-law abound in her columns, suggesting to American mothers that she understood their family concerns too. The role of daughter-in-law Eleanor Roosevelt herself played so long helped her, she said, to form an assertive self. If, as Marietta Tree commented, Eleanor Roosevelt had a natural politician's timing with an instinct for when to go for the jugular, she was also, Tree noted, a good and caring mother who wrote her sons once a week and visited every term when they were at Groton.[40] A more sophisticated public might have speculated that a father's behavior shapes children's attitudes toward marriage as much as a mother's.

"The most rewarding activity for any woman, young or old, is to meet the needs of those who are nearest and dearest to her," Eleanor Roosevelt wrote in 1954, a concession to the current definition of female fulfillment. But her feminist self intruded to add: "She will not meet these adequately if she has no interests and occupations of her own." Roosevelt concluded by extending her definition into age: "Young families should never have the feeling that the older members of the family are languishing for their companionship. This makes a duty out of something which should be a pleasure."[41] Independence became one of her ideals. Women had to be able to change and to stand alone.

In the 1950s Eleanor Roosevelt shifted her attitude toward the Equal Rights Amendment, which she had originally opposed as destructive to protective labor legislation for women: "I can see that . . . it does add a little to the position of women to be declared equal before the law and equal politically in whatever work a woman chooses," she wrote in "My Day" in 1951.[42] She had always believed in equal pay for equal work, and supported daycare. Although both political parties supported the ERA, it was not considered essential to establishing better pay and hours for women. Even the 1963 report of the Committee on the Status of Women, submitted after Roosevelt's death, did not consider an equal-rights amendment essential to the improvement of women's status.

In a speech delivered at Bryn Mawr in 1959, Eleanor Roosevelt declared that "women, more than men, will change the living conditions of the arenas in which they find themselves." She came to believe, as Anna Rosenberg reported in another oral history interview, that "there were many causes, many problems like the welfare system, that men really were not very interested in . . . and she saw that women were emotionally and otherwise involved with these causes. Therefore I think that she began to advocate the use of women. I think it was not only the justice that women should have equal rights, but more important to her was the fact that women can do things and be of use. . . . She didn't want this resource that she came to respect—because she knew what women could accomplish in the many areas in which she was interested—to be wasted."[43]

During the 1950s, when women were being pressured from many angles to stay in their homes, Eleanor Roosevelt's columns and public addresses continued to echo the complexity of women's right to work. In one article, she proclaimed the Wagner Act, which granted labor the right to organize for fair wages and hours, as important as the Magna Charta and the Bill of Rights.[44] Women, she idealized, might find fulfillment through such general protective legislation. Not to use more of the female work force, as Anna Rosenberg suggested, was to waste a great human resource. "My Day" describes a number of women's training programs and available part-time jobs for older women, who represented a particularly glaring waste to Eleanor Roosevelt, herself able to work tirelessly both as a volunteer and as a paid journalist until almost the moment of her death at age seventy-five.

If in her public utterances at the UN she agreed with the official United States policy of putting human political rights before economic ones, her personal vision, shaped by the deprivation she had witnessed during the Depression, was always more complex. Just as her columns helped many readers understand that the self-respect and self-reliance of people all over the world were connected with economic well-being, so her discussions of woman's role invariably championed fulfillment of social potential. "American women," she wrote in the Barnard College Bulletin in 1954, "had made more progress socially, economically, and politically than any other group whose rights and privileges were once restricted." Because domestic work had become easier, Roosevelt urged these women to play a larger part "in the broader life of the nation"—not to be intimidated by any "religious group critical of working mothers." "A woman can have a career even if she is a mother," Eleanor Roosevelt insisted in 1954—"if family members plan their lives together."[45]

Ultimately her feminism may be seen as one part of the liberal tradition that sustained her against the strident narrow-mindedness that characterized so much of this decade. She would be remembered by all people for her humanism, which was "feminist" as she saw it in its concern for social justice, but never ideological. In a 1960 address to the National Council of Women, she urged her listeners to challenge the new decade with their power as women to end war: "We have to deal in our countries with something which is called politics," she realistically declared. She insisted that women recognize the strength they had in voluntary organizations, and also support other women in government positions. She never stopped believing that women—as a political force—could "push our governments to deal with questions we think vital for the lives of our children." Eleanor Roosevelt's speech finally reflected her concern for all humanity. She spoke with the authority derived from being a woman and mother, not a political figure: "Many of the questions we deal with," she concluded, "transcend all party politics."[46]

Rachel Carson, Bethesda, Md.
Courtesy of Marie Rodell—Francis Collin Literary Agency, Brooks Photographers.

Chapter Six

Women of Letters: Apostles of Moral Indignation

In the introductory address he prepared for the conference on *Work in the Lives of Married Women*, in 1958, Erwin Canham wondered what Harriet Beecher Stowe would have said about the atomic bomb; he also lamented the existence of hate-filled white women harassing the black children pioneers who were integrating southern schools. The times were out of joint, he insisted; women were meant to be "apostles of moral indignation," not part of the forces of hate. That these hostile women were themselves victims of a social system that made integration a threat was not an issue. The need for all women to be better than men hounded every class throughout the decade, when in fact greater numbers of women were actually working behind the scenes to make integration a reality. In Canham's own field, journalism, for example, there remained a number of strong women recording moral indignation about injustices everywhere.[1]

Women newspaper publishers, also, appeared as a group to be especially interested in using their power to bring about social change. Katherine Graham, Dorothy Schiff, and Alicia Patterson joined Agnes Meyer in taking liberal stands on moral issues like McCarthyism and integration. Patterson became the only member of the McCormick newspaper clan to turn away from past isolationism to make internationalism a positive value.[2] Women culture critics appeared regularly in both newspapers and magazines discussing social possibilities and moral obligations as well as the "feminine" issues that defined the times. Canham could have taken more comfort from the visionary concerns of the liberal imagination.

Conditioned to be subtle and indirect instead of outspoken, the women writers of the 1950s often adapted their social awareness to the possibilities of the decade but they did not retreat from defining areas that needed attention. What mattered, as Richard Hofstadter pointed out in a Michigan lecture in 1953, was "the openness and generosity needed to comprehend the varieties of excellence that could be found even in a single and rather parochial society."[3]

At a time when outlets for political activity were limited, a number of gifted women transcended their parochial society in the critical journalism that has become an important part of American female literary tradition—from Margaret Fuller to Frances Fitz-Gerald. If women during the 1950s did not work together to establish their own magazines, as women had in the 1920s, or as contemporary male intellectuals were doing in founding *Dissent* and *Liberation*, a few powerful critics nevertheless found outlets for their concerns as individuals. Freda Kirchwey continued to write editorials for the *Nation* during the 1950s, even after relinquishing power as publisher; Marya Mannes reviewed regularly for the *Reporter*, helping people understand the tremendous importance of the new medium—television; Diana Trilling wrote social commentary for the *Partisan Review* as well as for the *New Leader*. Elizabeth Hardwick also began to write for the *Partisan Review* and for *Harper's*; she was quick to realize the value of the "glorious and fantastic new book" on the subjection of women, Simone de Beauvoir's *The Second Sex*.[4] Mary McCarthy confronted a wide audience in *Harper's*, *Commentary*, and the *Reporter*, while Aline Bernstein Saarinen, believing that the impact of the total environment shaped the human spirit, invested her *New York Times* art reviews with concern for the quality of life in the world around us. Although Dorothy Day's audience for the *Catholic Worker* may have originally been a committed radical group, by the 1950s its subscribers were catholic in the broadest sense. Mari Sandoz, after a lifetime of dedication to recording the lives of immigrant pioneers and American Indians, found herself by 1950 a popular national figure publishing Native American materials in both the *Saturday Evening Post* and the *Reader's Digest*.

Dorothy Thompson, who had contributed to almost every level of the American press, succumbed to the power of the *Ladies' Home Journal* in its celebration of domesticity after retiring from the newspaper world in 1958. Noting that she had written three columns a week, fifty weeks a year, over a period of seventeen years, her editor hailed her lifetime of journalistic responsibility: "Even her enemies or opponents have always been compelled to recognize and admire her honesty, strength of character, and disregard of possible injuries to her career."[5] Another important columnist who kept on writing three times a week during the 1950s was Eleanor Roosevelt.

Like Margaret Mead, who also continued to publish popular magazine articles, Roosevelt thought it important for the women who were better informed to keep speaking out, to help educate others who had not had opportunities to expand their horizons. She kept reminding her readers that most of the world did not have white skin and steadily criticized American lawmakers whose racist policies had an impact on the way the rest of the world perceived us. Well aware that men in positions of power often put down "popularizers" who attempt to clarify ideas without professional jargon, both Mead and Roosevelt thoroughly enjoyed communicating with all sorts of human beings. The give and take they encouraged taught them much about the concerns of women of all classes. When in the 1960s both women were chosen at different times to head the presidential commissions set up to explore the status of women, they were familiar with a vast range of social problems.

There were few areas of awareness during the 1960s that had not been set up for action by the group of gifted social critics from the preceding decade. Women have frequently been able to use their own sense of alienation—which distinguishes even the most socially prominent like Eleanor Roosevelt, or the most intellectually gifted like Margaret Mead—to define the social needs of other outcasts. Mari Sandoz emerged from the sandhills of Nebraska to call our attention to the history of the Sioux and the Cheyenne. Although her first book, *Old Jules*, a description of her father's life as an immigrant pioneer, had been rejected by fourteen publishers before it won the *Atlantic* nonfiction prize in 1935, Sandoz in the 1950s received a string of honorary degrees and literary awards. *Crazy Horse: The Strange Man of the Oglalas* was named in 1954 one of the "Ten Best Serious Books on the West"; in 1955 four of her other books were included among the "Hundred Best Books on the West."[6]

During the 1950s, Mari Sandoz continued to publish articles on the folkways and the Native American habits she respected. Her social consciousness had grown, Sandoz wrote, from "having at an early age become aware of the long struggle to obtain and defend a small and decent portion of individual liberty—as society became more and more complex." Moreover, she added, there was another determinant factor in her childhood: "the daily presence of an expropriated race, the American Indian. I was attracted to them very much, as children are always by men of grand bearing, graciousness, and wisdom."[7] Although political action would characterize middle-class involvement with the unjust treatment of the Native American in the 1960s, concern based on separating fact from myth, for consciousness-raising based on historical record, was part of another historical tradition reaching back to Helen Hunt Jackson. Documenting yet another century of dishonor became part of Sandoz's literary achievement as much as recording the triumphant and complex struggles involved in civilizing the West. It was during the 1950s also that Theodora Kroeber began to work on her classic of Native American anthropology, *Ishi in Two Worlds: A Biography of the Last Wild Indian in North America*. Appearing in 1961, this book would be in its seventeenth printing by 1976.[8]

Similarly, another regional author, Lillian Smith, managed to make readers confront the outrages of racism in every decade of her life as a writer. Battling cancer during the 1950s, consistently attacked by hostile reviewers, Smith continued to champion sexual freedom and racial equality. In 1954 she managed to publish an autobiographical memoir, *The Journey*, and a handbook for helping people live up to the 1954 desegregation decision: *Now Is The Time*. Since the 1944 publication of *Strange Fruit*, Smith had grown accustomed to having her work banned, but she was not prepared for the hooliganism of the vandals who set fire to her study in 1955, burning 13,000 letters and four publishable manuscripts.[9]

Aware that sexual stereotypes were as limiting to men as to women, Smith struggled in *The Journey* to define what being human meant. She believed her generation's historic mission was "to find and set up in a high place the human being revealed in his manifold differences and infinite possibilities for all to see, to be exalted by, and to identify with."[10] The human beings Smith encountered on her personal journey included the rejected of her own town: the mute, the paraplegic, and the retarded. Like Carson McCullers, whose work she had encouraged, Smith insisted on individuality, not on categorical compassion. Although Lillian Smith had always urged women to be assertive, she expressed concern for the young friend who, fearing the label "female," gave up her feminine resources and tried "to snatch from man his maleness, or his masculine privileges, and now and then his worst style of life."[11]

During the 1950s it was natural that Smith include some comment on the anxieties that made Americans appear to look "bloodkin to the Communists they claimed to abhor." In spite of, perhaps because of, all she had endured for personal beliefs, she concluded that "future generations will think of our times as an age of wholeness; when the walls began to fall; when the fragments began to be related to each other."[12] When intruders again set fire to the mountain on which she lived in 1958, she knew she was lucky to save her home, but she still refused to move. Finally, in the late 1950s, she confidently judged herself: "I am patient; I know my worth; I know my historical value to this country."[13]

Another woman whose historical value as a writer was not yet clear in the 1950s was Dorothy Day. The daughter and sister of journalists, Dorothy Day once explained that her whole life had been in journalism. Even her first experiences with poverty were literary: Upton Sinclair's *The Jungle* had made her notice the social inequities around her in Chicago. The written word was part of her spiritual calling. Indeed, even her conversion to Catholicism had been influenced by readings in St. Augustine, Dostoevsky, and William James. And James continued to help define the purpose of her life's work. In a television summation, she used his words to describe her own life: "I am done with great things and big things, great institutions and big success, and I am for those tiny invisible molecular moral forces that work from individual to individual, creeping through the crannies of the world like so many rootlets or like the capillary oozing of water, yet which, if you give them time, will rend the hardest monuments of man's pride."[14]

Along with feeding the poor and publishing the *Catholic Worker*, Day found time in the 1950s to publish an early autobiography, *The Long Loneliness*. From many angles she discussed her need to take action against life's injustices. Women, she felt, understood especially what the long loneliness meant; she was convinced that communal living and structured religion would help combat individual pain through purposeful commitment.[15] A practical viewpoint was her contribution to the *Catholic Worker*, in contrast to coeditor, Peter Maurin's consistently ideological stance. During the 1950s—the time of the Korean War and forced civilian defense drills—Day remained a dedicated pacifist. And during that period of growing affluence she continued to remind Americans of the poverty in our midst, and to suggest that giving without sacrifice had no moral significance. The *Catholic Worker* also attempted in the 1950s to extend American awareness of new nations looking for moral examples as well as for technical advice. In a period of isolated individualism and political suspicion, Dorothy Day managed to make the parable of the loaves and the fishes an astonishing reality: "We have all known the long loneliness and we have learned that the only solution to human problems was love and that love comes with community."[16]

Other critics, no less concerned with the quality of American life, were more worldly. Mary McCarthy published several eloquent essays on the dilemma of the liberal during the 1950s.[17] In a *Reporter* article based on a speech given to the American Committee for Cultural Freedom in 1952, Mary McCarthy responded to Joseph McCarthy's attacks on categories of intellectuals. People who favored racial equality, for example, plus progressive education, plus peace, minus Senators McCarthy and McCarran and teachers' loyalty oaths, were automatically regarded by the senator as security risks. Mary McCarthy was equally suspicious of the similarly easy approval by category of people who believed in cultural anthropology, or in the Sullivan school of psychiatry, or abstract-expressionist painting. She tried to make her readers realize that the emergency mentality of totalitarianism was taking over democratic options. "What we will do," she declared with logical insistence, "if we persist in our demands for loyalty . . . will be to create new underground men behind the facade of conformity, new lies, new evasions, new human beings who float like glittering icebergs on the surface of society, with the perilous eight-ninths submerged." We will end up a society of surfaces, she concluded, "where papers and books circulate freely, like so many phantom abstractions, while their human authors and readers have been suppressed or excluded from the country."[18]

Reinforcing a belief in "goods" (that is, values) rather than "rights" in a speech delivered to teachers in 1952, "The Contagion of Ideas," McCarthy urged that we treat individuals not in terms of what was owing to them by society, but in terms of what an open society owed to its own image. Urging "common sense" as the informing spirit of all democratic institutions "from the jury system to universal suffrage," she remarked that, far from being in danger of indoctrination by communism, American students seemed more in danger of "being stupefied by the complacent propaganda for democracy" which was "pious, priggish and groupy." Noting that we had not behaved toward Fascists during the war—rooting them out, demanding loyalty oaths—the way we were then acting toward Communists, McCarthy concluded trenchantly that we were genuinely afraid of the germ of truth in communist criticism of the injustices in our society. "And this germ-phobia will be with us as long as we ourselves try to sell the white lie of democracy abroad, to the starving nations who are in fact the 'children'—the ignorant and uneducated—whose allegiance we question, rightly, and whose judgment of us we, rightly, dread."[19]

Although she was quick to defend the United States from the clichéd, inaccurate, criticisms of a foreigner, Simone de Beauvoir ("Mlle. Gulliver en Amérique"), Mary McCarthy refused to condone the methods we were then using to protect our way of life. Just as Dorothy Day enjoyed thinking of the impact of small human gestures on large social goals, Mary McCarthy also speculated on the details of her own experience as sources of insight into broader political issues. One of her most powerful essays, "Artists in Uniform," an indictment of anti-Semitism published in *Harper's* in 1953, appeared to be an anecdotal encounter with an army colonel on a train. Proud of her "modest contribution to sanity in our times," McCarthy's self-analysis is masterful as she tries to imagine how the men in the club car place her as Communist or Jew, and how she herself, a quarter Jewish, must react: "It occurred to me that defense of the Jews could be a subtle and safe form of anti-Semitism, an exercise of patronage: as a rational Gentile, one could feel superior both to the Jews and the anti-Semites."[20] The essay remains a perceptive indictment of innocence as it explores the reality of prejudice in American life.

Never reluctant to confront the flaws in democratic mythology, McCarthy also used social class to measure the quality of women's lives. "Up the Ladder from Charm to Vogue," published in 1950, describes how American women were conditioned to see themselves. Ahead of many intellectual women in using popular magazines as an index of taste to reveal more profound changes in

American life, McCarthy observed shifts in vocabulary and styles that catered to the growing number of clerical workers. In contrast with the older generation of fashion editors who wore their hats to work at *Harper's Bazaar* and *Vogue*, the new editors were live-wires with no social pretensions. "Youth" and "fun" were becoming key words, McCarthy observed, in the "dream mentality of a civilization of office conscripts."[21] She realized that the whimsical aristocratic readers of the older magazines were being replaced by a growing world of women at work.

Convinced that an appeal to the fashion-minded was rarely serious, McCarthy mocked the decadent literature included in fashion magazines as tonic to the flabby personality; an ephemeral, gimmicky publication, *Flair*, she did not hesitate to label "an instrument of mass snobbery." She attacked American preoccupation with deodorants and "personal hygiene" for spreading the lower-middle-class fear that social failure was the result of lack of fastidiousness, a tendency she found in *Mademoiselle*. *Glamour*, on the other hand, earned her praise for publishing a commonsensical editorial suggesting that the working girl lived too much in dreams and illusions. In *Glamour*, working women were made more aware of their own worth; "maturity and dignity are valued," McCarthy wrote. "Photographs of secretaries of well-known persons, photographs of successful women who began as secretaries, a history of the secretarial profession, emphasize the dignity of office work and give it status through history and a tradition."[22]

Exposing the pretensions and illusions that were foisted on American women as essential to their self-esteem was part of McCarthy's contribution to feminist thought of the 1950s. Although fear of narrow ideology might have kept her from ever calling herself a feminist, the tribute to Vassar she published in *Holiday* in 1951 made it clear how much McCarthy's independent mind owed to those "intellectually elegant unmarried women professors" she had so respected at an isolated woman's college.[23] If in 1951 she saw the Vassar graduate in danger of becoming more often a volunteer than a career seeker, she herself remained part of another tradition—but both shared the seriousness fostered in an atmosphere of wholehearted commitment to women's minds.

Mary McCarthy was also one of the first critics to attack the notorious Lundberg and Farnham book, *Modern Woman, the Lost Sex*, when it appeared in 1947, urging women to return to the home. Her summary of the book's thesis, that "woman can recapture the orgasm by accepting her biological destiny," suggested to McCarthy that the authors were totally disingenuous. "No jot of evidence," McCarthy noticed, was "brought forward to support the crucial proposition that the large family and the orgasm are interdependent." At a time when homosexuality was rarely championed publicly, McCarthy went on to challenge Lundberg and Farnham: "And the unsexed career woman may be frigid with men and amorous with women—is the Lesbian orgasm not certified by these authorities?[24]" McCarthy's criticisms would be documented with evidence from the Kinsey report on the sexual behavior of American women when it appeared six years later, ending once and for all the ideas about women's "lost" sexuality.

Although Mary McCarthy labeled herself a humanist, there can be little doubt that she was trying to define women's possibilities in the richest possible way. So too was Marya Mannes, who wrote regularly for the *Reporter* during the 1950s, paying a good deal of attention to the effect of commercial interests on women's socialization. Mannes, primarily a TV reviewer, made her opinions felt, as women often have, by adapting to the new. Television, not yet considered intellectually respectable, became for Mannes a medium that deserved serious attention in terms of its future power, as well as a focus for her personal responses to many aspects of American life.

"The death of art," Mannes wrote in 1953, "is to please all and offend none." She remembered how responsive large audiences had been to the good music her father conducted at free concerts, and she frequently referred to the success of the BBC in using TV for educational purposes. Never sympathetic with the artists and intellectuals who preferred to avoid television altogether, Mannes wrote: "This communication—so direct and so limitless—is open to the thinkers and dreamers and creators of this country if they want it. If they relinquish it," she warned, "the wreckers will take over."[25]

During World War II Marya Mannes had undergone an investigation of her work by the Office of War Information, a procedure designed by certain congressmen to discredit FDR, and she therefore understood the anxiety and powerlessness connected with congressional hearings. When she found herself on the *Reporter* staff during the McCarthy era she knew there was plenty to write about and rage against. She gave credit to the few courageous commentators like Eric Sevareid and Edward R. Murrow, who made Americans aware of what was happening in our country; on Murrow's show, "The People v. McCarthy," she remarked, "the brave speak up." And she listed by name sponsors like Alcoa and Pontiac who were backing away from the fearless men who called the shots as they saw them. Urging that nonprofit foundations protect such guardians of the public conscience, Mannes eventually lost her own TV spot on the NBC news. She later remarked that she had paid the price of an independence that made it impossible to tailor her comments on air or in print for mass acceptability. When the Army-McCarthy hearings were televised in June 1954—"a picture that should obsess American memory"—Mannes emphasized the heroism of the army's lawyer, Joseph Welch: "A presence not easily forgotten—that of a civilized man in the tradition of an older law and society."[26]

Totalitarian behavior distressed her on many occasions. When she turned against our military intrusion in Vietnam in the 1960s (she left the *Reporter* ostensibly in disagreement over this issue), she did not automatically accept the government of Ho Chi Minh. Mannes labeled herself finally as *Out of My Time;* like many other women, she refused to compromise her values to fit more neatly into male systems of success. Her autobiography continued to insist on old-fashioned standards: "Perhaps our last duty," she argued, "is to fight for the civilization of reason."[27] She believed that society falls apart without the mind and heart and judgment that shape a code of civility and concern for others. During the 1950s Mannes clarified a number of social issues and public outrages to justify this point of view.

Perhaps her most eloquent essay was a detailed description of the 1955 murder of a Korean graduate student at the University of Pennsylvania by an aimless teenage gang. Knowing that violence grows out of violence, Mannes also described the plans for a new "house of youth" designed to prevent future similar crimes. People had to learn again and again that young criminals were "made to feel that they are nothing and nobody, and the only way they know to become something and somebody is to harm themselves and others." In connection with social problems, Mannes also wrote about overcrowded schools and the inequities of education in Harlem; and she also commented on books and programs related to mental illness with a liberal's belief in progress. She may have been the first critic to point out how strange it was at the time that "not one of the nineteen million Negroes in this country is shown on television as a consumer of products."

Afraid that TV might be "mesmoronizing" too many people, she took pains to praise serious shows such as "The Open Mind," which treated issues like anti-Semitism, homosexuality, and mental retardation, and "Omnibus," an intellectual variety show that presented a series of dramas on American history in 1956, reminding us that we had a tradition of heroes who combined knowledge and courage to prevail over politicians who were "ignorant, violent, and compromised."[28]

A number of other distinguished women journalists and critics, including Maya Pines, Claire Sterling, Mary McCarthy, Flora Lewis, and Nora Sayre, also wrote for the *Reporter* during the 1950s; the magazine was a natural outlet for Mannes's own self-conscious feminism. She had resigned from a promising future in fashion editing, and also refused to renew a contract for a TV talk show she thought would compromise her more serious self. Later feminists might interpret such behavior as an abdication of responsibility or fear of power rather than as an assertion of principle. But there can be little doubt that Mannes was ahead of her time in helping readers realize how extensively the image of American women was shaped by the media.

Her TV critiques deplored the assumption that women had no interest in ideas. She protested against shows such as "Bride and Groom," which urged young innocents to marry in front of the camera, "Ladies Date," which catered to "the unanswered girlish dreams of women over forty," and "Here's Looking at You," which pandered to the "almost desperate absorption of these women in externals which at their age should count least among their assets."[29] Shows like "Queen for a Day," "Chance for Romance," and "Strike It Rich" Mannes challenged for exploiting women's fantasy lives rather than helping them use their minds. She also looked critically at women commentators like Kitty McCaffery, Maggi McNellis, Martha Deane, Emily Kimbrough, and Marian Taylor, who too often chattered aimlessly and did not know how to interview an accomplished woman like Vera Micheles Dean, Research Director of the Foreign Policy Association, or I. Rice Pereira, the distinguished nonrepresentational artist. Mannes tried to show that the medium—not just

the commercials—was reinforcing women's domestic role by showing most situation-comedy heroines to be "weaker, softer, duller,
slower, dumber . . . and just as cold as their male counterparts."
Soap operas in 1954 made sure that career women were never happy,
Mannes observed—a strange commentary in a country where "sixteen million women were wage earners." The formulas for woman's
fulfillment consistently demanded that careers be sacrificed for
"split-level security," and that "no mother could express relief at the
absence of her children."[30]

When Mannes later attempted to write fiction for women's magazines she was asked to rewrite the ages of her characters because
readers were not supposed to be interested in stories about love over
thirty. Heroines could not be plump, foreign, or have bad teeth;
nor—in a country where the divorce rate was rising daily—could
they bemoan stale marriages. Although Mannes may have exaggerated somewhat, she is to be credited for pointing out how damaging
this youth culture was to those older women, who were not yet in
the work force but felt liberated by many appliances to watch programs with as little wit as "Queen for a Day." Unfortunately, the
satirical sketches she wrote about women for the *Reporter* absorbed
many of the stereotypical values she fought against in her critical
writing; her "lady-editor," for example, became a quintessential career woman who gave "left-overs of feeling" to her own family.[31]

The women of letters of the 1950s felt they had to resist such ten-
dencies in themselves. They were concerned above all that women
retain their own custodial feminine values; they valued the personal
relationships so often put aside in the world of masculine successes.
Eve Merriam, another voice of conscience at the time, articulated
with force the dilemma both she and Mannes confronted: "Today's
career women are at last becoming the equal of men. It can be reck-
oned as one of the greatest negative achievements of all time. They
can now be almost as ruthless, almost as selfish, almost as unpublic-
spirited." Committed feminists on one level, both Merriam and
Mannes nevertheless cherished the ambivalence that forced them to
make conditions for their own modest success. Marya Mannes called
herself, finally, "an intellectual hermaphrodite."[32]

Like the Beats and the psychoanalysts who acknowledged that we
all have a drive to become both sexes, Mannes believed that human
beings had differing degrees of sexual identity. She thought that admitting as much would liberate men as well as women; but andro-

gyny may also be threatening to both sexes. During the 1950s, although attitudes had begun to change, it was as hard for men to understand how they could be liberated by sharing women's values as it was for women to recognize that their commitments were not always of their own choosing. Working with words made Marya Mannes sensitive to the way men and women were labeled differently for the same qualities: "A man of strong opinions is defined as 'having deep convictions,'" she wrote; a woman so constituted is merely "opinionated," and, always, "aggressive." That the words "single woman" or "spinster" should imply inferior worth, she would insist, is only "one of the damaging by-products of our consumer-based, security-mad domestic pattern."[33]

Believing that large families should be viewed as an indulgence rather than a duty, Mannes addressed a hypothetical "Letter to a Girl" urging that she not assume from the cradle that she had only one road in life and one function: "For you are not one entity, but several, having masculine qualities as well as feminine." "Let us by all means love men," she argued elsewhere, "bear children and love them, cook well and like it; but let that not be an end any more than man's work is an end, but rather parts of an infinitely larger whole which is membership in the human race."[34]

As science and technology were helping women extend their worlds, Mannes could see that the status quo, "dearest to those who benefit by it," was changing. If her concern for individualism and good manners seemed out of place in the more ideological feminism to come, there can be little doubt that her articulation of many discriminatory attitudes toward women prepared the way for a more radical future.

Like the other women social critics of this decade who had developed strong egos at an earlier time, Diana Trilling also attempted to reach a broad variety of readers. She published articles in *Esquire* and *Redbook* as well as in the *Nation*, *New Leader*, and the *American Scholar*. Involvement in the world was essential to her self-definition.

In "Liberal Anti-Communism Revisited," an essay included with her writings of the 1970s, she takes pains to clarify the differences between anti-Communism and anti-McCarthyism in the 1950s, as a response to Lillian Hellman's references to both Trillings in *Scoundrel Time*.[35] Characteristic of Diana Trilling's writing is not only a fierce moral tone, more self-righteous and less self-conscious than Hellman's, but also an ongoing concern that history be interpreted as a complex repetitive force. Her efforts to make readers understand the 1930s origins of the split between Communist sympathizers and liberals provide valuable documentary materials for historians, although she might profitably have reached beyond personal involvement to identify a deeper tradition of dissent in American thought. As a political analyst, Trilling sees herself always attempting "to look beneath the appearance of things, especially the things which announce themselves as virtue."[36]

Lillian Hellman's 1952 refusal to tailor her conscience "to fit this year's fashion" in order not to betray friends became to Trilling "a masterpiece of moral showmanship." Although Hellman's eloquent letter to Congress made many Americans think more seriously about what the House Un-American Activities Committee was doing, Trilling thought it more important to point out that Hellman herself also pleaded the Fifth Amendment rather than go to jail. The fear of communism seemed more real on Claremont Avenue than the fear of totalitarian tactics within our own government. "No one can call himself a liberal who is not an anti-Communist,"[37] Trilling had written, dogmatically redefining liberalism to suit the times.

The clearly defined social-intellectual-geographic world centered around Columbia University made it easier for Diana Trilling to criticize Alger Hiss without similar emotional involvement; she saw J. Robert Oppenheimer, the child of European intellectuals, more sympathetically as a victim of his own political naiveté. Both Hiss and Oppenheimer emerged from the 1950s as examples of idealists unfortunately drawn into real political life. And in spite of Trilling's intense anti-Communist bias, she characterized both men as enormously complicated human beings. Trilling summed up 1950s liberalism as the refusal to countenance any abrogation of basic human and civic rights: "I saw in the McCarthy period . . . no contradiction, only an entire consistency in having been opposed to both Communism and McCarthy."[38]

Where other cultural realities were concerned, Diana Trilling remained more open-minded. It was she, for example, in 1958, who joined the crowd at Columbia to listen to the Beat poets Allen Ginsberg and Gregory Corso. In "The Other Night at Columbia: A Report from the Academy," her *Partisan Review* editors worried that she was giving a tasteless, irresponsible element of American life too much attention; when she told W. H. Auden that she had been moved, he responded that he was ashamed of her. She tried to make readers appreciate Ginsberg and his friends for their warmth and vulnerability in spite of their sophomoric rebellions.[39] If the Beats went on to mock this essay in parody, "The Other Night in Heaven," they could not deny its sympathy with their anti-institutionalism. Trilling helped establishment academics see the Beat poets—in their reactions against technology, suburbia, and organization men—as legitimate heirs of Walt Whitman. It could not have been easy for her to confront the reality, in another context, that "politics is today the least revolutionary aspect of social protest."[40]

Trilling's "feminism" appears as another facet of liberal complexity—both paralyzing and humane—that was so characteristic of the decade. As early as 1943, Diana Trilling wrote sympathetically about Alice James; she knew what it felt like to be overlooked, or identified with the more famous member of her family. She used her role as book reviewer for the *Nation* to call attention to new women writers like Jean Stafford, or the mature talent of sixty-year-old Isabel Bolton, designated in 1949 "the best woman writer of fiction in this country today." Although her later tribute to Marilyn Monroe saw the movie star as an example of the "revenge that life seems so regularly to take upon distinction,"[41] rather than as an exploited woman, she forced us to consider all the social factors involved in Monroe's untimely death, as well as to appreciate the quality of her abundant sexuality.

Trilling touched on many of the issues later feminists would dwell on in more political terms. She paid tribute to Margaret Mead and Karen Horney as important Freudian revisionists, acknowledging, in spite of her own frequent homage, that there was "small doubt that Freudian doctrine . . . has powered an anti-female movement in American culture." Later, too, she would recall how overwhelming was "the widespread propaganda designed to persuade women in the late forties and early fifties that their mental health lay in devoting themselves to motherhood and the art of gracious living."[42]

Her 1950 review of Margaret Mead's *Male and Female*, "Men, Women, and Sex," criticized Mead for not adequately clarifying "the polarities to which the educated woman of our day is subjected." Trilling felt it necessary to argue against the latest generation of college girls who were scoffing at the pretense of setting important work goals for themselves: "The tending of babies becomes the boasted rather than the lamented occupation of educated women." She understood Mead's concern to give women's biological role greater

dignity, but remembering the intense demands of the 1920s feminists who shaped Mead's own self-image caused Trilling to accuse
Mead of "pious sentimentality" for asserting that women merely be
encouraged "to bring to all their activities the special talents that we
assume pertain to their femininity, the patience, delicacy, and intuition we suppose they have learned in tending the young and sick."[43]

Accepting "uncertainty" as the unfortunate essence of this stage of
woman's development, Trilling well understood the problem of
Mead's relationship to her audience—"now patronizing, now flatter-
ing its intelligence . . . a natural if excessive response to the ambivalent regard in which our society holds the woman who would dare
to be ambitious and successful as a man." The conceptual incoher-
ence in *Male and Female*, she perceived, derived from similar internal
sexual conflict. Indeed, one of the most incisive observations in this
essay applies to other articulate women as well: "If we look at the
work of our most talented women writers of fiction, we see how
commonly it is obscured by private reference, hidden patterns of rea-
soning, excessive discursion, over-modification of idea, and other
forms of non-declarativeness. Individual temperament cannot account for something this endemic in culture. We must conclude that
the American woman has reason to fear speaking in a way which
cannot be misundertood."[44]

Personal struggles to avoid such style-traps often make Trilling's
style dogmatic. In the Mead essay, she labels *Modern Women: The Lost
Sex* a book of "dull meanness of spirit," as she concludes with praise
for Margaret Mead's underlying effort to guarantee to women "full
participation in the life of culture."[45]

Looking at her own Radcliffe education in "Are Women's Colleges
Really Necessary?" (1951), Trilling reflects the same painful ambivalence she had described in Margaret Mead. In remembering how
outraged she was by a Dean's speech urging women to think about
Keats and Shelley as they washed dishes, Trilling translates momentary anger into the pain of the human condition; the purpose of all
education, she rationalizes, is to help "transcend the mean circumstances of ordinary existence." She had thought her Harvard education good because it flattered female intellects and "gave woman a
scale to measure her defeats"; but later she noticed that such traditional schooling "trained in us too much humility before authority as
a corollary of our humility before learning." She was clearly arguing
against the functional education for women that had started to take
hold in the 1950s. Differing from many of her contemporaries, Trill-

ing insisted that the only "practical way to treat women is *im*-practi-
cally—that is to treat them as if they were the full and absolute
equals of men."[46] That the tools given to the women educated as
equals of men enabled them to challenge the authorities that trained
them remains clear. Women of letters during the 1950s sustained the
valuable American feminist tradition—of moral dialogue with the
world.

In a review of uncollected writings, *Janet Flanner's World (1932–
1975)*, Stephen Spender singled out a quality that might be said to
define the entire group of women of letters. He wrote that Flanner
did much more than describe events: "She maintained standards of
civilization."[47]

Like Smith, Trilling, and Mannes, Janet Flanner also wrote sympathetic and penetrating criticism about other women. As a foreign
correspondent from France, Germany, and Italy, she used her Indi-
ana-trained common sense to make us aware of what we shared with
the rest of the world, as well as what was different. Like Eleanor
Roosevelt, in the 1950s, she contributed more to our renewed commitment to internationalism than to our ongoing domesticity. Aware
of the intense intellectual lives of French women, Flanner was one of
the first American woman to take note of Simone de Beauvoir's classic, *Le Deuxième Sex*, when it appeared in 1950. Living in France, she
thought the book would seem archaic to American women who
believed themselves on a more equal footing with men; but she
defended it from the "rough, unjust reviews" of the French. Recognizing the importance of *The Second Sex* as a complex vision of civilized women, Flanner described it as "a dry wry job written
straightforwardly by an intelligent, determined woman, a practical
observer who, having inherited three thousand years of European
civilization, has something conclusive on her mind that she wants to
say." De Beauvoir, she neatly summarized, "thinks that women's defects and limitations are precisely what society has desired of her."
Flanner praised the "instinct for liberty" that characterized the first
volume of de Beauvoir's autobiography when it appeared in 1958.
And she also perceived the worth of Simone Weil, as "spiritual refreshment—noting, as early as 1950, the power of Weil's appeal to
the "lay-religious soul," which would later make her a significant cult
figure.[48]

In 1959, when the United States Information Agency put on a
display called "The Twenties: American Writers in Paris and Their
Friends," Flanner found opportunity to stress the importance of the

tradition of American women expatriates—in which she might have included herself. Europe continued to provide an escape for creative American women. Like Sylvia Beach and Gertrude Stein, Flanner saw Marguerite Caetani de Bassiano, American-born editor of *Botteghe Oscure*, continuing to shape contemporary literary taste from Europe in the 1950s.

Janet Flanner paid special attention to the arts perhaps in reaction to the aesthetic starvation of a Quaker Hoosier childhood, but she commented also on every important political and moral issue of her time. During the 1950s, she recorded the French reaction to our behavior at Little Rock, and their amused bewilderment at the antics of Cohn and Schine—sent by McCarthy to clean out "communist" writings in our USIA libraries—to the obvious detriment of American prestige abroad. After the Soviet suppression of the Hungarian revolt in 1956, she called attention to Jean Paul Sartre's "great modern corrective pamphlet" on communism; but her more personal comment that the puppets in *Petrouchka* represented the Russians' "perpetual search for personal liberty " may have had as much impact. In the same decade that appeared to sanction Farnham and Lundberg's insistence on the domestic orgasm, Janet Flanner celebrated Colette for her serious analysis of "sex and the sexual response and of sexual variety and ambiguity."[49]

The indexes of the volumes of Flanner's collected essays suggest her amazing versatility. William Shawn, editor of the *New Yorker*, remarked that her reporting methods were "eccentric and seemingly haphazard." Like many women's writings, he said, "they appeared more intuitive than logical." But, he concluded: "as if by inadvertence, she wrote political, social, and cultural history of the first order." Like many other distinguished women, Flanner refused "to allow her thoughts to fall into molds or patterns." Shawn's final tribute suggested a more important dimension: "Although nominally a journalist, . . . Janet Flanner was above all, and abidingly, a poet."[50]

Another significant voice among the women of letters in the 1950s was a critic of art and architecture, Aline Bernstein Louchheim Saarinen. Like Janet Flanner, she consistently managed to invest the particulars of her journalism with a personal moral viewpoint. Although no editor has yet bothered to collect her commentaries on American art and culture, published regularly in the *New York Times* after 1947, her work remains a valuable part of the feminist heritage of culture criticism which embraces art not just as aesthetic satisfaction, but as part of the riches of everyday living. Saarinen looked at everything: playgrounds, postage stamps, stage sets, jacket designs for records, and war memorials. She tried to make everyone aware of the impact of the total environment.

Although a Junior Phi Beta Kappa at Vassar, Saarinen chose not to be a professional scholar, but, like other women of letters, to be a journalist, a popularizer of good taste. Not reluctant to name the "six worst man-made objects,"[51] she received more than one award for her efforts to maintain high critical standards, but she was not snobbish about amateurs, and she also defended the new abstractionists who were having a hard time becoming accepted in the general culture. In 1955 Saarinen praised an outdoor exhibit sponsored by the city of Boston, which included works of both amateur and professional and displayed the artifacts of local craftsmakers next to the fine arts. During the 1960s she became a TV personality, discussing women's issues along with the social dimensions of art.

When Aline Saarinen published *The Proud Possessors* in 1958, a book about the lives of American art collectors, she not only recorded the idiosyncrasies of a group of powerful individuals but also made readers accept the seriousness of the collector mentality. A number of women emerged as leaders in the establishment of great American collections of art. From Mrs. Potter Palmer and Isabella Stewart Gardner in the nineteenth century to Katherine Sophie Dreier, Electra Havemeyer Webb, Gertrude Stein and the Cone sisters, Peggy Guggenheim, Lillie Bliss, Abby Aldrich Rockefeller, and Edith Halpert (the gallery owner) in the twentieth century, Saarinen made it clear that women found useful social roles in extending their private tastes to educate the public.

With consummate aesthetic judgment and literary skill, Aline Saarinen, so like the women she wrote about, extended the reality of art to a large audience.[52]

Even the decade's most popular sentimental collection of essays, Anne Morrow Lindbergh's *Gift from the Sea*, although it glorified "patience and faith," suggested the need to reevaluate woman's role. "Woman must come of age by herself," Lindbergh wrote.[53] But she too warned that she must not become competitive in order to do so. From her private island, Anne Lindbergh's prescription for enriching life was to turn inward, an idea that harmonized with the interior life more competitive writers were also exploring. At a time when opportunities for women were limited, *Gift from the Sea* sold hundreds of thousands of copies. Many women clearly wanted to identify with Anne Morrow Lindbergh's vision of personal choice. Her view of herself as *both* writer and mother must have reinforced thousands of housebound women's dreams of their own possibilities.

What is impressive about all these women of letters is how loyal they remained to their individual visions of what really matters in life. Although they tried to reach a broad audience, they did not pander to it or shift their viewpoints to modify the moral concerns that meant much to them. But they did not represent any group ideology, and their feminism never limited their humanism. What they yearned for was a world in which women's greater social sensitivity improves life for everyone. In articulating personal moral concerns during the 1950s, not only did they register the ongoing indignation Erwin Canham overlooked, but they also kept an important literary tradition alive.

Shirley Jackson.
Photograph by Laurence Jackson Hyman.

Adrienne Rich.
Reprinted from Radcliffe Yearbook, 1951.

Harriette Arnow.
Courtesy of Harriette Arnow.

Gwendolyn Brooks.
Courtesy of International Portrait Gallery.

Chapter Seven

Writers of Imagination: Private Worlds and Social Visions

U nlike the moralists, the women of letters who continued to confront America with outright criticisms of its flaws, many imaginative writers chose a less direct way to assert themselves. The cheapness of paper, as Virginia Woolf pointed out in her famous essay "Professions for Women," made it possible for women to succeed as writers before they succeeded in other professions; society did not have to invest much in their talents. Although personal struggles to kill the "Angel in the House"—the spirit that was always urging women to put the needs of other people before their own—were often fierce, words remained an effective weapon. During the 1950s the pen and the typewriter became the most powerful means women had to assert their individuality and their social imagination.[1]

Our most distinguished woman writer, Katherine Anne Porter, published only one long story during the 1950s. About a crippled servant girl disdainful of pity, "Holiday" celebrated the vitality available to the most limited members of American society. Porter contributed as well to the 1950s body of women's critical writing. Challenged for entering a field dominated by men, she shed dazzling light on the creative process in her 1956 essay on "Noon Wine." Sex, she insisted, had no more to do with critical expertise than it did with

art. If we do not expect artists to be good at everything, she responded to Robert Penn Warren, why should we expect critics to be
so? Forced to defend her attitudes in a debate with Donald Sutherland in 1959 over an attack on Gertrude Stein's autobiographies, Porter asserted her own artistic credo. Never an active feminist, she
became outraged that Sutherland saw her criticism of Stein as female
malice rather than as testimony to her belief in writing as a statement
of order designed to make sense out of the confusion of life.[2]

"You are welcome to disagree with me as much as you choose,
criticize my work as severely as you like," she challenged; "but please
don't expose yourself by putting it on the grounds that I am a
woman." Typical of women at this time, Porter did not hesitate to
acknowledge sexual differences; she believed that women felt less
need for asserting themselves by analyzing and judging everything:
"they do not, in a word, feel a need to be God." She concluded that
women writers don't seem "to need to classify themselves, or join a
trend, or name their school." The most complex vision informed her
own literary practice. Celebrating the "human faculties" both sexes
shared, she declared: "What I always hoped for myself was that I
might keep a warm heart and cultivate a cool head."[3]

That a writer of Porter's prodigious talent should have found it
necessary to justify herself suggests the extent of the decade's hostility to the competitive creative woman. In 1958 Porter took care to
stress how important it was to encourage gifted artists: "I have no
patience with this dreadful idea that whatever you have in you has
to come out, that you can't suppress true talent. People can be bent,
distorted, and completely crippled." When she declared her disappointment in the "middle-classness" that was dominating the times,
and driving young artists to get married and "have lots of children
and live like everyone else," we can easily believe that gifted women
were foremost in her mind.[4]

Writing by Region

Other southern writers more specifically concerned with ideas of
alienation also flourished during the 1950s. Katherine Anne Porter
added her encouraging appreciation to the critical enthusiasm about
Flannery O'Connor, who published *Wise Blood* in 1952[5] and an unforgettable group of stories, *A Good Man Is Hard to Find*, in 1955. In
1954 Eudora Welty published *The Ponder Heart, The Bride of Innisfal-*

len, and a collection, *Selected Stories;* and Caroline Gordon published *The Strange Children* in 1951 and *The Malefactors* in 1956. These were visions of personal intellectual worlds affirming the mystery in life and the reality of individual salvation. Shirley Ann Grau revealed a talent for local color in *The Black Prince* and *The Hard Blue Sky*—both published in the 1950s. In 1951 Carson McCullers brought out *The Ballad of the Sad Café,* perhaps the most extreme example of literary identity with outcasts. In 1954 Ellen Glasgow's publishers posthumously presented *The Woman Within,* a fictionalized summary of her life emphasizing the willpower Glasgow used to overcome southern cultural rigidities. In spite of domestic and political limitations, the female imagination managed to flourish in the south. Mary Lee Settle also began in the 1950s to record the southern past in *The Beulah Quintet,* a series of carefully documented historical novels that would win her the National Book Award in 1978.

Perhaps the most overlooked southern writer of the period was one whose metaphors were drawn directly from everyday realities. Harriette Arnow described Kentucky workers' families dominated by women who display incredible strength. In *Hunter's Horn* (1949), Arnow articulated a woman's reaction to the monomaniacal hunt that defines so much male mythology in American literature. Along with Jean Stafford's *The Mountain Lion* (1947) and Kay Boyle's *The Crazy Hunter* (reprinted in 1958) this atomic age story reinforces a female literary tradition that demands a more complex respect for nature than many male writers—identifying with primitive hunters' initiations—have been able to imagine. Although the courage to face death and disaster has been part of the American woman's literary heritage since Anne Bradstreet, so too has been a more insistent dependence on nature. The intellectual arrogance of an Ahab is rarely available to any woman concerned with the survival of her children.

Although *The Dollmaker,* published in 1954, focused on the lives of the poor rather than on the newly affluent, it may still be the most representative woman's work of the decade. The novel describes the pains and conflicts involved in an American family's migration from the hills of Kentucky to the industrial world of Detroit, as well as the tensions of a loving mother who is also an artist. Gertie Nevels, the heroine, is gifted and responsible; she does not want to adjust to the new environment because she sees so clearly the price her family pays for economic survival. But the Nevels cannot go back to the hills where Gertie derived so much of her own strength from an earlier closeness to nature. By making Gertie a talented woodcarver as well as a reliable mother, Harriette Arnow suggests also that art may be a means to women's spiritual survival in an industrial world of confining ugliness. That Gertie must finally destroy the beautiful block of wood she has been saving for carving the figure of Christ becomes almost as much an indictment of the culture as the physical disasters that befall her children.

Joyce Carol Oates's tribute to *The Dollmaker*, "our most unpretentious masterpiece," suggests that "the social dislocation of these Kentucky 'hillbillies' is an expression of the general doom of most of mankind." She sees the corruption of Arnow's successful characters as "more basic to our American experience" than the failure of the other characters.[6] The compromises that many women refused to make, Arnow reminds us, are not a matter of choice for the poor. Not every American, even in 1954, was affluent. As many women writers have managed to do, Arnow translated traditional responsibilities for families into metaphors of greater problems in American life. Her early concerns about women working recorded in "Washerwoman's Day," reappeared in the 1950s in Tillie Olsen's work.[7] Although these women, writing in a decade of consumerism, were striving to bring a greater range of female sensibility into print, the audience for feminine social realism remained small. As a nation we seemed more concerned to make domestic myths.

The southern literary renaissance included some sentimental writers who also played useful social roles. Frances Gray Patton's books were examples of attacks on the smugness of white supremacy. The enormously popular *Good Morning, Miss Dove* (1954) paid tribute to the strong spinster teacher whose inner self-confidence permitted her to reject trendiness and make the most of being single.

The peculiar dilemmas of southern women, so long part of a tradition of ladies on pedestals—from which they watched their husbands make love to unwilling blacks—enabled them to articulate sharply an alienated perspective characteristic of the entire South. Many of the ironies of southern history were always part of a woman's sensibility. Another gifted writer, Elizabeth Spencer, who left the South in 1953, devoted her first three novels to exploring its meaning. *The Crooked Way* (1952) and *The Voice at the Back Door* (1956) dealt specifically with the individual's problems in coming to terms with the social heritage of the Civil War: "My grandfather could remember the close of the Civil War, and my elder brother's nurse had been a slave."[8] By no means was her writing indifferent to the moral anguish involved in the contemporary restructuring of race relations in the South.

Elizabeth Janeway wisely suggests that the post–World War II women writers' interest in eccentric characters reflects the social and economic circumstances of a South haunted by memories of defeat, occupation, and powerlessness: "An analogy can be drawn between these conditions and the normal subordination that has been the or-dinary lot of women and that was becoming increasingly the subject of literature." It was natural for southern women writers to feel this connection, Janeway concludes. "The idea of another sort of life, tangent to that of the mainstream, but running its course according to different rules, is familiar to literature."[9] Writers like Flannery O'Connor, Carson McCullers, and Eudora Welty, while in no way specifically feminist, are indirect critics of society who have moved a long way from the mythology of the southern lady as they explore the narrow roles available to modern southern women.

O'Connor's preoccupation with theology might link her techni-cally with many women of the 1950s who sought religion as solace, but her refusal to accept easy consolation over historical reality makes her theological dimension hard for many to identify with. Evil in O'Connor's world relates not to solvable social problems but to ongoing mystery. Her Catholic faith transcended the very real so-cial tensions of her stories. The belief in dogma, she said, liberated her power of observation and guaranteed her respect for the myster-ies of existence. Attacked by *Life* magazine in 1957 for not celebrat-ing more of the "joy of life," she replied that what interested her more was "the redeeming quality of spiritual purpose." Perhaps demands for joy, O'Connor countered, would not be so strident, "if joy were really more abundant in our prosperous society." She pointed out also that she was writing about people who are poor, "who are af-flicted in both mind and body, who have little—or at best a distorted sense of spiritual purpose"—whose actions would not naturally give the reader any assurance of "the joy of life."[10]

The religious women O'Connor identified with—not unusual for an artist—were ascetics like Edith Stein and Simone Weil; she also wrote feelingly about Rose Hawthorne's commitment to victims of incurable disease. In her approach to her own art, like Katherine Anne Porter, O'Connor expressed a distrust of theory; she disliked the logic that made categories smaller and smaller. Her letters con-

tinue to mock "interlekshuls." The integrity of everyday detail dom-
inates O'Connor's aesthetic. Yet "quotidian" is a word often used
pejoratively to define women's writing regardless of deeper purpose
or symbolic resonance.

A sense of humor also helped make life bearable for Flannery
O'Connor. On one level the South appears as a gigantic spectacle for
amusement, as it does also in the writing of Eudora Welty. Welty,
later challenged, as Flannery O'Connor had been, for not writing in
a more polemical way about racial issues, answered her critics in secular terms in "Must the Novelist Crusade?" What she had been striving for, she insisted, was an integrity in capturing feelings that
"stands outside time." "The novelist's work is highly organized," Eudora Welty wrote, "but I should say it is organized around anything
but logic." Out of the writer's personal moral conviction will emerge
a richer human vision, she insisted, that would be neither black nor
white, nor particularly southern. "If our stories are worth the reading," she summarized, "we are writing about everybody."[11]

During the 1950s Eudora Welty also published a number of critical reviews, including the essays "Writing and Analyzing a Story"
and "Place in Fiction"; she has always been a self-conscious artist.
Insisting that writing was a career that women could pursue with a
minimum of disadvantages, she believed that "all that talk of wom-
en's lib doesn't apply *at all* to women writers. We've always been able
to do what we wished." (Tillie Olsen might have commented that it
was easier if we remained childless.) Welty also found ways to pay
tribute to a number of women writers who influenced her craft: Jane
Austen, Isak Dinesen, Virginia Woolf, and Elizabeth Bowen. Her
appreciation of Katherine Anne Porter, another southerner, is especially eloquent. In Porter, Welty sees the artist as she wanted to be
seen, one who has made order and form "out of their very antithesis,
life."[12]

A much later essay, "The House of Willa Cather," may well be the
most distinguished example yet of the shock of recognition between
women writers. As a culture, we cannot exist without a sense of the
connections and traditions in American writing. In the 1950s new
paperback classics brought writers like Willa Cather and Sarah Orne
Jewett back onto the contemporary literary scene, inspiring many
women who valued the sense of a female literary heritage. When
Emily Dickinson's three volumes of unabridged, unbowdlerized po-

etry also finally appeared in 1955, American women were forced to confront their capacity for greatness.[13]

The South had no monopoly on remarkable women writers. And consensus was not by any means the distinguishing mood for most women writing during the decade. Evan Connell's 1958 heroine, *Mrs. Bridge*, who would not take off her gloves in a bookstore to scan a copy of *The Theory of the Leisure Class*, may have suggested the confused side of suburban motherhood to many readers, but there were also women writers struggling with compassion to record a variety of equally real environments. Out of New York City came the literary testimonies of Hortense Calisher *(In the Absence of Angels,* 1951), and Grace Paley *(The Little Disturbances of Man: Stories of Men and Women in Love,* 1959).

Calisher's *Tale for the Mirror,* a collection of stories written in the 1950s, insisted on the value of individuality. She understood the anguish of many women who made the choice between marriage and career, asking if the denied half of their lives would persist, "venomously arranging for the ruin of the other." The Communist she described turned out also to be a southern lady, an "arch-individualist just as much as Stalin." In "The Woman Who Was Everybody" Calisher was able, too, to write with sympathy about a young woman department-store section manager, a "queer chick" whose love of books had made her major in philosophy and fine arts in college. "We'd rather have it business administration," the hiring office said; Miss Abel saw herself "acquiring that whole vocabulary of pretense forced upon those who must make themselves commercially valuable or die." "The Rabbi's Daughter" captured the pain of a young woman pianist—talented enough to have dreamed of a concert career—as she takes her new baby home. She feels sympathy for her young husband, now a father, "dented" with fatigue. The story is a feminist documentary, albeit implicit. "So many of them," Calisher sighed, "the shriveled talented women." Her pianist heroine thinks jealously: "A man can be reasonably certain it was his talent which failed him, but the women, for whom there are still so many excuses, can never be so sure." Hortense Calisher frequently concerned herself with "the sad consanguinity" of many women who refused to stay in their traditional places.[14]

Grace Paley stressed the same theme even more obviously. These writers, not usually discussed along with the rich gallery of post–

World War II male Jewish writers, deserve greater attention. Hailed as "unladylike" by Philip Roth, *The Little Disturbances of Man* demonstrated, Herbert Gold believed, "a girl's charm and a woman's strength." Susan Sontag labeled Paley's collection of stories an example of "the unity of the art of consciousness and the naturalness of conscience." When Donald Barthelme remarked that Grace Paley was a wonderful writer and troublemaker, concluding that we are fortunate to have her in our country,[15] he may have been pointing up the role Paley subsequently played as a social critic, but there can be no question of the individuality—the strength and the vulnerability—of her women characters. During the 1950s she explored the bravery of single mothers, adolescent girls, and aging maiden aunts; she wrote of the passions of a woman so happy with a man that she threw all precautions to the winds, and of the suspicions of another woman whose husband gave her a broom for Christmas: "No one can tell me it was meant kindly."[16] Humor, notably rare in angrier feminists, remains, as in O'Connor, one of Paley's great strengths.

The 1950s liberal tradition associated with the rich ethnic heritage of New York City produced a number of competent writers of thesis fiction, like Laura Hobson, whose exposé of tacit anti-Semitism, *Gentlemen's Agreement*, had been a best-seller in 1947. Hobson went on to write two novels about conflict in urban life, as did Jo Sinclair (Ruth Seid). Like Lucy Freeman, whose *Fight Against Fears* (1951) remained the most popular autobiographical novel about psychoanalysis, Sinclair continued to write books—fictionalized and journalistic—about the therapeutic experience, reflecting the way women during this period saw their problems stemming from inner flaws rather than from social conditions. Sinclair's best work, however, may well be her 1956 biographical sketch of a woman who defied the state during the Hungarian uprising, seventy-four-year-old Anna Teller, an inspiration for less assertive Americans. In the 1950s too, a few strong women like Ilona Karmel who had survived the earlier horrors of Nazi Europe, began to create remarkable fiction out of their past.

Cynthia Ozick published a novel, *Trust*, in the 1950s, a record of contemporary changing mores, not as sharply sociological as the vision of the 1950s Marilyn French would later create in her best-seller *The Women's Room*. Ozick's identity as a Jew, another kind of outsider, contributed to the richness of her personal definition of woman's possibilities.

A westerner, Tillie Olsen, started to overcome the silences imposed on her by the obligations of work and family. Most of the stories collected in *Tell Me a Riddle* in 1960 had found audiences in magazines like *Prairie Schooner* or *Pacific Spectator* in the 1950s. Out of poverty and hardship, noted the *London Tribune,* Olsen, who would become a heroine of the 1970s, created "a working class America that few writers have known or realized existed." Her eloquent articulation of the *silences* that often define writers as surely as their words would later become a classical tribute to the force of creativity struggling against social odds. "We who write are survivors," Olsen insisted. [17]

Another western radical survivor, Meridel LeSueur, famous for descriptions of social conditions in the 1930s, was one of those forced underground by the political pressures of the McCarthy era. Shunned by publishers, blacklisted, repressed, LeSueur nonetheless kept writing diaries, experimental prose, novels, and poems, all stored in the basement of her Minnesota home. "Unseen—like the seed buried underground (LeSueur's favorite image)—her work waited for its time." [18] The pattern of her career, forced by political rather than by biological pressures, remains strangely identified with the lives of other fifties women who were also waiting to play more active roles.

Josephine Herbst, the successful leftist novelist of the 1930s, made more extensive use of the seed image in the 1954 tribute to the botanists John and William Bartram, *Green New World.* Harassed during the 1950s for her continuing radicalism, Herbst too found in nature a source of strength more important than family or man's institutions. [19]

Kay Boyle, another westerner, contributed to the continuing literary achievement of American women. Born in St. Paul, shaped in the 1920s as Olsen had been in the 1930s, Boyle continued to add to a prolific body of work; by the 1970s she had written fourteen novels, eight volumes of short stories, three children's books, four collections of poetry, an anthology of writings about peace, and two volumes of memoirs. In the early 1950s she published a valuable fictional documentary of the postwar occupation army in Europe, *The Smoking Mountain.* Many American women, as journalists and teachers as well as GI wives, shared an unusual military life from 1945 to 1955; they were all part of the army of occupation in Europe. Personally involved with government occupation policies, aware of the fragmented ideologies remaining in the minds of conquered peoples, Boyle captured in writing the experiences that American men and women had never had before.[20]

The 1950s postwar reality was a sobering one for Americans abroad—a far cry from the self-indulgent hedonism of the 1920s. Notable among the non-fiction pieces of this period was Kay Boyle's vivid account of the trial of Heinrich Baab, a minor Nazi official responsible for killing fifty-seven people. In fiction Boyle described women enriched by the value struggles they shared with the still-drafted United States soldiers; the European background she reconstructed underlined the inescapable international involvement that had begun to touch every class of American and every part of American life.[21]

No more searing indictment of early 1950s institutionalized racism exists than Kay Boyle's story "The Lost." A Czech war orphan dreams of going to America to work in the garage of a GI he has learned to love. Because the garage is in Chattanooga, and the GI is black, the United States government denies the homeless boy permission to emigrate; he is forced to write to the man who wanted to help him, pretending he has found an unknown relative. The remnants of Nazism that scarred the Germans also touched Boyle's morally sensitive imagination; her motherly awareness of the plight of the young, strong in these tales, perhaps reflects her experience with her own six children. Involved during the 1960s in a number of social protests against war, jailed at least once, she wrote: "It is *always* the writers who must bear the full weight of moral responsibility."[22]

Another westerner who often found herself part of the European scene, but kept her roots "in the semi-fictitious town of Adams, Colorado," was Jean Stafford. Although Stafford published her two best novels at the end of the 1940s, in 1952 she produced *The Catherine Wheel*, about a passion-tormented imperious woman. In 1953 she brought out an impressive collection of all her previous works, *The Interior Castle*, along with a new collection of short stories, *Children Are Bored on Sundays*. Stafford was criticized for being too feminine, for not making enough effort to understand the male psyche. Her gallery of female characters includes women of all ages and emotional ranges—from adolescents struggling toward independent identities to ladies in old-age homes "animated and rejuvenated" by wrath. She wrote with equal insight of New England aristocrats and of western chambermaids. Like Katherine Anne Porter, Stafford insisted on avoiding abstractions without descending into what she believed to be mindless realism; and like Mark Twain, one of her personal heroes, she explored the fate of innocence—but in female terms. Imitating Henry James, another literary model, Stafford examined the experience of dislocation and the psychological challenge of different cultural settings. Her stories bring regional identities to life as well as human dilemmas: Europe and Boston, Manhattan and Colorado become testing grounds for the independent spirits of her heroines. She cannot, however, permit the unforgettable tomboy Molly Fawcett to grow up; and the strong old maid she creates, Katherine Congreve, must die a martyr's death. The contrast De Tocqueville noted long ago, between the free-spirited young woman in America and the wholly dependent wife she is doomed to become, remains a challenging theme in women's writing.[23]

Popular Writers

One way to deal with the sacrifices involved in turning the capable independent girl into a responsible mother was deliberate humor. Shirley Jackson's *Life among the Savages* (1953) and *Raising Demons* (1957) delighted baby-boom readers, who also enjoyed the dramatic whimsy of Jean Kerr and the domestic verses of Phyllis McGinley, a believer in housewifery as woman's most honorable profession.[24]

In Jackson's amused descriptions of pajama parties, Little League games, den mothers, sneaker crises, and children's homemade chemistry experiments, women in the 1950s often saw their own lives. Whether they also saw their unconscious anxieties and tensions in her ghost stories—so often told in a banal tone—remains worth thinking about. Jackson's most famous story, "The Lottery," coincided in 1947 with Truman's intensification of anti-Communist security investigations; she continued to explore the paranoia that seemed to live side by side with harmless domesticity. During the 1950s she also published *Hangsaman, The Bird's Nest, The Sundial,* and *The Haunting of Hill House,* novels about witches, ghosts, and multiple personalities; she also wrote *The Witchcraft of Salem Village* for children in 1956. Further analysis might reveal how much Shirley Jackson's split literary personality reflected the complex fears of other civilized mothers. During this decade women could also witness a cinematic case study of split personality in *The Three Faces of Eve.*

Love stories like Maud Hutchins's *Love Is a Pie* and *Honey on the Moon* and Elaine Dundy's *Dud Avocado* were bound to be popular in a decade when early marriage was stylish. Dundy's heroine, the very opposite of the "new woman" of the 1920s, gave up her free Parisian life to return to America, to become a librarian and bask in the shadow of her husband's success.

Although Ayn Rand continued to gather converts to philosophical narcissism with the publication of *Atlas Shrugged* in 1957, few women writers attempted in a similar manner to translate personal dilemmas into ideology. And few attempted in any fictional way to comment on the real political anxieties of the times. A courageous exception was May Sarton, whose novel about the suicide of F. O. Matthiessen—a Harvard professor who had been involved with Communists—*Faithful Are the Wounds*, tried to appraise in 1955 the heroic quality of an intensely caring life in a world of social indifference. Sarton, a self-conscious if not always successful writer, produced three other novels during the decade. Her struggle to articulate how a solitary individual managed to cope with her own loneliness and her homosexual preferences would make her a heroine for a later generation of women looking for models less bourgeois than the conventional family.

Mary McCarthy's *Groves of Academe* also focused on the academic world as a target for Communist witch-hunts—although her main character, Henry Mulcahy, is an opportunist lacking any of the real social concerns that might have identified him with the victims of the times. It is indeed hard to find a good *man* in any of McCarthy's novels. Her ability to expose human pretension manages to penetrate every male establishment. Intensely intellectual, McCarthy nonetheless manages to ally herself with writing women like Porter and O'Connor and Welty who profess suspicion about theorists and ideologues. During the 1950s McCarthy not only wrote a great number of nonfiction articles for magazines, she also published a collection of short stories, as well as *A Charmed Life*, a novel that included the dilemma of unwanted pregnancy. Like M. F. K. Fisher and Eleanor Clark, who were also writing in the 1950s, Mary McCarthy added to the literature of travel meant to define civilization. *The Stones of Florence* and *Venice Observed* were among her achievements for the decade, which included what may remain her most lasting literary work, the 1957 autobiography *Memories of a Catholic Girlhood*. It was in the 1950s too that Mary McCarthy published the first section of the controversial documentary novel *The Group*, about a group of Vassar graduates from the 1920s to the inauguration of Eisenhower. She described the period after World War II as a time when "everyone was trying to live in a very principled way."[25]

Some women made good livings writing detective novels and film scripts. Mary Highsmith and Margaret Millar (Ellis Sturm) flourished. Cid Ricketts Sumner wrote a fine film, *Pinky*, out of her novel about an educated black girl who "passed" as white. Sumner also published a successful novel, *The Hornbeam Tree*, in 1953 about a fifty-year-old woman free of responsibility who falls in love.

And women continued to produce enormously successful bestsellers. Edna Ferber, Fannie Hurst, and Pearl Buck were still on the scene. Jessamyn West not only wrote compassionately about adolescent girls in *Cress Delehanty* but also wrote a filmscript based on *The Friendly Persuasion*, a story of pacifism and inner strength derived from her own Quakerism, Rona Jaffe's contemporary novel about career women, *The Best of Everything*, provided vicarious adventure for many housewives. By far the most astonishing work of the decade, however, was Grace Metalious's *Peyton Place*, which appeared in 1956. An exposé of the decay of small-town morals in New England, *Peyton Place* sold six million copies in its first six months; by 1970 it had earned a place in the world book of records, with sales totaling 11,919,660. More than any other American novel of the times, *Peyton Place* demonstrated how great was the discrepancy between American moral myth and reality; the classical New England town remained as powerful a setting for hypocrisy in 1956 as it had been for Hawthorne. Totally unprepared for the effects of instant fame, Grace Metalious merits the kind of sociological attention that has been given similar male cult figures like James Dean, Jack Kerouac, and Ross Lockridge, Jr., the author of *Raintree County*, whose lives, like hers, ended prematurely, damaged by coping with success.[26]

Peyton Place remained a long distance from the disappearing elegant world Nancy Hale evoked in *A New England Girlhood*, also published in 1956. How much any level of regionalism would remain in the American novel after the 1950s—the decade defined by highways, cars and constant moving, and by televised standardization of the American dream—also remains worth exploring.

Other Forms of Writing

In 1955 Elizabeth Stevenson was the first woman to win the Bancroft Prize in History with her biography of Henry Adams, a man who defined himself in terms of feminine sensibility and powerlessness.[27] A number of women found writing biographies to be a new source of power as well as a means to self-identity. It was possible to create vicarious lives of action by writing biographies of vigorous women. Katherine Anthony told about Susan B. Anthony and Mercy Warren; Amy Kelly produced her classic on Eleanor of Aquitaine; Louise Hall Tharp celebrated *The Peabody Sisters of Salem;* and Faith Chipperfield even wrote a "romantic" biography about Margaret Fuller, who would become a rediscovered heroine of the feminist 1970s. Some remarkably gifted women, including Mary Handlin, Ruth Painter Randall, Elizabeth Schlesinger, and Marion Pottle gave their energy to helping their husbands' scholarly achievements, playing the traditional subordinate role behind the scenes— as many women scientists similarly worked in their husbands' laboratories. Like Mary Beard, Ruth Painter Randall also wrote books on her own; while her husband wrote his monumental books about Lincoln and the Civil War, she wrote about Lincoln's personal involvements. Disturbed by Herndon's unsympathetic account of Mrs. Lincoln, Ruth Randall in 1953 wrote *Mary Lincoln: Biography of a Marriage.* She also published during the 1950s *Lincoln's Sons, Lincoln's Courtship,* and—for children—*Lincoln's Animal Friends,* subjects considered trivial by historians more interested in Civil War battles.

To overlook the authors who gave their primary energies to children's writing would be a serious omission in trying to understand the means women use to assert themselves. Writing for children has been an important way to nurture, reinforce, and preach values; it was a way to offer the young a more complex vision of reality. If there were an insufficient number of books about women working outside the home, or becoming doctors, lawyers, and mayors, there were still a good number praising heroic women and trying to help children value themselves as individuals as they adapted to a pluralistic society. The public library is often a more important source of American education than the public school. During the period that fostered an unconscious mandate to educate children for democratic choice, books continued to appear that exposed little girls to possibilities other than mothering; women recorded the lives of adventure-some heroines as well as the lives of women who felt serving others their means to self-definition. Writing was a way of extending experience for the author, too. Jean Latham, a Newbery Medal winner who wrote about both Elizabeth Blackwell and Rachel Carson, remarked that she chose subjects who "managed to achieve something worthwhile despite overwhelming setbacks."[28]

"I write about survivors," echoed Ann Petry, too, when she published her young people's biography of Harriet Tubman in 1955.[29] The 1950s produced a surprising number of books for children about the underground railway, unconsciously illustrating how a network of behind-the-scenes activity could be powerful in dealing with an immoral establishment. In *Freedom Train: The Story of Harriet Tubman* (1954), Dorothy Sterling made much of the "omissions and distortions in history written concerning black people."[30] After the Supreme Court decision declaring separate schools unequal, Sterling traveled through the South interviewing black children who were entering white schools. *Mary Jane*, the award-winning book that grew out of these experiences in 1959, was translated into seven languages. Another important children's biography related to integration was Elizabeth Yates's *Prudence Crandall, Woman of Courage*, about a nineteenth-century Quaker schoolmistress persecuted for admitting black children into her boarding school. Children who read the decade's new books would have discovered the idea of integration strongly reinforced by courageous individuals in America's past. They would also have realized that when occasion demanded action, women who *seemed* politically powerless knew how to play useful dissident roles.

The most valuable ethnic storytelling of the period was probably Ann Nolan Clark's, derived from long experience with the Native American. Clark, a writer of bilingual primers, had worked with the Bureau of Indian Affairs since the 1930s. As she wrote stories about tribes living in harmony with nature trying to weave beautiful blankets and hammer silver for survival, she attempted to remind young people of the dignity of the Native American's nontechnological civilization. In 1952 she too won the Newbery Medal, and the government made her an adviser for the Institute of Inter-American Affairs.

Women outside the conventional power structure have often been successful in articulating the feelings of other secondary cultures. In

storytelling they tried to help children respect the rights and humanity of people whose external lives were different from their own. Just
as the great anthropologists Ruth Benedict, Margaret Mead, and
Ruth Underhill defined richer female identities through their work
on foreign cultures, so women writing for children managed to con-
vey a broader range of values and possibilities than their more mechanical daily lives would suggest. To minimize the value of the
imagination is to diminish any society.

Marchette Chute of Minnesota awakened children to another kind
of world. That her two 1950s books on Shakespeare for young people remained in print thirty years later is testimony to the versatility
of the young.[31] Mary Lee Kingman not only wrote nine books of her
own during the decade, but also directed *Hornbook* magazine, which
provided teachers and librarians with critical standards for judging
children's literature. Women were also beginning to contribute personal visions to the new age of science fiction.

Andre (Mary Alice) Norton wrote six volumes about intergalactic
conflict during the 1950s; she managed to emphasize the earthly values of resourcefulness, loyalty, courage, and sensitivity in the battles
between good and evil taking place in space. Ursula LeGuin started
to write the fantasies that would bring her a raft of awards in later
years—not simply for her children's writings. One of LeGuin's most
imaginative ideas, perhaps nourished by both the frustrations and
satisfactions of childrearing, was "ambisexuality"; she would imagine
a world where each person was capable of choosing gender for purposes of reproduction only, the rest of the time we would all be
neuter.[32]

Although Madeleine L'Engle's children's classic, *A Wrinkle in Time*,
was not published until 1962, she added to the 1950s writing about
girls' struggles to achieve independence with *Camilla Dickinson*.
"When I have something important to say which I think is going to
be too difficult for adults," she wrote, "I write it in a book for children. . . . They have not yet closed the door and windows of their
imaginations."[33]

Poetry

No decade has any monopoly on the expansion of the imagination, but in periods when opportunities for action seem limited,
good minds often turn to what De Tocqueville called "interior with-

drawal." The image of Saint Teresa of Avila's *Interior Castle* was the one Jean Stafford chose in compiling one of the most distinguished story collections (about women) of the decade. Anaïs Nin called her 1959 collection of novels *Cities of the Interior*. If writers like Flannery O'Connor, Carson McCullers, and Eudora Welty identified with eccentrics and freaks, as Leslie Fiedler has suggested, because they were outside of the world of power,[34] they nevertheless converted their internal experiences into images that many people understood. The women writers of this decade managed to mine astonishing riches from limited soil.

Intense images of private emotional life contributed also to the wealth of remarkable poetry. No decade has nourished a greater variety of talented women poets. If some of these poets were shaped in earlier periods, their poetic ideals could not be contained by time, and they were—like Emily Dickinson—very much a part of the 1950s literary scene.

Elizabeth Bishop, for one, won the Pulitzer Prize in 1955 for *North and South*, together with *A Cold Spring*. Her work, "wryly radiant, more unaffectedly intelligent than any written in our lifetime," James Merrill thought, reflected an unconventional mind. Poet and critic Robert Pinsky believed several of her poems "great works of art."[35] In 1951 Bishop's good friend, Marianne Moore, similarly enchanted with the precision of language, won not only the Pulitzer Prize but also the National Book Award and the Bollingen Prize. Moore's work was assumed to be part of the durable body of poetry written in the twentieth century. Asked by Howard Nemerov if the changing world preoccupied her work, Moore replied, "Not as timely topics, but fundamentally and continuously." Her writings suggested "how endlessly various, how ingenious, and idiosyncratic and inexplicably fascinating, how sheerly *interesting* the world is."[36]

Louise Bogan presented her *Collected Poems* in 1954; and two books of her essay reviews also enriched the 1950s. Theodore Roethke thought Bogan's work would stay in the language as long as language survived; and Adrienne Rich saw Bogan's poetry as part of a feminist literary heritage: "a graph of the struggle to commit a female sensibility, in all its aspects to language."[37]

Although H. D. (Hilda Doolittle) added little to her poetic canon when she returned to America in 1956, other women whose identities were formed in the 1920s and 1930s, including Leonie Adams, Babette Deutsch, and Marya Zaturenska, continued to publish valu-

able books in the 1950s. Janet Lewis and Josephine Miles also continued to write in preparation for the collections that would appear in
the next decade.

Strong new voices began to be heard. May Swenson published
two books in the 1950s; and Mona Van Duyn brought out *Valentine
to the World* in 1959. May Sarton, praised by James Dickey for
"womanly assurance and judiciousness," published three books of
poetry during the decade, and Jean Garrigue produced two. Barbara
Howes, who proudly defined herself as "a poet, a wife, a mother,"
gave us *In the Cold Country* in 1954 and *Light and Dark* in 1959.[38]
Katherine Hoskins, greeted by general critical acclaim, also managed to bring out three books in less than a decade.

Nor was Gwendolyn Brooks (see chapter 8) the only poet using
words to awaken readers to social problems. During the 1950s New
Yorker Muriel Rukeyser continued a vital career among those Kay
Boyle called "the great poets of human concern and compassion of
our time." Rukeyser wrote of civil liberties, split atoms, the Long
March, and Wendell Willkie's vision of one world. In *Body of Waking*
in 1958, she contributed an elegy for F. O. Matthiessen:

> Angel of suicides, gather him in now,
> Defend us from doing what he had to do
> Who threw himself away.[39]

Poets like Adrienne Rich and Denise Levertov, who would later
be identified with radical women and peace movements, began in
the 1950s to solidify their craft and test their ideas. Rich saw women
then as taking the world as it was. In "Aunt Jennifer's Tigers," which
addressed the unconscious aggression embroidered by a meek
woman into a panel of "prancing, proud and unafraid" tigers, Rich
acknowledged that her craft had enabled her to speak: "In those years
formalism was part of the strategy—like asbestos gloves, it allowed
me to handle materials I couldn't pick up bare-handed."[40]

In *Snapshots of a Daughter-in-Law* (1958) Rich continued to look at
how gifted women were taught to regard themselves:

> Bemused by Gallantry, we hear
> Our mediocrities over-praised,
> indolence read as abnegation,
> slattern thought styled intuition

every lapse forgiven, our crime
only to cast too bold a shadow
or smash the mold straight off.

For that, solitary confinement,
tear gas, attrition shelling
Few applicants for that honor.[41]

One of the applicants was already in the solitary confinement of
what she called *The Bell Jar*. The tremendous female anger that
would burst forth in the next decade through the words of Sylvia
Plath and Anne Sexton became a comfort to many women. As Elizabeth Janeway noted, they read confessional poetry eagerly "for re-
assurances that their own similar sensations have been
shared . . . that someone has faced them and struggled to understand them." Madness appeared for these poets a part of the revolt
against normality. Like the eccentrics of fiction, "those who have
fallen into madness measure and criticize the values of orthodoxy."[42]
There were other ways.

Denise Levertov preferred to remember Anne Sexton for those
moments when she found her own depression boring: "I would be
better to make / some soup and light up the cave." Levertov herself
continued to celebrate the possibilities of life.[43] She saw the "every-
dayness" of women's existence "coming to symbolize a connection to
reality" instead of representing—as men saw it—"the triviality of
their existence." Full of the wonder and joy of living, the experience
of the mystery that denies arrogance she had praised in the early
poetry of H. D., Levertov's poems seem a rhythmic complement to
Rachel Carson's prose or Barbara McClintock's science. "If I speak of
revolution," Levertov would later write, "it is because I believe that
only a revolution can save that earthly life, that miracle of being,
which poetry conserves and celebrates." But she was not an ideo-
logue; during the 1960s, when more women were writing poetry
than ever before, Levertov would lose patience with the writing that
was "feminist first and poetry afterwards."[44]

Among the Beat poets of the decade who wanted no identity with
any one region or any traditional institutions, or any formal poetic
tradition—except Walt Whitman—was Diane Di Prima.[45] The life
of freedom Di Prima tried to invoke in California spoke to few
women in this period of dominant domesticity. And it would take

more than another decade before many readers were ready to accept Denise Levertov's assertion that poetry was intrinsically revolutionary.

Theater

A few women playwrights contributed to the more modest distinction of the American theater. In 1951 Lillian Hellman produced *The Autumn Garden*. Continuing to exorcise sentimentality, Hellman forced audiences to examine the meaning of the too comfortable existence that leads to "social inanition and disaster."[46] Labeling Hellman a moralist, Harold Clurman summed up her achievement as one that reminded us of high ideals and a scorn for the phony. During the 1950s Hellman also adapted Jean Anouilh's play about Joan of Arc, *The Lark*, for the American stage and wrote the script for Leonard Bernstein's musical, *Candide*. Joan of Arc, boyish and bright, who sacrificed herself for her country and a mediocre king, was a reappearing female image during the 1950s. Ingrid Bergman, Julie Harris, Siobhan McKenna, and Jean Seberg played the martyred Joan during these years that celebrated both female fortitude and selflessness. That Joan had to dress and act like a man to gain political attention was always clear.

Carson McCuller's most popular work, *A Member of the Wedding*, not only opened the decade's theater but later also became a successful movie. The teenage girl Frankie Adams, and her black mentor, Berenice, seemed a momentary challenge to alienated innocence. Although Frankie was lonely she appeared capable of change and growth. McCullers extended national mythology beyond the development of adolescent males such as Nick Adams and Holden Caulfield to include female sensibilities. In print, each of four successive volumes of *A Member of the Wedding* sold over 500,000 copies. Elected to the National Institute of Arts and Letters in 1952, McCullers never matched her earlier level of artistry in *The Heart Is a Lonely Hunter*, but she continued to write in spite of a number of personal tragedies. The 1958 production of *The Square Root of Wonderful* was, however, an almost immediate failure.[47]

Lorraine Hansberry's *A Raisin in the Sun*, winner of the "Best American Play of 1958–59" award, became the first work by a black woman ever to appear on Broadway. In a run of over 500 performances Hansberry managed to speak out against racism and also to suggest that a black woman should be able to go to medical school. When the heroine's brother challenges:

Who the hell told you you had to be a doctor? If you so crazy 'bout messing around with sick people—then go be a nurse like other women—or just get married and be quiet. . . .

the determined Beneatha Younger replies: "I'm going to be a doctor. I'm not worried about who I'm going to marry yet . . . if I ever get married."[48] Whether the insistent Beneatha will have to go to Africa to fulfill her ambition remains a question at the end of the play, when she has also changed her attitude toward marriage. But the reality of her potential was surely convincing to the many women in audiences who had been dissuaded from similar vocational determination.

More typical of the decade's vision of women was Dorothy Parker's last play, *Ladies of the Corridor.* In 1953 Parker gave us a gallery of culturally paralyzed women who could not act or change. Although known for her wit, a common female defense, she was often, as Ann Douglas remarked, "more profoundly political as an artist than she was as an activist."[49] In spite of her successes she continued to identify with outsiders and left the bulk of her estate to Martin Luther King, Jr.

The most popular woman dramatist of the period was Mary Chase, whose unrealistic *Mrs. McThing* starred Helen Hayes in 1952. She produced another fantasy, *Bernardine,* in 1953 and adapted her 1940s success, *Harvey,* about an imaginary rabbit, to the screen. Fantasy remained one way to escape the pains and suspicions of contemporary life. In 1958 Clare Boothe Luce suggested another way, mysticism, in *Child of the Morning.* In that same year the always avant-garde Djuna Barnes produced *Antiphon,* celebrated in Europe but neglected by her fellow Americans. It was during the 1950s, too, that Elaine May perfected the trenchant cabaret humor that would identify Nichols and May with the best topical satire by the end of the decade. And Megan Terry, a founding member of the Woman's Theatre Council, was getting her start in 1955 in Seattle community theater. Experimental theater also began to reawaken in New York, too, as Judith Malina, with Julian Beck, formally launched the Living Theatre in 1951. Margo Jones carried her interests in new playwrights and theatre in the round to Broadway in 1955. In Cambridge, Massachusetts, with inspiration from Violet Lang, the

Poets Theatre prospered. Before the decade was over, a number of women also established the San Francisco Mime Troupe, which helped the next decade to dramatize many of its social tensions.

The disproportionate space allotted here to women writers (by no means all the talented women who might have been included) suggests how successfully women in the 1950s found freedom and power through the literary imagination. Language became for them a means to move the world as well as to reflect it. But many of the writers mentioned in this chapter were also testimony to the *silences* Tillie Olsen eloquently defined. Long periods between books characterized the work of Eleanor Clark and Grace Paley; Hortense Calisher's first novel appeared thirty years after her graduation from college. Long anticipatory preparation also defined the work of Barbara Howes and later, Ruth Whitman and Amy Clampitt, who published first books of poetry in mid-life, not at all in the romantic tradition of young men. Many women, Olsen asserted, need "the sudden lifting of responsibility to make writing necessary, to make writing possible."[50] Encouragement was not always easy to find. Yet the incredible variety of literary talent on the scene during this fearful and discriminatory period proclaimed writing as one of women's most valuable roles. Words may indeed make nothing happen, but they bestow a sense of power on those who learn to use them well.

Rosa Parks being fingerprinted, Montgomery, Alabama, 1955.
Courtesy of Wide World Photos, Inc.

Chapter Eight

Black Women: Activists, Artists, and Athletes

Activists

The black women of America did not share either the complacency or the anxiety of the 1950s. Not only did they remain in the post–World War II work force as more than domestics—in 1956 the NAACP reported that the New York telephone company had begun to hire Negro women; in the Far West, even black teachers were finding jobs—but they also emerged as leaders in the renewed struggle for civil-rights legislation. The 1950s, so stultifying for women on many levels, must ultimately be seen as a decade of progress for blacks.

When Martin Luther King, Jr., declared that the history books would have to say, "There lived a great people—a black people who injected new meaning into the veins of civilization," he was right.[1] The behavior of blacks in America in the 1950s remains inspirational in the best sense; their humanity—their reasonable courage and compassion—stands out in contrast to the McCarthy hysteria that stains the white history of the decade. Over thirty percent of all the people polled for political opinions in 1954, the year that "under God" was added to the pledge of allegiance, supported the paranoid anticommunism of the Wisconsin senator.[2]

Yet 1954 also marked the historic anti–school-segregation decision of *Brown* v. *Board of Education of Topeka, Kansas*—the beginning of a long period of renewed concern about social discrimination that would mark the attitudes of the decades to come. That Linda Carol Brown was eight years old at the time of the decision that bore her name makes it difficult to attribute any feminism to her contribution to black equality, but it is a tribute to her parents and lawyers that they realized that a daughter's education was as important as a son's. For black women education has been a means to social mobility, a source of opportunity not available to black men. As Gerda Lerner pointed out, black families, "who expected their daughters to work most of their lives, would make greater sacrifices to educate their daughters than their sons," in noticeable contrast with the general white American pattern of "educationally depriving daughters for the sake of sons."[3]

Although the strength of the black movement in the 1950s lay in the community support behind every gesture—the extent of group commitment, including many whites, was enormous—there were also real heroines, like Rosa Parks. The forty-two-year-old department-store seamstress arrested for refusing to give her bus seat to a white man will be remembered in spite of her protests: "Many black people before me were arrested for defying the bus laws," she insisted. "They prepared the way." Yet Mrs. Parks's challenge was as brave as any military hero's in Alabama, where legal protection was not easy to find. Many threatening phone calls menaced Parks, a former NAACP secretary, who had been educated by northerners and long involved with "attempts to bring about freedom."[4] The department store where Rosa Parks sewed closed its alterations department; her husband later lost his job as a barber. And finally the Parkses were compelled to move away from Montgomery. Yet the 381 day bus boycott triggered in 1955 by Rosa Parks's defiance remains one of the most productive acts of civil disobedience in our history. The reason it succeeded, Parks believed, was that everyone involved had experienced the same kind of humiliation.

Eighty to ninety percent of the Negroes in Montgomery supported the boycott. Walking to work every day was especially hard on the women who did physical labor: "the cleaning women, the cooks, the washerwomen, the children's nurses," Louise Meriwether noted. Some women had to get up at three in the morning and walk twelve miles to and from work."[5] Forty-two thousand people walked to work; they stuck it out. One woman picked up by the improvised taxi system the blacks eventually organized to help each other remarked: "My soul has been tired for a long time. Now my feet are tired and my soul is resting." Another mother of six commented: "We know now that we're free citizens of the United States. Now we are aiming to become free citizens of Alabama. Our state motto, you know, is 'We Defend Our Rights.'"[6] Such sharpened political awareness reminded other Americans of the range of democratic commitments neglected for almost a hundred years. The United Auto Workers sent $35,000 to help run the car pool. Private donations came in from all over the world. Although Parks realized that the final gains were modest, she felt pleased that blacks had "acquired enough freedom to be able to be vocal and to . . . act as human beings."[7] It may well be true, as one of her admirers insisted, that "if Mrs. Parks had got up and given that white man her seat, you'd never aheard of Reverend King."[8]

When Autherine Lucy, a twenty-six-year-old black woman, tried to apply to the University of Alabama in 1956 to study library science—the first black in 125 years—she was labeled as "too old to have any honest interest in education." Mobs tried to kill her. "Miss Lucy said she was not afraid," reported the New York Times, "and would not break down."[9] A lone woman besieged in a classroom by a howling mob, she said she had prayed. One of ten children, Lucy sought this education without any kind of support from her parents, who told reporters that they had taught their children to stay their distance from white folks.

"She didn't get her new ideas from home," her disowning mother cried. "Why, I keep asking myself, out of all the colored folks in Alabama did this have to fall to my baby daughter's lot?"[10] The NAACP provided Autherine Lucy with excellent lawyers, including Constance Baker Motley, who counted on the Constitution to restore dignity to the black citizen—in contrast with the irrational behavior of the white mobs. "Don't ever let anyone pull you so low as to hate them," Martin Luther King, Jr., was urging: "This is not a war between the white and the Negro, but a conflict between justice and injustice."[11]

Naturally, many Americans at that time suspected her of being a pawn of the Communists—"Miss Lucy Denies Communist Ties," a New York Times headline reported on 8 March 1956; she generously agreed to broadcast a statement on her position for the Voice of

America. "I know very little about Communism," she began; "I am an American and I believe in the American system of government. I am also a Christian. . . . In my struggle for recognition as an American student, I have approached it in the American spirit and without the help of any enemies of our country."[12] Hanoi, nevertheless, exploited this contemporary example of racial injustice by forging a letter from Autherine Lucy to all Vietnamese students underlining the heritage of racism, not the ideal of equality Lucy was willing to die for.

Because she had been suspended "for her own safety" (one of the trustees admitted she would "probably be killed") she acknowledged at one point that she was "completely disheartened." But she would not give up: "At the same time I cannot see any reason to abandon my sole purpose of obtaining an education within the meaning of the decision of the Supreme Court." With Thurgood Marshall's steadying support, she confronted a summons to appear before the Alabama House of Representatives for an investigation of possible Communist affiliations, saying, "I still maintain my faith in my country, and there is nothing that anyone in Alabama or any place else can do that will check my faith in ultimate justice within the democratic principle."[13] Subsequent decades would be slow to vindicate this faith, but before the 1960s were over a number of other blacks would challenge southern schools; one brave woman, Charlayne Hunter, would go on to become a distinguished journalist and TV commentator.

There have always been a few remarkable black women on the American political scene. Barbara Ann Morris was sworn in as the first woman United States Assistant Attorney in New Jersey in the same year that Autherine Lucy was struggling for her education in Alabama; and Barbara Jordan began her career with a law degree from Boston University in 1959; Shirley Chisholm, the first black woman in Congress, was shifting her vocation into party politics in the 1950s after twenty years as a nursery-school teacher; Dorothy Kenyon became a judge; and Charlotta Bass, the editor of the oldest Negro paper in the West, who had run for vice president on the Progressive ticket, ran again for Congress in 1950. Patricia Harris's recognizable achievements as a diplomat helped her to gain power within the political establishment. But there can be no doubt that in the 1950s the greatest impact on society was achieved by those black women who put their lives on the line outside the party system to dramatize injustice. Their inspiration would continue to influence 1960s civil-rights workers like Ella Baker (Hodgson), a founder of the Student Nonviolent Coordinating Committee (SNCC), and Fannie Lou Hamer, active in voter registration at the end of the decade. Behind the scenes of the civil rights action during the 1950s were valuable women like Constance Baker Motley, who worked steadily as counsel for the NAACP legal defense fund, and Ida Wells Barnett and Georgia Caldwell Smith and Marguerite Belafonte and Irene Diggs, ardent workers for the NAACP. By 1959, one out of ten branch presidents (108) of the NAACP and more than 50 percent (669) of the branch secretaries were women. Black women's voluntarism was no less important in the 1950s than white women's.

Although conventional history may justifiably give credit to the brilliant black lawyers like Thurgood Marshall who masterminded the movement for civil rights in the 1950s and 1960s, it is important to recognize the brave and legitimate dissenters who grew weary of standing in the back of the bus and started demanding "Freedom Now"—with, as Shirley Chisholm later defined it, "the patience, tolerance and perseverance" more needed in politics—after years of suppression.[14]

Perhaps the most memorable battle in the civil-rights wars of the decade—because it forced the president to take action—was the attempt by nine black teenagers to integrate Little Rock Central High School in September 1957. The names of these students, like the names of Civil War veterans, should be recorded for posterity on a memorial tablet:

Minnijean Brown	Thelma Mothershed	Terrence Roberts
Elizabeth Eckford	Melba Patillo	Jefferson Thomas
Ernest Green	Gloria Ray	Carlotta Walls

Six of them were girls; and the guiding spirit who advised and protected all of them and dealt with their daily harassment was Mrs. L. C. Bates—Daisy Bates, the "besieged and courageous president of the Arkansas State Conference of the NAACP."[15]

Daisy Getson Bates, a "fighter for integration," went to school daily with the nine teenagers and remained near to make sure nothing happened to them. It was she who demanded the intervention of federal troops to combat Governor Orville Faubus's misuse of the National Guard to keep the students out. In exchange for her activity, the *New York Times* reported that "she has been vilified, abused, threatened, and intimidated. Her phone rings constantly."[16] When her adopted son was also threatened, friends managed to remain with her nights. She was arraigned for not revealing NAACP members' names; and finally her white townsmen deprived her of her livelihood by taking all advertising out of the *Arkansas State Press*, the newspaper she and her husband had run for eighteen years; yet Daisy Bates did not give up.

Her success at getting federal protection to allow these students to go on with their education was no easy accomplishment under a president who did not believe morality could be legislated. Eisenhower, like many people in Little Rock, suspected foreign agitators as the source of all the trouble. As late as May 1958 he would still be urging Negroes to be patient—to depend on better education instead of "simply on the letter of the law to gain rights."[17] Where was better education to be found?

Thelma Mothershed wanted to go to Little Rock High to learn to become an elementary-school teacher; she said she expected to be jeered at and insulted but not to be denied admission by Governor Faubus's troops. Mrs. Hosanna Mothershed, her mother, acknowledged anxiety, but also clearly articulated her democratic ideals: "I just had to let her go. There is a principle involved. If our boys and girls enter the white school now it will be easier for others to get in later. It's not easy to be a pioneer though."[18] Elizabeth Eckford, fifteen at the time, understood well what Mrs. Mothershed meant; white citizens made a point of tormenting her for the thirty-five minutes she had to wait for the bus and managed to get Mrs. Lee Lorch, an onlooker who tried to comfort the girl, subpoenaed. Minniejean Brown was kicked constantly, threatened with a knife, and had hot soup spilled on her. Daisy Bates provided continuing group discussions to help the black children talk out their anger, and she supported other brave neighbors (including Mrs. Grace McKinley, hit on the head by a soft-drink bottle) who worked to keep the students in school; by 3 October, the *New York Times* reported that black morale was still good.

The *Times* reporting of the Little Rock ordeal continued to underscore the prejudices of older whites such as the woman whose maid ate from a shelf in the kitchen while she sat close by, knowing for certain that God did not want the races to mix. The young, on the other hand, the *Times* stressed, simply wanted to get on with their educations. Sixteen-year-old Judith Nahlen, aiming to become a nurse, said, "I think it's all senseless. If the Negroes come in, I'll just mind my own business. I won't quit."[19] Other students admitted, though, that social pressure would keep them from befriending the blacks. The record of white student behavior in Daisy Bates's published memoir, *The Long Shadow of Little Rock*, is far from honorable. And although by the end of the decade integration appeared inevitable, the black individuals involved in Little Rock had paid a heavy price for their heroism. Of the original nine children, five were driven out of the city. Rather than comply with the Supreme Court's desegregation order, the governor eventually closed all the high schools; the students who remained had finally to get their diplomas through correspondence courses from the University of Arkansas. Twenty-five years later, however, a black student from reopened Central High would be at Yale.[20]

By 1959, in Florida, the NAACP in *Crisis* reported a number of schools accepting black students without friction; and Oklahoma had even integrated faculties.[21] Although the continuing strength of the NAACP and the growing charisma of Martin Luther King, Jr., helped blacks to become more demanding in the 1950s, there can be no doubt that a number of strong black women saw the temper of the decade suited to their own talents for leadership. In the area of labor organizing, as early as 1950, Moranda Smith became the first woman regional director of the International Tobacco Workers Union, encouraging sit-down strikes for improvement of working conditions and wages. Her union would register over 8000 voters; it is no surprise that at age thirty-four she died of overwork.[22] One after another, similar women inspired each other to use the patience and endurance American injustice had taught them, in order to seek the freedom and equality that were also part of their heritage. The strength of their insistence on their Americanism when their enemies found it so convenient to label them Communists remains one of the moving truths of the period.

In 1951, in spite of attacks by the loud radio journalist Walter Winchell, Josephine Baker, the sensational "French" cabaret performer, would not appear in any place that was not integrated; the NAACP made her Woman of the Year. By May 1959, when Irene Dobbs Jackson, the sister of Mattiwilda Dobbs, the Metropolitan

Opera singer—who at that time refused to sing in Atlanta because her father would have to sit in the second balcony—offered to make herself a test case for getting blacks into Carnegie Library in Atlanta, she never got the chance. The trustees agreed at once to give the extraordinary woman, who had six children and a doctorate from the University of Toulouse, a library card. They thereby opened all the libraries of Atlanta to the Negro population. A white Atlantan wrote to the local paper acknowledging his embarrassment at never having realized that the libraries were segregated. Many whites were similarly shamed by the dignity and self-sacrifice they saw.

If the next decade would reveal some of the weaknesses as well as the strength of passive resistance, there was good reason at the end of the 1950s to accept Howard Zinn's conclusion to Irene Dobbs Jackson's story that "the twentieth century may, eons from now, be viewed as the time when purposeful peaceful social change came into its own."[23]

Artists and Athletes

In February 1952 Dorothy Maynor gave a concert at Constitution Hall, thus ending the era of discrimination that the Daughters of the American Revolution had begun in 1939 by denying Marion Anderson the right to perform on their stage. American Negroes, unstinting through most of our history in their willingness to share their talents, began during the 1950s to be judged more seriously for their achievements than for their color.

In 1955 Marion Anderson became the first black woman to sing with the Metropolitan Opera. And although critics remarked that it was too late for Dorothy Maynor's career to flourish, it was a mark of progress that during the 1950s she was also the first black woman to sing on the Lyric Theater stage in Baltimore. These women confidently led the black procession of brilliant classical singers who proclaimed the richness of American talent in interpreting European music to the rest of the world during the second half of the twentieth century: Leontyne Price, Mattiwilda Dobbs, Grace Bumbry, Adele Addison, Shirley Verrett, Jessye Norman, Felicia Weathers, Clamma Dale, and Carole Brice, among others, proved themselves versatile and skillful artists in the highest competitive sense. Distinguished among black classical musicians in the 1950s was also Phi-

lippa Schuyler, a concert pianist and composer whose work
Manhattan Nocturne was performed by the Detroit Symphony.
Schuyler's death in a plane crash in Vietnam in 1967 remains a nota-
ble loss.

More important, perhaps because it demanded more imagination,
was the acceptance by the white intellectual establishment in the
1950s of popular "black" music as an American form of art. The
1950s marked a resurgence of many different popular musical forms:
blues, jump, rhythm 'n' blues, jazz, swing, bop, cool, rock 'n' roll,
folk, country, and bluegrass—even the names suggest the richness
characteristic of the period—a mixture of African roots and European folk traditions never confined to any one style or narrow interpretation. For the first time in 1956, the State Department saw what
a cultural asset our eclectic musical heritage could be, and began to
send American jazz musicians on tour all over the world.

In 1956 the government would even lift its travel ban against Paul
Robeson so he could sing in Wales as a guest of the National Union
of Mine Workers. Sydney Bechet's clarinet caused audiences to go
wild in France; Louis Armstrong would use his great popularity
abroad to bargain for intervention in the Little Rock crisis at home.
In the 1950s, too, the Newport Jazz Festival heralded the beginning
of serious jazz concerts; and jazz criticism, like Stanley Edgar Hyman's discussion of the blues, began to appear in magazines like the
Partisan Review.[24] The beginning abundance of LP re-releases, along
with the acceptance by music educators of the idea that jazz was
worthy of scholarly attention, helped re-create an earlier decade of
high musical achievement at the same time that it enhanced the self-
respect of younger musicians.

The great tradition of black women singing the blues reaching
back to Ma Rainey and Bessie Smith thus became accessible to white
middle-class audiences in the 1950s. The complexity of the form
suited the steady ambivalence of the times; Ralph Ellison defined
blues as expressing "both the agony of life and the possibility of con-
quering it through sheer toughness of spirit. They fall short of tragedy," he wrote, "only in that they provide no solution, offer no
scapegoat but the self."[25] Lawrence Levine, in his fine book *Black
Culture and Black Consciousness*, agreed that blues were never fatalistic—quoting a classical Bessie Smith refrain about a woman whose
man has left her: "And I'm a good woman, and I can get plenty

men." It seemed clear, when Ethel Waters won the "Woman of Achievement" award in 1951, that it was not just for her performance in *A Member of the Wedding*, but for a lifetime of contribution to our awareness of other dimensions in American life. Langston Hughes wrote: "Ethel Waters could pour all her own memories of grief, sorrow and loneliness / into her songs / and make them unforgettable vignettes of great dramatic intensity."[26]

In 1950 Mahalia Jackson gave a concert in Carnegie Hall; and in 1952 she toured Europe as a gospel singer not wanting, she said, to exploit her talents just for secular success. Although her music seemed to carry people back to the painful reality of slavery, she made a point of not being part of the blues tradition because she felt the refrains too despairing. She chose to emphasize the more sustaining spiritual aspect of American life—the powerful consolation of religious folk music, the evangelical, mystical quality of the hymn or spiritual that singers like Marion Williams continued. Finally Mahalia Jackson saw her role as a political-religious crusader alongside Martin Luther King, Jr., as did Eslanda Robeson, who had been driven by Senator McCarthy to living abroad.

Koko Taylor, singer of songs about independent women, found Chicago unreceptive in the 1950s: "It took more than ten years of waiting around, hanging out in clubs and sitting in with whoever would ask her before she was able to make a record."[27] But in Europe the blues remained a lively part of the repertory of Alberta Hunter, who sang for the United Services Organization until 1953 as well as in European concert halls. Hunter, who had written songs for Bessie Smith and later composed scores for movies, also left jazz singing in 1956 to practice professional nursing—perhaps another example of the decade's failure to reward adequately the talents of powerful women. When Alberta Hunter returned to jazz singing in New York in 1977—then in her eighties—she became still another "new old woman," an example of woman's capacity to play many roles with vitality and to change identity at different stages of her life.

The most popular black woman singer of the 1950s was Ella Fitzgerald, who won the *Metronome* poll twice and the *Playboy* and *Down Beat* awards as well. She toured Europe several times during the 1950s, singing musical-comedy songs. People who could not attend her jazz concerts with Duke Ellington could see her in *Pete Kelly's Blues*, a 1955 movie.

In the 1970s another movie, *Lady Sings the Blues,* based on the autobiography of Billie "Lady Day" Holiday, reminded us of the tragic
life and death, in 1959, of the most extraordinary blues singer of
modern times. During the 1950s, Holiday, who had begun her singing career much earlier with Benny Goodman, became an accepted
celebrity. Her message was "the miracle of pure style," Elizabeth
Hardwick wrote: "That was it. Only a fool imagined that it was necessary to love a man, love anyone, love life. Her own people, those
around her, feared her. And perhaps," Hardwick concluded, "even
she was often ashamed of the heavy weight of her own spirit, one
never tempted to the relief of sentimentality."[28] Billie Holiday gave a
number of European concerts, including one for 6,000 people at
London's Royal Albert Hall, which she ended with the song that
may have been her best-known musical testimony to the agony of
being black in America, "Strange Fruit." If the lyrics of her songs
often seemed not to matter as much as her style, what was certain,
as Levine noted, was that her grandmother's slavery remained a part
of Billie Holiday: "She used to tell me how it felt to be a slave, to be
owned body and soul by a white man who was the father of her
children."[29]

In 1954, *Down Beat* gave Holiday a special award as "one of the
all-time great vocalists in jazz." She too had not wanted to be known
as *just* a blues singer. After the 1956 publication of her autobiography, the high point of her life was a Carnegie Hall concert during
which Gilbert Millstein read passages from the book in between her
songs. Nat Hentoff wrote: "it was a night when Billie was on top,
the best jazz singer alive. . . . What Billie had to say," he went on,
"should be said aloud, and precisely in those places where good manners and 'taste' have been substituted for the courage to see."[30] "How
many symphony orchestras, for example, have played Carnegie Hall
with not one Negro in the ensemble, and who cried on stage then?"
If Billie Holiday refused—as she once told Hazel Scott, another
black musician—to let the whites see her cry, she would still let her
audiences feel the tears in her music.[31] And the extension of feeling
we all experienced made America, momentarily at least, more
human.

During her final hospitalization in 1959 Holiday remained—perhaps like Bessie Smith—a victim of hostile prejudice. Police found
an envelope of heroin in her hospital room; they planted guards out-

side and sent men to fingerprint her even as she was dying. She had once said that she liked singing in England because there she was respected as an artist, not just as a singer; here she could never commercialize her style adequately "to achieve the acclaim that the insecure side of her character needed so desperately."[32] The alienation that has tormented so many gifted artists in this country was Billie Holiday's, yet so was the ultimate acceptance. After her death sales of her records continued to mount; she became part of the Smithsonian's collection of classic jazz immortals.

Ethel Waters had won an award for her autobiography, *His Eye Is on the Sparrow*, in 1951. Lena Horne wrote hers, *In Person, Lena Horne*, in 1950; and Eartha Kitt added hers, *Thursday's Child*, in 1956. Together with the 1956 *Lady Sings the Blues* and Pearl Bailey's later volumes, *The Raw Pearl* and *Talking to Myself*, they represent a written testimony to the versatility, courage, and achievement of black women singers in America in the period immediately following World War II. Bailey, it must be noted, unlike Billie Holiday, saw herself as a traditional rags-to-riches success story—she was proud to sing at Eisenhower's second inauguration. Mary Lou Williams, a musical arranger, would have seen herself in similar terms; working behind the scenes, she was valued as a gifted composer-arranger for a great variety of black and white musicians. Never again, in any case, would the level of artistry these black women represented be questioned. The written word—the Western white man's measure of accomplishment—was able finally in the 1950s to record the extent of the black musician's influence.

"A people must define itself," wrote Ralph Ellison in 1953, "and minorities have the responsibility of having their ideals and images recognized as part of the composite image which is that of the still forming American people."[33] That Ellison and James Baldwin produced their finest work during the 1950s may have tended to distract public attention from the black women who were also writing then, especially because black women writers have been more concerned with their identity as blacks than with their identity as women. But there would be little dispute that a woman wrote the most distinguished Negro play of the decade, *A Raisin in the Sun*: "Never before in the entire history of the American theater," Baldwin wrote, "had so much of the truth of black people's lives been seen on the stage."[34]

In 1959 Lorraine Hansberry was given the Drama Critics Circle Award for having written "the best play of the year"; she was the youngest American playwright, the fifth woman, and the only black writer ever to have won the award. Although never despairing—Hansberry said her vision of man was basically good—she nevertheless felt the absurdities of life as most blacks lived it in America, and appreciated the moral dilemma of the Negro writer's position: she could not take refuge in the comforting illusions—or underlying assumptions—of our society. "She made no bones about asserting that art has a purpose," James Baldwin wrote, "and that its purpose was action: that it contained the energy which could change things."[35] Yet in keeping with the liberal imagination that defined the age, Hansberry abhorred the idea that even the painful realities of Negro life should be oversimplified: "Ours is a complex and difficult country and some of our complexities are indeed grotesque,"[36] she wrote to a student at Little Rock. Committed to using her specific experience to clarify a more universal suffering, she believed that if "blackness brought pain, it was also a source of strength, renewal and inspiration, a window on the potential of the human race."[37] She relished the challenge of putting on paper—or on the stage—all the "infinite varieties of the human spirit" that her own black experience revealed. Although a subsequent generation of black writers would be less responsive to her optimism, they could not ignore the sincerity of her attempt to record that spirit which "invariably hangs between despair and joy."[38] When she died of cancer in 1965 at the age of thirty-four, a sense of impoverishment remained. She would not have tolerated platitudes, yet her literary aim, to create many-sided black characters—to counteract a heritage of stereotypes—was barely fulfilled.

James Baldwin wondered if Hansberry's complex and compassionate vision had grown out of her sense of "vulnerability as a woman in a violent universe," or "perhaps because of her multifold experience as a *black* woman," or simply "perhaps because of her intuitive view of human frailty."[39] The black woman's compulsion to write seems to grow out of all these forces, enriched by a need to legitimize herself in the consciousness of the white culture she also shares.

If it was not until the late 1960s and 1970s—with the acceptance in feminist journals of critical articles on black women writers; with the publication of Mary Helen Washington's excellent anthologies of classic stories by and about black women;[40] and with the Feminist Press's reprints of seminal thinkers like Zora Neale Hurston—that black women writers were finally accorded special recognition for their own feminine sensibilities, they had, nevertheless, been exploring and recording their experiences for many decades.[41]

When Gwendolyn Brooks won the Pulitzer Prize in 1950 for *Annie Allen*, she admitted to being shaped by European models and by Langston Hughes. But she kept her Chicago mind receptive to cultural liberation and the black pride that accompanied the new civil-rights movement. Flexibility almost defines the many strong women who were already mature in the 1950s, but did not stop growing. Like Adrienne Rich, Gwendolyn Brooks quite consciously redefined herself in mid-life. As Rich shifted to define her sensibility first as a woman, so Brooks turned to make her consciousness black. She grew tired of being just a "poet who happens to be black."[42] In the 1970s she gave up her long-standing connection with a white publishing house as a gesture of support to the black cultural community. "It frightens me to realize that, if I had died before the age of fifty," she would proudly say, "I would have died a 'Negro fraction.'"[43] Yet that fraction remains a vivid part of all her early work.

To be a black woman is to be doubly disadvantaged in American society; but being both black and a woman, Gwendolyn Brooks was doubly free to look critically at the values of the groups that refused to recognize her as an equal. Even Lorraine Hansberry had stopped to wonder if it was worthwhile integrating oneself into a burning house. Brooks would go on to question the price of the education that had so often been the key to liberation for black women:

> Maud, who went to college,
> Is a thin brown mouse
> She is living all alone
> In this old house.[44]

Would the mother's agony in "The Last Quatrain of the Ballad of Emmett Till" seem a more worthy human experience than the less vulnerable educated isolation of "living all alone"? Black women writers, even the most intellectual, were generally less eager than white women to identify with the emotion-controlled world of successful white men. They continue to debate the value of severing their feelings for any illusory power they might gain. An example of such feeling might be the black woman's ambivalence about abortion. Brooks had reflected: "Abortions will not let you forget / You remember the children you got that you did not get."⁴⁵ White women also feel such pain; but the issues of birth control or sterilization as genocide continue to haunt the black community surging toward social mobility in a manner that is unreal in its intensity for whites. Nikki Giovanni, in an autobiographical statement on her first twenty-five years of being a black poet—*Gemini*—would declare that one thing she knew for sure about white people was that they *hated* children.⁴⁶

Although there can be no doubt that many of Gwendolyn Brooks's poems reflected a fundamental concern with what it feels like to be black in America, many of these poems are also outspokenly written in women's imagery, or from a woman's point of view. The dramatic monologue about "Mrs. Small"—trying to pay the insurance man as she takes care of ten children, makes apple pies, and attempts to bolster her self-esteem by remembering the good cup of coffee she can brew—should speak to as many readers as the better-known T. S. Eliot portrait of a lady serving tea to friends. In describing "the children of the poor," or "A Bronzeville Mother" in Mississippi, domestic imagery fills her poems. Even in writing about Little Rock, Brooks stresses the banality of evil: "The *Chicago Defender* Sends a Man to Little Rock—Fall 1957":

> In Little Rock the people bear
> Babes, and comb and part their hair
> And watch the want ads, put repair
> To roof and latch. While wheat toast burns
> A woman waters multiferns
> . . . .
> And after testament and tunes
> Some soften Sunday afternoons
> With lemon tea and Lorna Doones.

But brutality breaks through:

> And true they are hurling spittle, rock,
> Garbage and fruit in Little Rock.
> And I saw coiling storm a-writhe
> On bright madonnas. And a scythe
> Of men harassing brownish girls,
> (The bow and barettes in the curls
> And Braids declined away from joy.)
> I saw a bleeding brownish boy. . . .⁴⁷

Gwendolyn Brooks's female black conscience was clearly alive and growing in the 1950s even as Rich's lesbian awareness was taking root. In *Maud Martha*, the autobiographical novel first published in 1953, Brooks gave us a classic early example of a young black woman's identity search, but as the *Chicago Tribune* perceived, she also gave us a book that could be read as "vividly, intensely racial," a novel "more illuminating about racial relations than hundreds of books which discuss them."[48]

Mary Helen Washington remarks that such novels provide knowledge of how a black girl grows up in an unprotected world. Another 1950s novel, Paule Marshall's *Brown Girl, Brownstones*, similarly reflected how a developing woman learned to deal with a harsh environment. These books "show the black girl developing self-reliance and resilience in order to deal with the hostile forces around her, quite often assuming adulthood earlier than she should have to because of the external pressures around her." Although it may be true, as Washington asserts, that sociologists can back up literary illustrations with statistical examples of the coping strategies and resources that have enabled many black women to exhibit "an unusual degree of emotional stability and strength,"[49] it can be dangerous to accept these writers complacently as arguments for benign neglect. Not many black women emerge from environments of pain with the strength of Naomi Madgett, who produced *One and the Many*, a collection of poetry, during the 1950s; or of Ann Petry, who published *The Narrows* in 1953 and celebrated the bravery of Harriet Tubman in *Conductor of the Underground Railroad* in 1955; or with the will to achieve of either Paule Marshall or Gwendolyn Brooks—both products of strong, supportive families.

The tradition of black women's autobiographical writing, which would flower in the second half of the century in the skillful hands of Maya Angelou, Kristin Hunter, Louise Meriwether, Nikki Giovanni, Alice Walker, and Toni Morrison, was rooted in the 1950s. Were there new ideas in these books as well as strong female characters? The loss of childhood innocence; the generational conflicts, the stories of failed romantic love—so embedded in the tragic side of our vision of social mobility—are all part of a broader American literary tradition. The constant concerns about how each individual relates to outside society—even the continued concern about being black—reflect general anxieties in American life. If the pain of having dark skin has made black women more continually vulnerable to the white world's insistence on judging all women first by surfaces, white women nevertheless identified with their feelings in other ways. To be a fat woman or an old woman or an ugly woman may be no less difficult in a society that worships mythical physical ideals and depends so much on appearances.

But the conflict between black and white women as it begins to be articulated in the writing of the 1950s does indeed represent an important new dimension in literary expression. Alice Childress published *Like One of the Family . . . Conversations from a Domestic's Life* in 1956, a series of dialogue confrontations between mistress and maid that clarified how such relationships were perceived by bright blacks. Too often white women, because of the more subtle putdowns they experienced, did not realize that their pedestals were all too real—and offensive to the black women, who saw their own daily work the base of the middle-class white's standard of living. Although the black writers of the 1950s believed in integration as a goal, they also wanted to help white liberals confront their limitations.[50] Gwendolyn Brooks wrote critically about white women's fears of black ostentation in "The Bronzeville Woman in a Red Hat," and again of their condescension in "The Lovers of the Poor," in which the "Ladies from the Ladies Betterment League" . . . "Keeping their scented bodies in the center / Of the hall . . . Try to avoid inhaling the laden air."[51]

In *Maud Martha* Brooks wrote also about the pain of being "invisible" while listening to a white saleswoman talk about "working like a nigger," or being patronized by a lady selling hats; she had to use the back entrance if she wanted to go on being a maid for Mrs. Burns-Cooper of Winnetka. For the first time, Maud Martha understood what her husband was enduring daily when his boss just looked at him as if he were a child. Brooks did not mean to suggest ever that the black woman's lot was harder than the black man's; and Maud Martha's final self-discovery through marriage was as full of love and forbearance as any romance in the 1953 *Ladies' Home Journal*: "And in the meantime, she was going to have another baby," the novel concluded affirmatively; "the weather was bidding her bon voyage."[52]

Brooks knew what a demanding institution marriage could be. "If you're a woman, you have to set yourself aside constantly," she later wrote, describing her agreeable separation from her husband of thirty years. "After having a year of solitude, I realized that this is what is right for me, to be able to control my life."[53] But she urged

younger black women to stick with their men during their tempes-
tuous black identity crisis. And she remarked that she had felt no
regrets for all the time and attention she had given her children—in
contrast to the complaints about children of 70 percent of Ann Lan-
ders's newspaper-column readers in the 1970s. In one interview,
Brooks acknowledged that she also did not like to be labeled a
"professional writer" or to be defined in terms of her "ambition." Yet
her perfectionist concern for the quality of her work suggests that
she will be valued as more than a black polemical poet. Gwendolyn
Brooks relished the complexity of the decades that shaped her consciousness. If black poets end up being fortunate for having both the
richness of being African and of being American behind them,
Brooks would add to the definition of her own wealth the pleasure of
being a woman.

The more specific her writing was, she realized, the more depth
could be extracted from it. The celebration of urban life—with all its
exploitation, injustice, and humor—helped to extend the range of
poetic possibility. Black Chicago had as much to say to the contemporary Negro as the classics of black folklore turned up by Zora
Neale Hurston under Franz Boas's supervision in an earlier decade.
The fate of Hurston in the 1950s, in fact, became still another example of painful paradox in American life.

Among the best Negro writers of the first half of the century,
Hurston had so little money by 1950 that she took a job as a cleaning
woman. She was discovered only when her employer chanced upon
one of her articles in the *Saturday Evening Post:* "Famous Negro Author Working as Maid Here Just to 'Live a Little,'" the local paper
declared. Interviewed, Hurston declared proudly: "I like to cook and
keep house—why shouldn't I do it for somebody else a while? A
writer has to stop writing every now and then and just live a little."[54]

The pressure to earn money and the terrible publicity she had received in connection with a false morals charge at the end of the previous decade left Hurston drained and desperate. An article
published in the *Negro Digest*, "What White Publishers Won't Print,"
discussed survival techniques, and her own reaction to stereotypes:
"As long as the majority cannot conceive of a Negro or Jew feeling
and reacting inside just as they do, the majority will keep right on
believing that people who do not look like them cannot possibly feel
as they do."[55] By 1950 Hurston had abandoned the folk material that
distinguished her early work—the rural mythology parallel to

Gwendolyn Brooks's city descriptions of the people "farthest down." Her new political role confounded many of her former admirers because she became an ardent reactionary, reflecting the decade's tendency to foster complex reactions in sensitive individuals. Hurston supported the conservative Taft in the election of 1952, and even questioned the value of the 1954 desegregation decision. Roy Wilkins and Harold Preece of the NAACP accused her of forgetting the economic conditions of the people she was writing about; and Ralph Ellison and Richard Wright attacked her for "turning her writing into caricature."[56]

But Robert Hemenway, Hurston's biographer, reasonably attributes her 1950s conservatism to three factors: her obsessive individualism—that self-confidence that emerged from growing up in an all-black, self-governed community, Eatonville, Florida; her suspicion of communism, which was fed by the hysteria of the McCarthy era; and the pride of her long-standing commitment to the strength of black cultural heroes. In her own mind, Hemenway points out, she had already "liberated rural black folk from the prison of racial stereotypes and granted them dignity as cultural creators."

Disliking liberals for seeing blacks as victims, Hurston had made a point of celebrating "the black folk who had made a way out of no way, like their folk heroes."[57] She refused to accept what she saw as the prejudices of American social science, which reported Negroes as pathological or deviant because of their deprivations. In the white middle class she saw a different kind of "ideological and esthetic poverty." As early as 1937, Hurston had asked the Guggenheim Foundation to establish a college of *black music*, a plea not seriously echoed again until 1971, when Ishmael Reed called for an end to the "Western Established Church of Art." But in the 1950s Hurston's demands for cultural pluralism came across as political stagnation: "one could not both celebrate Afro-American culture and deplore many of the conditions that helped to shape it."[58]

In 1951 Hurston joined the anti-Communist crusade by publishing in the *American Legion Magazine* "Why the Negro Won't Buy Communism," a polemical refusal to see blacks as victims of their economic opportunities. A letter to the *Orlando Sentinel* in 1955 protested the pathological stereotype behind the 1954 antisegregation decision—the idea that black students could learn only if they sat next to whites. Had not *she*, after all, received an excellent education in all-black Eatonville? In a decade struggling toward integration when, in fact, 66 percent of black children lived in poverty, her racial ideas seemed unreal. Hurston found it hard ever to admit that discussion of the grimmest social realities amounted to more than self-pity. Yet a strong sense of individual racial injustice remained eloquent in her 1956 account of the murder trial of Ruby McCollum, incorporated by William Bradford Huie as a section of *Ruby McCollum: Woman in the Suwannee Jail.*[59]

When fate turned circumstances against Hurston, pride remained. Did not tourists stop to take pictures of the artistic flower display she had planted around her one-room rented cabin in Eau Gallie? She wanted to laugh at the whites who saw her "shack" in the pitying terms of black poverty. It would still be hard to argue with the minister who gave her funeral sermon: "Every time she went about," he said, "Zora Neale Hurston had something to offer; she didn't come to you empty." Because she was buried in the city's segregated cemetery when she died in 1960 at the age of fifty-nine, the Miami paper reported that she had died "poor"; but the minister rightly insisted that she died "rich"—"She did something."[60]

The strong ego of Zora Neale Hurston managed for a long while to assert itself on its own terms—to side-step the dilemma W. E. B. DuBois found so anguishing to Afro-Americans torn between their own folk culture and the white male European norms our technological society uses for final judgments. If, like Jean Toomer, she finally abandoned the folk tradition in her writing, she did not, like Toomer, also abandon the black system of values that remained apart from the other America. She enjoyed being black and acting like a woman. And in finding much satisfaction in her flowers and in the phosphorescent beauty of the river that coursed near her hut, Hurston asserted a lifelong identity—like Thoreau's—that challenged the technological civilization that had also become part of her life.

Zora Neale Hurston's anthropological excursions helped many blacks extend the dimensions of their lives. Negroes continued to explore the separateness of black culture. In 1955 Shirley Graham Dubois published her biography of Booker T. Washington as part of a series that was to include Paul Robeson, George Washington Carver, Phillis Wheatley, Frederick Douglass, and W. E. B. DuBois. And, in 1956, Pauli Murray published a distinguished genealogical history. *Proud Shoes: The Story of an American Family* recounted the story of Murray's own ancestors at a time when such studies were hardly fashionable. Interrupting her law practice for four years to research and write this book was Pauli Murray's individual response to the hysteria of the moment:

> The fear of Communism was rampant; anyone who championed a liberal cause was vulnerable to the charge of disloyalty. . . . As a civil rights activist fighting against racial segregation when challenges of segregation policy were few and defeats were customary I found it imperative to declare my American heritage. Not Communism, but the ideals and influences within my own family had made me a life-long fighter against all forms of inequality and injustice.[61]

Again, although racial conflict in America is at the heart of the story, she shows that there is more to her family than any ideology. Especially important are the characterizations of "several remarkably brave and independent women," not, as Murray describes them, "conscious feminists, but women who in coping with the intolerable tensions of their time "assumed responsibilities and performed actions which quietly defied convention and transcended 'a woman's place.' "[62]

When Pauli Murray, herself a triumphant example of such a woman, retired from a life in law and in university teaching, she went on to study for the ministry. At age sixty-seven she became one of three women ordained at Washington Cathedral. Although her special talents may make the imitation of such a life difficult, Pauli Murray's achievement must also be recorded as an example of a woman who managed to overcome three different institutional barriers: color, sex, and age. From the women in her own family she had learned not to be easily discouraged in efforts to manage this variety of successful careers.

Black women excelled in other fields during the 1950s as well. Pearl Primus and Katherine Dunham, also an anthropologist, danced. Jackie "Moms" Mably kept up a folk tradition of Negro comedy that influenced the later popular entertainers Bill Cosby and Godfrey Cambridge. Relying on "recognition" as the main source of humor, as Lawrence Levine noted, her material was topical and general enough to be hilarious to more than just blacks. In the next decade two records of her comedy routines sold over a million copies each.

At a time when students were earnestly trying to integrate lunch counters, Moms could still jest about being stared at when she entered a fancy restaurant: "I don't want to go to school with you," she assured the other diners, "I just want a piece of cheese cake."[63]

Dorothy Dandridge experienced more of the difficulties than the triumphs of being a black woman in a Hollywood she perceived as racist in the 1950s. She called her biography *Everything and Nothing: The Dorothy Dandridge Tragedy*.

Visual artists like Lois Maillou Jones, Barbara Chase—whose work was bought by Ben Shahn—and Alma Thomas produced a number of gallery shows during the decade. Elizabeth Catlett turned her studio into a Harlem museum. The idea that "black is beautiful" appeared in her prints long before it became a fashionable slogan. Catlett's work also celebrated the beauty of pregnancy and motherhood—that part of the feminine mystique so valued during the 1950s that one art critic went so far as to insist that the Mona Lisa's smile revealed her secret pregnancy.

And black women excelled in more competitive worlds. Althea Gibson brought the pride of black achievement to tennis, at that time still an elite sport, when she won both Wimbledon and the United States Lawn Tennis Association championships twice (1957–58) as the first black participant. In her autobiography, *I Always Wanted to Be Somebody*, Gibson apologized for not being as racially conscious as Jackie Robinson had been in integrating baseball, but she was proud to note that her individual triumphs had resulted in extending privilege to her race; by the end of the 1950s there were many more blacks playing professional tennis. Another talented athlete, Wilma Rudolph trained during the 1950s to win three gold medals as an Olympic runner in 1960.

Overall, the 1950s represented a decade of important achievements for the Negro woman. A great wave of strength spread out at the beginning of the civil-rights movement enabling individuals to define themselves with pride. "Black women have never been the silly little Christmas tree ornaments—fragile and false—of the Western woman myth,"[64] Eugenia Collier would later write. What these women, the lowest-paid workers in America, shared with white women during the 1950s was their alienation from the power structure of the white male—and their capacity for survival.

Speaking in *Gemini* of the forces that shaped her own life, Nikki Giovanni paid tribute to Gwendolyn Brooks's exhortation: "This is the urgency—live." The younger poet concluded: "We Black women are the single group in the West intact. And anybody can see we're pretty shaky. We are, however (all praises), the only group that derives its identity from itself."[65] White women continued to profit from the black woman's example in American society.

Mrs. Elsie Truesdell playing with children on the grounds of the old age
home where she lives in Stony Brook, Long Island.
Photograph by Eve Arnold. Courtesy of Magnum Photos, Inc.

Chapter Nine

Health: New Old Women and "Neurotic" Mothers

In San Francisco, the city where Imogen Cunningham would continue to photograph the wonder of living beyond the age of ninety, physicians at the University of California Medical Center held a symposium in the early 1960s on *The Potential of Women*. They were then just beginning to assimilate the statistical changes over the first half of the twentieth century that documented women's capacity to live longer. In a report on *Health Progress in the United States 1900–1960*, figures demonstrated that the sex differential in mortality was wider than at any other time in American history. In 1957–59, male mortality exceeded female by 142 percent at ages fifteen to twenty-four and by 92 percent at ages fifty-five to sixty-four; male mortality from heart disease in 1958 was more than twice the female rate over the entire age range from thirty-five to sixty-four. Even cancer in 1958 showed an excess of male mortality by 25 percent; diabetes was the only disease with a higher death rate for women. The accidental death rate for males—always higher—exceeded the rate for women by 177 percent.[1]

Instead of celebrating this achievement of longer life, a number of male doctors appeared unnerved by it. Typical of such was Edmund W. Overstreet, a gynecologist who did not hesitate to express his

anxiety over women's life expectancy at the San Francisco conference: "When you come right down to it," Overstreet jocularly declared, "perhaps women just live too long! Maybe when they get
through having babies they have outlived their usefulness." This was
no Jonathan Swift but a serious physician raising a question he said
many of his fellow gynecologists were asking: "Is a woman's post-
menopausal status a normal physiologic condition, or is it actually a
pathologic disease state?"[2] A quick glance at the statistics gathered
by the National Manpower Council in 1957 would have told these
gynecologists that many of the pathologically diseased women they
were talking about were an important part of the labor force. By
1970, over 54 percent of all American women between the ages of
forty-five and fifty-four would be at work. Whether some of the
women on the panel with Dr. Overstreet were also beyond their
years of "usefulness" was a question that did not trouble him. He
managed to cast doubt upon the capabilities of younger women as
well by discussing the traumatic aspects of premenstrual tension. It
was clear that Overstreet, belonging to the dominant school of gynecology in the 1950s, also saw menstruation, pregnancy, and childbirth as illnesses, rather than as natural functions. There were few
women doctors on the scene when 5 percent medical-school admissions was standard policy, and even fewer women gynecologists to
take issue with his point of view. (Gender statistics for the 1950s are
hard to come by. We do know that as late as 1971 there was but one
woman gynecologist each in Alaska, Nevada, New Hampshire, and
Wyoming; and five or fewer in each of eleven other states. To say
that 95 percent of all gynecologists were men would not be an exag-
geration.) But it may be noteworthy that when the physicians in
charge planned to call this symposium "The Control of Women"
there was enough of a protest to change the title that many doctors
seemed to prefer.

Fortunately, the symposium also included speeches by Eleanor
Maccoby and Esther Peterson, who understood clearly the growing
need to redefine women's biological potential in terms of cultural expectations. They, and Marya Mannes—whose feminism consistently transcended the popular opinions of the 1950s—argued
eloquently for the need for extensive social change. If women were
an essential part of the labor force who often managed both home
and children as well as a job—if they were reentering the world of
work when many men were ready to retire, and still outliving

FIGURE 3

Percentage of Women Workers over 45

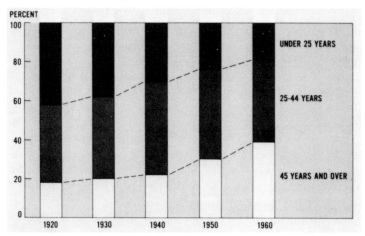

Reprinted from American Women *(Washington, D. C.: U. S. Government Printing Office, 1963).*

them—women could hardly be described as physiologically weak or biologically inferior. Facts spoke louder than physicians' fears.[3]

Yet most women in the 1950s readily accepted the "scientific" opinions of the medically trained. Although they may have been uneasy about some medical attitudes, they did not even question the radical surgery being performed on their own bodies. A National Health Survey (1960–62) reported that five million American women—more than a quarter of the total between the ages of fifty and sixty-four—had had surgical rather than natural menopause. As early as 1953 Dr. James C. Doyle published an article, "Unnecessary Hysterectomies," in the *AMA Journal*. In over six thousand operations studied, Doyle found 30 percent of women age twenty to twenty-nine had no disease when their wombs were removed; 39 percent of the operations were open to criticism, and 12 percent had no indications whatsoever that hysterectomies were necessary.[4]

An article in *Obstetrics and Gynecology*, also published in 1953, noted that almost 80 percent of the operations performed in five different hospitals to remove women's ovaries, between 1947 and 1951, were unjustified. When the United Mine Workers Medical Care Program in the mid-1950s required that all gynecological operations be endorsed by specialists, the number of hysterectomies performed dropped by as much as 75 percent. A 1956 survey, *Family Medical Costs and Voluntary Health Insurance*, by O. W. Anderson and J. J. Feldman, regrettably demonstrated that the number of hysterectomies performed on insured persons—guaranteeing the surgeon payment—was double the number for the uninsured.[5]

Similarly extreme surgery was usually prescribed for lumps in women's breasts. Radical mastectomy—the complete removal of breast, lymph nodes, and pectoral muscles—was standard procedure during the 1950s, although there was no controlled study to demonstrate that it was any more successful than the less extreme surgery used in Britain. A few daring surgeons like George Crile in Cleveland and Oliver Cope in Boston were willing to perform more focused operations, but choice was rarely available for most patients.[6]

It is easy to understand how "our bodies, ourselves" would become a natural outcry in the next decade—against the numbers of Overstreets wanting to control such crucial areas of women's lives.[7] Organized demands for change brought about by the women's health movement would help to make the number of practicing women obstetricians and gynecologists an improved 20 percent by the end of the 1960s, but during the 1950s there was little choice for women about anything involving their bodies.

Even birth control was an area that women had little to say about. Although available for decades, birth control was not, in fact, officially sanctioned by the American Medical Association until 1959, the year before the Pill was put on the mass market. How much of the general legitimization of birth control grew out of the new conservative concern to limit the fertility of undesirable populations rather than from any interest in giving all women more control over their own bodies may be worth more extensive study. The original experiments on the birth-control pill in the 1950s were all made on Puerto Rican women (132 had taken the Pill for one year or longer; 718 others had taken the drug for less than a year; three died with symptoms suggesting blood clots.) When later public opinion demanded more adequate studies of the Pill's side effects, Chicano women were used. Dr. Joseph Goldzieher, who directed these studies at the Southwest Foundation for Research and Education, neglected to tell the women that he was also using placebos; ten became pregnant.[8]

Most medical schools felt no responsibility for training future doctors in the quality of different birth-control methods, or in their dangerous side-effects, or in problems related to sexuality and fertility. Two states—Massachusetts and Connecticut—continued throughout most of the decade to make the distribution of materials related to birth control illegal.

Abortion, the ultimate measure of woman's ability to control society in terms of self, was generally defined as a criminal act—unless performed to save the life of the mother. By 1958 there were modifications of some abortion laws in a few states to preserve the health of the mother, or to permit abortion on "medical advice as well as the peril of necessity,"[9] but in general women needing abortions had to see themselves as criminals. When Dorothy Day published her autobiography, *The Long Loneliness*, in 1952 she knew that to mention her own abortion would destroy her credibility, perhaps even demolish the possibility of getting her book published; readers have to imagine the quality of the sin for which her life atoned so eloquently.

A 1959 legal study of the abortion problem revealed a "dramatic variation between a legal norm and social fact." Many nonclandestine abortions were in fact being performed to protect a woman's health as opposed to her life. Because of the criminal laws there was also an enormous black market in abortions of over ten million a year, resulting, by 1962, in the deaths each year of between five and ten thousand women. Contrary to social expectations, statistics available in 1958 made it clear that most illegal abortions were performed on *married* women who already had children; such women were willing to risk both life and criminal prosecution to avoid the lifetime stress of dealing with an unwanted child.[10] Those doctors who argued against legal abortion as involvement with destruction rather than preservation of life steadfastly refused to confront the vast numbers of women's lives already being lost in illegal operations.

After Mary Calderone, "the high priestess of sex-education," became Medical Director of Planned Parenthood in 1953, she designed a conference on abortion to take place in 1955. The meetings were prepared in absolute secrecy for fear of a hostile press. *Abortion* was an unspeakable word. Calderone knew that sex education, like fluoridation and daycare, was often considered a communist plot to undermine American health. She also knew that the educated middle class had continual access to many services denied the poor (one-fifth of the women interviewed by Kinsey had had abortions) and she urged more social concern on the part of the medical profession: "The underprivileged group needs consideration principally because it is inarticulate and unable to ask for either abortion, or the preventive service of contraception."[11]

When the Planned Parenthood Federation of America published *Abortion in the United States* in 1958, a collection of the opinions of forty experts, a number of medical journals expressed anxiety about even reviewing the book. At a time when only two states permitted therapeutic abortions to preserve a woman's health, and neither rape nor incest, even if the victim was a very young girl, was considered valid ground for abortion, to publish such a text was a heroic act. A Baltimore abortionist who had served 350 doctors over a period of twenty years could not find one among them to testify on his behalf when he was called before the courts. Calderone's principled moderation did much to prepare the way for the angry radicals of the future who could not understand why she had not gone further, or, more surprisingly, attacked her efforts to extend birth control as a form of genocide. The liberal proponents of more easily available birth control and legal abortion in the 1950s did not foresee how extensively their reforms would be identified with the eugenics movement in America. When in the early 1960s Planned Parenthood shifted its emphasis from maternal and child health to population control on a grand scale, its leaders were still concerned about maintaining quality in life. Although there were, at the end of the 1950s, only 150 agencies in the entire country dispensing birth control information, by 1972 there would be over three thousand.[12]

Childbirth, as Margaret Mead continued to point out, was yet another of woman's functions conditioned by society. During the 1950s when the birth rate was high, the circumstances for bearing children probably produced more "feminists" than any other single demeaning experience women had. Most women hospitalized for birth during the 1950s were isolated from their husbands, tied down, and knocked out with strong medications. Many had childbirth artificially induced for convenience—without any knowledge of the effects of additional drugs on their infants; some who did not even have fertility problems were given a dangerous hormone, DES, to ensure the stability of their pregnancies. Doctors rarely felt obliged to discuss what they were doing with patients. In 1958, when the *Ladies' Home Journal* published a note from a registered nurse urging an investigation of the delivery-room abuses she had witnessed, the response was greater than for almost any full-length article the *Journal* had ever printed.[13]

Indeed, the *Ladies' Home Journal* articles on "Cruelty in Maternity Wards" were probably the decade's most important contribution to female consciousness-raising. Although the editors of the *Journal* were clearly reluctant to attack the medical establishment, they received so many responses to this one small note from a Chicago nurse that they felt compelled to publish not one but two articles documenting abuses in maternity wards. They reported getting "hundreds and hundreds" (not "thousands") of letters from women all over America relating experiences so shocking that they felt "national attention should be focused on such conditions wherever they exist in order that they may be ended."[14]

Trying to be as fair as possible—the *Ladies' Home Journal* was not eager to become an outlet for muckrakers—Gladys Denny Shultz, the editor of "Cruelty in Maternity Wards," reported that these letters had come in from both rural and urban America, and that women who moved often found great contrasts from one hospital to another; she tried to counterbalance the majority of responses with a few reports of happy births, assuring readers that the "majority of both obstetrical and maternal hospitals resent such practices and want them ended." The editors, nevertheless, felt compelled to report "incidents that would be unbelievable if they had not come so spontaneously from such obviously intelligent mothers." Many readers, they noted, had accepted indignities or abuses as unavoidable until they read the nurse's indignant letter.[15]

If only one such cruel abuse had taken place, a reader wrote—typical of the mentality of a time that did not rely on numbers for action or authority—it would have been one too many. During a decade when the birth rate soared (births hit a peak in 1957 with almost 123 per thousand women between the ages of fifteen and forty-four), it seems a particular irony that childbirth was so frequently a degrading experience: "Far too many doctors, nurses, and hospitals seem to assume that because a woman is about to give birth to a child she becomes a nitwit, an incompetent reduced to the status of a cow," one woman wrote. To their credit, the *Journal* editors refused to accept the implication that their readers were "spoiled and hysterical," but they could not imagine any way to pressure the profession. Ultimately, they said, the "responsibility for careful delivery of your unborn child lies with you."[16]

Finally, the magazine did make some timid recommendations ("We earnestly urge the medical profession to review the rule which bars the husband from his wife's side") and they invited an unusual doctor, John Whitredge, Jr., of Johns Hopkins—who believed in training 400 nurse-midwives a year—to express a radical opinion. It was hard to argue with the fact that 97 percent of all women survived maternity no matter what the psychic scars were, or the damage to infants might be.

Before the decade was over, the idea of "natural childbirth," a concept that Dr. Overstreet labeled "fad and fancy," would take hold. The few happy births the *Journal* reported were almost always the result of this new flexibility, which gave women much more control over their bodies. Even Helene Deutsch, later much criticized for urging women not to emulate her professional choice but to accept Freud's definition of woman's passive role, tried to make other doctors understand how important it was for women to have more control over the process of childbirth. A change in attitude was long overdue. By the 1960s a few distinguished hospitals, like Grace–New Haven in Connecticut and Jefferson in Philadelphia, were willing to commit themselves to the idea of childbirth without fear, encouraged by Grantly Dick-Read, a successful British gynecologist. Although more conservative cities like Boston tended to see natural childbirth as a return to the primitive, by 1959 Marjorie Karmel's *Thank You, Dr. LaMaze*, celebrating the French alternative to Dick-Read's childbirth training, was a national best-seller.[17]

Perhaps a society committed to equality of opportunity has much to fear from women's gaining power over themselves in any sphere; we seem to have a hard time admitting that 50 percent of our brightest citizens are women—also designed to have babies. During the 1950s a dispassionate technological orientation to chidbirth managed to deprive many sensitive women of satisfaction in the great experience of having a baby. Women had to look to Europe for more sensitive theories of child delivery and, perhaps more important, they finally had to look to each other for help in having babies on their own terms. Before the decade was over women formed classes away from hospitals to teach each other about natural childbirth. Contrary to the advice of the *Ladies' Home Journal*, they learned that they had to stick together to make sure that practices they believed in were professionally available. As husbands took more part in bringing children into the world, another of Dr. Overstreet's fears was also realized: childbirth was no longer simply an experience of women.

Having husbands present during labor not only made it less likely that women would be abused, but also allowed men access to another of women's worlds. Natural childbirth became another way for men to experience androgyny.

It may seem astonishing that so many women during the 1950s accepted the pronouncements of the gynecological establishment as absolutes. The greater number of educated women appeared eager to demonstrate their capacity to respect scientific "experts"; they did not even openly question the use of estrogen in helping to alleviate symptoms of menopause or wonder about the effects of DES or oxytocin on their children. Often separated from their mothers and sisters, they were slow to realize the importance of forming women's support groups like the ones in favor of natural childbirth. There were no visible self-help health programs then, and no midwives. An organized league to help the few women who wanted to nurse their babies was not publicized in either hospital or obstetrician's office; most doctors were indifferent to nursing. Dr. Benjamin Spock's enormously popular paperbound book, *Baby and Child Care*—designed to help women rely on their common sense—made it clear that the pediatrician was far from indispensable. The great success of the book owed much to the young mother's sense of isolation. In reinforcing the hesitation many women naturally felt about leaving their young children to go out to work in the world, Dr. Spock also made them more reliant on his own kind of expertise.[18]

By the end of 1957 in any case, the birth rate began to drop. The women staying in the labor force felt no compulsion to have large families even if they saw the work they were doing as "jobs," not as careers; the women committed to motherhood may have had a more difficult time coping with a house full of young children than they anticipated when they made their original choice. On the back page of a medical journal advertising Mary Calderone's collection of essays on abortion appears an ad for a tranquilizer for mothers. This pill (Pacatal) would "release the housewife from the grip of neurosis," the drug company claimed, so she could live normally and play with her family. What becomes clear is that the mental health of women in the 1950s was thought to be "more precarious than their physical well-being."

Although the introduction of antipsychotic drugs did indeed begin to empty out the asylums, many women less seriously ill, depressed, and confused about their roles continued to be guided to seek help from psychiatrists. Many personal problems that might have been cured by more extensive social programs—by better daycare or more equitable work arrangements, or by more available organized activities outside the home—were treated as mental deficiencies in individual women. Postpartum depression, a cause for institutionalization at the time, as one example, might have been eliminated if "mothers" had been able to be more "self-selective"—to examine more thoughtfully whether or not motherhood was appropriate for everyone.[19] Had there been available networks of competent nurturing outsiders to help women with raising young children, tranquilizers like Pacatal would not have been so necessary. If we had had the "excellent" daycare available in Europe, which a number of gifted women later acknowledged as important, many yearning talented mothers would have played a second role in society as often as talented young fathers did.

The Farnham and Lundberg book, *Modern Woman: The Lost Sex*, which had such an unfortunate impact on defining women's mental health during this period, employs an almost obsessive repetition of the term "neurotic" to describe all women who struggled to define themselves outside of contented motherhood.[20] Appearing as it did right after the war—a time of bustling activity—it tried to persuade women that their mental health depended on remaining in the home. Mirroring other messages from the popular culture of the 1950s, it attempted to make the independent woman suddenly appear sick. Heroines of earlier decades, especially Mary Wollstonecraft, were to Marynia Farnham, the psychiatrist-author, the source of modern women's problems. Taking pains to include an appendix of fragments of the "corrosive ideology" of a number of important feminist thinkers like Charlotte Perkins Gilman, Elizabeth Cady Stanton, Olive Schreiner, and Margaret Sanger, Farnham may, ironically, have helped convert a number of readers to the opposite side. After all, like Helene Deutsch, she too was a doctor recommending for other women a path she herself did not follow. Women in this analysis are invariably described as "they," never as "we."

Called "the most valuable book we have concerning women," by Philip Wylie (inventor of the pejorative term "momism" in the 1940s to challenge women for *over*-involvement in their children), *Modern Woman: The Lost Sex* emerges historically as a source of confusion as well as of guilt. The text seems to grope toward some domestic solution to world revolution focused on the production of children as a cure for "the destruction of the home" and the "increase of neurosis" throughout society. Women, the main targets for attack, were not entirely alone—bachelors over thirty were also to be recommended for psychotherapy "unless physically deficient." No one laughed.[21]

Personal anger characterizes so much of the tone of this writing focused on women's "modern unhappiness" that we cannot help wondering about the degree of self-justification invested in the examination of female "neurosis," a term that would become as obsolete as neurasthenia by the 1980s. How such neurosis might relate to civilization, a question of major importance to Freud, was not examined by Farnham and Lundberg in connection with women's intellectual contributions, which are never taken seriously. The authors chose to identify with that part of the psychiatric establishment that tends to trivialize all human achievement by labeling it sublimation.

Although Farnham continued to stress the penis-envy of the feminists, who wanted to "eradicate men," her tone was more concessive in 1956 when she took part in a symposium on "The Way of Women" sponsored by the Cooper Union in New York City. At that time she acknowledged that it was "impossible to conceive that woman being every bit as clever, and as intelligent as her brother and husband, should be consigned to a life in which she has no function outside of childbearing." More pointedly, in spite of her resentment of the feminists, who had managed to secure her own right to vote, she perceptively noted that modern women were unable to organize themselves to get what they wanted. And she went on to define two real social causes for female discontent: "the implacable and obstinate opposition of employers to part-time workers" and "the tendency to close ranks" against a woman who takes time off from her job. Ten years after writing her critical analysis of modern women, Farnham had been forced to make greater allowances for social discrimination. By the mid-1950s, also, she could not close her eyes to the numbers of older women pouring back into the work force: "It cannot be expected that a woman after the time of rearing her children, is necessarily going to fold her hands and play the role of Whistler's mother," she declared. "In this day and age she is not. She is very chipper indeed, and very able to get around in the world and do the world's work." "But," she insisted, unaware of how many women with children were already working, "if she wishes to take enough time to fulfill her function in the home, and thus to fulfill herself, she must of necessity be out of the operations of a full-time professional, or a

business task for a certain amount of time.[22] This has made a "powerful conflict" in women, Farnham rightly concluded—this time
without using the term "neurotic."

The mixed messages of such "experts" did little to alleviate the
conflict; they did not clarify how emphasis on personal domesticity
and the natural isolation of the nuclear family would necessarily in-
terfere with any sense of political solidarity among women. They
did not point out that self-fulfillment and family demands were frequently at war in women's minds. Although the experts paid tribute
to the exceptional women who should be using their brains for the
good of society, they did not pursue the broad social reinforcements
necessary to bring about such usage.[23] And they refused to urge such
exceptional women to identify with *all* other women—perhaps the
most damaging decision in a democratic society.

Psychotherapy existed for middle-class women to bolster a lack of
self-esteem that Farnham understood to be the root of women's (and
therefore the modern world's) problems. That Lucy Freeman's *Fight
Against Fears*, a laudatory description of her own psychoanalysis,
would become a best-seller in 1951 suggests how seriously such individual solutions were entertained; in 1953 Freeman published a
second popular book on mental health, *Hope for the Troubled*. Women
who would once have sought clergy to help deal with the ongoing
tensions of family responsibilities turned in droves to psychiatrists.
Afraid of the disasters that might befall young children if mothers
were not perpetually available, believing that "latchkey children"
would turn into juvenile delinquents, apprehensive at the same time
about "momism," many young mothers may have also sought psychiatric dialogue for the simple satisfaction of talking over problems
with an adult outsider. But there can be little doubt that the profession often reinforced rather than dispelled women's lack of self-esteem; women became dependent on their psychiatrists as often as
they were liberated by them.

Indeed, the standards of mental health for women during the
1950s stressed dependency. "Normal adult" behavior for women was
apt to be defined quite differently from what was socially desirable
for men. The healthy woman was supposed to be submissive, dependent, emotional, and subjective. As the research of Inge Broverman and her associates has since demonstrated, there was—and
often remains—a clear-cut double standard of mental health for men
and women related to their adjustment to the roles society wants

them to play. Women, rarely encouraged to seek maximum fulfill-ment of their individual potential as a primary goal, had to decide whether to exhibit the "positive characteristics considered desirable for men and adults," and thus be "deviant in terms of being a woman," or "to behave in the prescribed feminine manner, accept second-class adult status, and possibly live a lie to boot."[24] The women who *had* to earn a living were spared this dilemma, but the conflicts of many middle-class women kept the psychiatric establish-ment prosperous at a time when many sociologists were looking at personal fulfillment in a broader sense.

The 1950s produced a number of sociological classics that grew out of the need to explore the relationship of individuality to an in-creasingly totalitarian world. These books were written for and about men; but any woman could see herself as *Growing Up Absurd*— in spite of Paul Goodman's remarkable belief that the role of mother was the only goal women had. The ideals of self-actualization, mas-tery of environment, and fulfillment of potential explored in texts like Abraham Maslow's *Motivation and Personality* in 1954, Gordon Allport's *Becoming* in 1955, and Erving Goffman's *The Presentation of the Self in Everyday Life* in 1959 might well have made thinking women begin to wonder about their own patterns of adjustment—in much the same way that Emerson's essay on *Self-Reliance* permeated the thinking of earlier advocates for women's rights. Domesticity in its most extreme forms provided the bonds and security of any total thought system. Young mothers, from one point of view, could have defined themselves as the loneliest crowd of all; and some might even have identified with the "other inmates" Goffman would describe in *Asylums* in 1961.[25]

When the Kinsey report on *Sexual Behavior in the Human Female* appeared in 1953, however, anthropologist Clyde Kluckhohn noted that it revealed women to be less conditioned than males were by the social groups in which they lived. There appeared to be a much greater variety of sexual activity among women than most people suspected. Kinsey had interviewed nearly 8,000 women, a tremen-dous number for such a survey, even though self-selected. Of the actual 5,940 females who supplied the data for the 1953 volume, 17 percent were high-school graduates; 56 percent college graduates; 19 percent had done graduate work; and a small number attended only grade school. The interviewers found that education had less impact on women's sexual habits than on men's. From businesses, factories, prisons, labor unions, YWCA groups, the armed forces, the Salvation Army, and random housewives, the Kinsey staff questioned females about their sex lives. Included on the list of women interviewed were artificial-flower makers, circus riders, drill-press operators, laboratory technicians, telephone operators, stewardesses, salesclerks, welders, policewomen, robbers, a labor-relations counselor, a paleontologist, and a judge. It would be hard to describe the range of experience the Kinsey report included as narrow.[26]

Some psychiatrists welcomed the survey as a valuable contribution to women's mental health. But many members of the psychoanalytic establishment were hostile to the 1953 report, which destroyed their efforts to establish norms. *Kinsey's Myth of Female Sexuality: The Medical Facts*, by Edmund Bergler, M.S., and William S. Kroger, M.D., attempted to speak for the profession. These doctors were justified in objecting to Kinsey's indifference to the unconscious and to the ideal of love as conditioning factors in women's sexuality, but their outrage blinded them to realities that were also medical facts. The Kinsey team established once and for all the dominance of clitoral eroticism; and the Kinsey interviewers also refused to label female homosexuality "perverted," thereby enabling homosexuals, as Bergler and Kroger protested, "to spread their perversion without conscious guilt."[27] By the 1980s, a book like Bergler and Kroger's would seem to be a historical artifact, one of the last efforts by men in America to control women with dogmatic male definitions of what the female orgasm should be. But subsequent decades, sated with the experimental statistics of Masters and Johnson (who began laboratory research in the late 1950s) and the polemics of Ann Koedt and Alix Shulman, tended to forget the pioneering value of the 1953 Kinsey report.[28] Suggesting as it did that women could control their private lives regardless of society's strictures, the Kinsey report stood for a much broader range of female sexuality than appeared on the social surface of the 1950s. Fannie Hurst, the popular novelist, in a *Life* review aptly called it "nourishing."

In the field of health, as in most other areas, although male-dominated institutions did little to encourage women to fulfill their potentialities,[29] a few exceptional individuals managed to represent a high level of humanity; a number of women doctors trained in other decades, like Sarah Murray Jordan or Martha May Eliot, commanded the respect of the entire medical world. And a few new doctors with a feminist awareness forged out of the institutional rigidities of the times began to emerge with a concern to change much that seemed inhuman in medical practice. Such a new doctor was Mary Howell, later called the godmother of the woman's health movement.

Mary Howell, a brilliant student, named the first woman associate dean at the Harvard Medical School in the 1970s, might well be understood in terms of her own 1950s education. Hers was the training that included solid intellectual discipline and offered opportunities side by side with institutional obstacles and, most important, socially conditioned self-denials. At Harvard-Radcliffe Howell refused membership in Phi Beta Kappa in order not to overshadow the man she would marry, who was not doing as well; although her grades and thesis warranted her graduating with a *summa* degree, the chairman of the Linguistics Department, known for hostility to women, argued against her that she had not been in the field long enough. Howell subsequently gave up a chance to go on studying linguistics with Noam Chomsky in order to learn secretarial skills useful for finding work in Hawaii, where her new husband had been sent by the army. Shortly after their first baby arrived, this husband ran off with a neighbor. Deciding to go to medical school to be able to support herself, Howell was warned she would have to do premed work *full time* in order to be a competitive candidate for medical-school admission. The state of Minnesota, the dean told her, was reluctant to waste money on women's education. At that time she was fortunate to have her mother available as a babysitter.[30]

Admitted as one of seven women in a class of 100, a somewhat larger percentage than most medical schools were then taking, Howell only later became aware that the women never stuck together; all felt themselves exceptional. But when she remarried, and adopted three children—besides having two more of her own—she identified with the many other mothers in the 1950s who enjoyed the responsibilities of motherhood. Later she remarked that she could never have been anything but a mother first and a medical student second, an attitude that differentiated her clearly from many female professionals who put other values first. She remembered that she had never wanted to "distance" her feelings as many men in medicine aspired to do. Her dreams of reforming the system included enlarging opportunities for men as well as women to spend more time with their families.

As a dean at Harvard in the 1970s, Howell became interested in collecting statistics on female medical students, a process that made her aware of how widespread and complex the resentment against

women students of medicine remained. Ultimately she would publish her findings as *Why Would a Girl Go into Medicine*, under the pseu-
donym Dr. Margaret A. Campbell.[31] Although she found herself
becoming more and more feminist, she characteristically gave up the
job as Havard dean when her husband sought better opportunities
for his own work in the state of Maine. Like Betty Friedan and Adrienne Rich—also shaped by the attitudes of the 1950s—Howell
nevertheless managed later to extend the meaning of her personal
experiences into a broader social analysis. She dramatized her resig-
nation with a statement pointing out the dangers of the kind of tokenism she herself had represented.

Believing that female doctors who identified with the male em-
powered group would not defend women patients "against harmful
obstetrical practices, unnecessary surgery, unsafe contraceptives,
and forced sterilizations," Howell expressed a concern for women's
health that would not be felt necessary by a generation of women
doctors less conscious of institutional prejudices. Out of the contra-
dictions of her own life, Mary Howell forged a medical philosophy
that insisted on greater human concern as well as technical skill.
Women who denied their own alienation would, she believed, lack
compassion: "If you're a member of an oppressed group, and you
don't see it, you block the ability to see other kinds of oppression
too," she explained in an interview. "These women may be even less
feeling than men about patients' rights, and the rights of blacks and
poor people."[32] In a speech at an all-girls school in Rhode Island she
later declared: "I am confident that if we can undo sex-role inequities, touching each and every one of us at the most intimate places of
our lives, we can and will undo all other inequities as well."[33]
Whether getting more women into medical school has made any difference in the quality of health care for other women remains to be
studied.

When President Kennedy appointed Janet Travell his personal
physician in 1961, tokenism was not a political issue; it was obvious
that Travell, who had done a study in the 1950s proving that 91 percent of all women doctors made good use of their educations, was a
competent doctor.[34] For a number of Americans who had never even
seen a woman physician, the public presence of Janet Travell suggested widening opportunities.

Whatever progress was made in the health of American women
during the 1950s may have emerged finally from greater bureau-

cratic consciousness of general need. With the founding of the department of Health, Education and Welfare in 1953 came more organized attention to public problems. Shortages of nurses and technicians prompted the HEW in connection with the Department of Labor to publish a *Health Careers Guidebook*, which made citizens aware of available work and services in both public and private health sectors. In 1956 *Progress in Health Services*, a monthly statistical abstract, also began to appear. The Bureau of Labor Statistics published *Working Life for Women* in 1957, calling attention to the challenge to public policy of maintaining women's skills and well-being during their child-bearing years; but few significant institutional changes were made. Keeping women healthy contributing members of society—both physically and mentally fulfilled, not just well-adjusted mothers—would also remain a goal for another decade.[35]

Helen Frankenthaler, Basque Beach, July 1958.
Courtesy of Hirshhorn Museum and Sculpture Garden, Smithsonian Institution, Washington, D.C.

Chapter Ten

Artists and Scholars: The Identity of Profession

Like the writers sustained by private emotional worlds, a number of serious visual artists created extraordinary personal work during this decade of mass hysteria and domestic imperatives. Our most imaginative woman artist, Georgia O'Keeffe, produced a number of sweeping landscapes that may well be judged her most profound creations although critics were slow to perceive her abstract talents; she gave four one-woman shows during the 1950s, and her work was included in the 1958 display "Fourteen American Masters" at the Museum of Modern Art.[1] Isabel Bishop and Loren MacIver, also well-recognized artists, continued to paint profitably. Louise Nevelson ignored being ignored to produce her finest indoor environmental constructions—perhaps an artist's version of the interior castles that were so real at the time to literary women.

Shaped in the bohemian 1920s, or in the WPA-supported 1930s, these women had found small communities of soulmates and had managed to develop powerful individual styles. They had learned to ignore much social reality. Nevelson went so far as to remark that recognition of being enslaved was a condition of freedom. During the 1950s she used her own house as a gallery, filling even the bath-

tubs with monumental closed-form sculptures not yet considered respectable contributions to contemporary art. The size and style of
her work, judged revolutionary at the time, helped liberate the
American conception of modern sculpture. By 1979 a triumphant
success, Nevelson would dedicate one of her pieces to her home-
town, Rockland, Maine, proud that she had fulfilled an unusual destiny. Her very life had become a defiance of the influential Hans
Hofmann's smug 1950s declaration that "only men had the wings for
art."[2]

At a moment in American life identified with political fear and
social alienation, America was producing an astonishing group of
nonrepresentational artists who were well aware of the outrageous
public significance of their work. The women who became part of
the New York School of abstract expressionist painters shared the
excitement. In a private world where everyone stood so far outside
of establishment taste, it was easier for women to feel imaginative
equals with the creative men; "You had this feeling of a group against
the world," Joan Mitchell noted; "it was exciting."[3] There was in the
air, wrote Irving Sandler, a pervasive "feeling of work, great work,
being done" fostered by the intense community spirit.[4]

Although the abstract subject matter of a number of women artists suggested traditional feminine connections—children, wed-
dings, flowers, etc.—often fifties women wanted their abstract art to
connect with the broader intellectual traditions that shaped all talents. They did not see themselves as a group of women but joined
with the men as individuals reacting against more specific European
academic taste—as Americans frequently have. Grace Hartigan remarked that it was no coincidence that Jackson Pollock, their leader,
was a westerner: "We had a very strong sense of being American, of
being pioneers again, creative pioneers." Hartigan would not allow
outside criticism to make her retreat from her own subject matter—
"that which is vulgar and vital in American life."[5] Our artists were
turning a decade of impossible restraint into the wildest kind of individual freedom.

Elaine de Kooning, Lee Krasner, and Helen Frankenthaler (like
Jean Stafford, Sylvia Plath, and Caroline Gordon) were not just talented wives of distinguished men but important artists in their own
right. Their professional commitment was never in doubt. To be
sure, the women who were a part of both generations of abstract
expressionist painters often felt left out of the original conceptualiz-

ing; they were rarely given one-woman shows; and they sometimes felt, as Joan Mitchell put it, a sense of "being allowed to join."[6] Remembering reactions to her own realistically rooted *City Life* shows of 1954 and 1958, Grace Hartigan complained: "They made me feel it wasn't serious." Still, in the first major abstract expressionist display of 1950, both Hartigan and Elaine de Kooning were included. And by the 1970s other artists like Jane Freilicher, Joan Mitchell, Jean Follett, and Nell Blaine contributed to the important redefinition of visual reality. With private showings every year between 1951 and 1958, Helen Frankenthaler had achieved a high level of recognition before the 1950s were over.[7]

After Jackson Pollock's death in 1958 the women artists in New York continued to thrive. Looking back at the East Hampton community where so many talented members of their group had painted during the decade, Lee Krasner concluded that it was "being able to concentrate and being cut off that made this such a wonderful place to paint."[8] To insist that the abstract expressionists were more cut off from mainstream society than any other group of artistic revolutionaries might be hard; yet the radical nature of their work suggests an astonishing degree of personal freedom. American politicians and Communist cultural authorities alike agreed on labeling them all "decadent."

Other women artists not part of the abstract expressionist movement also contributed new works to the world of 1950s art. I. Rice Pereira's geometric spaces earned a large spread in *Life*; Anne Ryan, who took up painting at the age of forty-nine, created remarkable collages; and Alice Neel, working on her own, produced a number of highly original portraits. "Beautiful is a term that rarely can be applied any more," Elaine de Kooning wrote: "The struggle with oneself that now produces art is more likely to leave harsh even ugly tracks."[9]

Struggling with herself not only to paint but also to support two sons, Alice Neel drew strength from the tradition of social realism that seemed remote from the abstractionists; she tried to capture human intensity in portraits like the one she painted of Emmett Till's mother, Mamie Bradley. But Neel derived inspiration from just being in New York City during the 1950s; she enjoyed the vitality of her insecure wild life. She would later remark that she had found it impossible to read Betty Friedan: "I couldn't identify with the housewife in Queens. I didn't have her aids—her washing machine, her security. . . . But I realized that at the same time that was snobbish of me."[10]

Among the artists of New York were also a number of imaginative and dedicated women dealers or gallery owners, perhaps inspired by the early contributions of Peggy Guggenheim and Edith Halpert. Elaine Benson, Elizabeth Parker, Eleanor Ward, Martha Jackson, Eleanor Poindexter, Betty Parsons, Grace Borgenicht, Margaret Brown, and later Paula Cooper, played an important role in helping the public see that the new paintings were of value. A number of receptive women critics: Katherine Kuh, Eleanor Munro, Sonya Rudikoff, Anita Ventura, Barbara Rose, and Barbara Guest also did much to try to explain what abstract artists were doing and to help them become accepted throughout America. Betty Parsons went so far as to promote the work of female artists including Agnes Martin, Hedda Sterne, and Anne Ryan during this decade, when there was little interest in fostering women's creativity as such.

As in every sphere during the 1950s, a few women in the art world were victimized by conservative suspicions. Louise Bourgeois, investigated by Senator McCarthy, subsequently sequestered her work until she felt liberated by the feminists of the late 1960s; Hilla Rebay, who founded the Museum of Non-Objective Art in 1939, which had given support to distinguished artists like I. Rice Pereira and Alice Turnbull Mason, was fired in 1952 from her job as director.[11] The undeniable injustices of the decade served not only to drive artists into themselves in the ways of modernist expression but also created a public taste for nostalgia. The most popular artist in America during the 1950s was clearly Grandma Moses.

Although Moses had become prominent in the 1940s among collectors (her work was bought by the Metropolitan Museum of Art and the Museum of Modern Art, as well as by other museums all over America), during the 1950s she played a more public role. She published an autobiography in 1952 and later appeared on the Ed Murrow TV show to demonstrate her artistic techniques. A classical example of a "new old woman," Moses had not begun to paint until the age of sixty-seven. She produced an astonishing number of fine primitives, sometimes on order, just as she had produced the preserves and afghans of her earlier life as farmer's wife. In her nineties during the decade, Grandma Moses kept producing; even after her centennial she completed twenty-five paintings. The *New Yorker* described Anna Mary Robertson Moses as "one of those old people who, as old buildings civilize a city or spindly church spires bind up a landscape, make the world seem safer."[12] Our yearning for a Currier and Ives America found expression in her work—which was also an enormous commercial success.

Along with the renewed interest in primitivism and folk music, the crafts movement experienced a modest renaissance. In 1956, under the direction of Aileen Osborne Webb, the American Crafts Museum opened in New York as a showplace for the skills of talented women who have always defined themselves in terms of services to others. Making useful articles did not necessarily limit self-expression or creativity. Lucy Morgan and LeGette Blythe called attention to the Penland School of Handicrafts in 1958, with *Gift from the Hills*. Anni Albers, whose weaving had flourished in yet another North Carolina community of artists, Black Mountain, valued the decade's materialism in artistic terms; she saw the 1950s as a time of "truth to materials."

Every decade of American life has supported communal groups that sustain creative individuals against mainstream hostility or indifference. The Black Mountain Community, admittedly inspired by distinguished men, encouraged a great range of creative activity over twenty years among the women who lived there. Included in the gifted women nurtured at Black Mountain were Ann and Natasha Goldowski, Charlotte Schlesinger, Anni Albers, Trude Guermonpriz, Mary Callery, Francine Du Plessix Gray, Mary Gregory, Carol Brice, Mary Caroline Richards, Marguerite Wildenhair, and Hilda Morley—singers, writers, sculptors, potters, and finally dancers: Carolyn Brown, Viola Farber, Marianna Preger, Katherine Litz, Jo Anne Melsher, Louise Lippold, and Sara Hamill. The years 1953–56, according to Martin Duberman, the historian of the community, were "years of innovation and accomplishment equal to any period in its history."[13] Although the group spirit waned, the level of individual achievement remained significant—suggestive of the importance of such eccentric communities in fostering talents which subsequently turn back to enrich the broader culture.

Modern dance has been from its beginning a field in which American women excelled. Comparable to black jazz in its international impact, contemporary dance became a gift of twentieth-century American women to the world. During the 1950s modern dancers continued to celebrate the uncorseted female body glorified by Isadora Duncan and Loie Fuller, along with the woman of strong self-discipline exemplified in the dances of Martha Graham.[14]

The fragile fairy-tale maidens of traditional ballet, choreographed by men, withered back to their European roots as Graham explored the formal feelings that grew out of Emily Dickinson's repression, and the passions of pioneer women in Appalachian Spring, designed in the 1940s as part of a growing repertory of dances with strong heroines. During the 1950s Graham created new interpretations of Joan of Arc and of Mary Queen of Scots and Elizabeth I, along with powerful heroines from Greek mythology. Her most ambitious work (some think it her greatest) was a 1955 dance drama on the character of Clytemnestra, the Greek queen who murdered her husband. Roger Copeland, the dance critic who believes that women are "not only prominent but dominant" in modern dance, suggests that many postmodern choreographers continue to imitate Martha Graham's vision of women as "austere, cerebral and anti-voluptuous," reflecting every serious woman's desires not to be seen solely as a sex object.[15]

During the 1950s the Martha Graham Dance Company was sent by the State Department both to Europe and to the Far East as cultural ambassadors; and in 1950 Harry Truman himself awarded Graham the National Press Club award for theatrical entertainment extending beyond mere diversion. Although there was less social content in the dances of this decade when Graham turned more often to mythology and classical tragedy for themes, she was socially ahead of her times in encouraging integration of black and Native American dancers. In the Santa Barbara of her youth, she said, she had discovered the "power of the Indian and the freedom of the Negro." Her choreography made use of the black presence in American life in a way that classical ballet could not. To Alvin Ailey, on the verge of creating the American Dance Theater, Martha Graham represented as important a force in liberating the dance as Picasso had been in painting and Stravinsky in music. It was in the 1960s that a less imaginative State Department declared her unfit to receive government aid; they thought her dances "obscene" and found her "too old" to perform. By 1973, though, a new biography would advertise Graham as a woman who "emancipated both women and the dance—the most militant feminist who ever lived."[16]

Another art form in which women had pioneered—photography—continued to provide outlets for their skills and values. Margaret Bourke-White recorded the Korean War through a photo-documentary of the life of a young guerrilla fighter. The price of an ideological conflict that split families apart was what she wanted to illustrate. In her autobiography, *Portrait of Myself* (1963), she regretted that Americans had not been ahead of the Communists in teaching Korean farmers—then being indoctrinated with Bolshevik history—about the Declaration of Independence. Exposed to an encephalitis epidemic in the course of her 1950s work in the Far East, Bourke-White developed Parkinson's disease later in the decade. Risk, she understood, was part of the excitement of photo-journalism. She had climbed on skyscrapers, and was one of the first photographers to use the helicopter; she had intended to go to the moon. Domesticity was never part of her self-definition.

"If I had had children," she wrote, "I would have charted a widely different life, drawn creative inspiration from them, and shaped my work to them. Perhaps I would have worked on children's books, rather than going to wars. . . . One life is not better than the other; it is just a different life." Bourke-White was a classical example of the American woman who testified to enjoying independence as part of the either/or choice:

I have always been glad I cast the die on the side I did. But a woman who lives a roving life must be able to stand alone. She must have emotional security, which is more important even than financial security. There is a richness in a life where you stand on your own feet although it imposes a certain creed. There must be no demands. Others have the right to be as free as you are. You must be able to take disappointments gallantly.[17]

Some equally distinguished photographers did not see their lives so clearly in either/or terms. Imogen Cunningham stated dogmatically in 1951: " I feel that no woman has really lived without the experience of motherhood." She also regretted, however, that a number of women who could have been good artists, made their children "a reason for NOT working any more." Cunningham (who had to cope with twins along with two other children) managed to work steadily. After she had reached the age of ninety—another "new old woman"—she told an interviewer that she most liked to photograph individuals older than she was. Always an outspoken individualist, Cunningham made her eloquent comments on fifties domesticity, a picture of an unmade bed and of a woman artist with her children.

But she had to wait until the 1970s for any recognition beyond the West Coast.[18]

Berenice Abbott, best known for 1920s portraits of Parisian notables and for dignified cityscapes of New York, was commissioned in 1954 to photograph U.S. Highway No. 1 from beginning to end. When she reached the state of Maine she said she felt she had come back to life. Like Marguerite Yourcenar, the first woman ever elected to the Académie Française, she chose to continue working in Maine, far from the conventional world of success. "It's such a problem to live half-way decently," she declared. "You hear a lot of talk about who's talented and who isn't, but I believe that people can be great in themselves and not just for what they do." Along with local landscapes and pictures of Maine industries, Abbott began to photograph scientific enterprises. She lamented the prejudice against age that kept her from fulfilling her ambitions: "Everything possible and impossible was done to stop me. The young physicists didn't see what an old woman like me was doing in their laboratories. I was doing a good job, but the world wasn't ready for it." Her final put-down may have been a common one: "When they saw that it was worth doing after all, they got me out and hired my assistant instead, because he was younger and cheaper." Although Abbott would say, in 1980, that she felt "a total flop," there can be little doubt that her work will be included among the best of the century; and that, as John Russell asserted, she managed to project "a complete and unmistakable world of her own."[19] Other female photographers continued to profit from the example of her "armored ego."

By 1959 Diane Arbus decided to give up fashion photography to study with Lisette Model. She too would seek to project a world of her own—an extraordinary portrait gallery of human beings who had come to terms with their peculiarities. Her work became a commentary on the need to look beyond the conventional and "normal" for a more complex vision of reality, and complemented the creation of literary freaks during the 1950s. Women too often find it easy to identify with total outsiders.[20]

But they have rarely been intimidated by changing technology. Many women enjoyed taking pictures from the first, and they continued in the 1950s to develop and master special skills. Some became well known for expertise in special fields: Laura Gilpin, for her industrial work; Eve Arnold, who documented men picketing a woman bartender in 1952, focused on photo-journalism; Ylla, killed while working in a fall from a jeep in 1955, recorded the dignity of wild animals; Lotte Jacobi became known for her spontaneous pictures of children; Consuelo Kanaga captured the beauty of black women; and Rollie McKenna and Inge Morath and Ilse Dorfmann began to create portrait galleries of writers and artists, in the tradition of Barbara Morgan, whose earlier photographs had immortalized Martha Graham. By the early 1960s, when an entirely new photographic process became well established, Marie Cosindas proved eloquent with Polaroid color prints.

Women photographers followed the pioneering tradition of Gertrude Kasebier in not letting their strength betray the woman; their adaptability to this important democratic art form suggested a degree of receptivity that some later feminist critics labeled passive and feminine—entirely vicarious. Annie Gottlieb thought women's portrait photographs of the great, "poignant expressions of their longing to participate in genius."[21] But surely Susan Sontag's analysis of the art of photography remains equally true. "To photograph is to appropriate the thing photographed," wrote Sontag: "It means putting oneself into a certain relation to the world that feels like knowledge—and therefore, like power."[22]

During the 1950s Eve Arnold photographed not only Senator McCarthy ranting, but also blacks and whites eating together at the beginnings of the Congress for Racial Equality. "What I knew in America," she wrote later, "was free and adventurous." A friend agreed that photographers during the decade were most interested in human beings; and that later they would be more interested in photographic techniques.[23]

For Susan Sontag, the idea that knowledge and power were identical was not questionable. But Sontag, a 1950s defector from academe, would also have more impact on the culture as a critic (as did Betty Friedan) than as a professor of philosophy. The graduate school was no less stultifying for women in the 1950s than the world of the corporation. Quotas set up to keep women out of the professions, bolstered by male mentor systems and institutional rigidities made many women graduate students feel entirely out of place. Yet institutional hostility could not extinguish intellectual fire. And a few gifted, determined women gained attention in the world of ideas in spite of the obstacles put before them. If they could not derive social power from their learning, they found inner power in the mastery of knowledge and in the pleasure of personal accomplishment. If there were not enough intellectual women visible during a decade that celebrated domesticity, there were nevertheless a few important thinkers who sustained society's acceptance of the intellectual equality hard won in the early years of the century.

The academic world could not ignore a woman whose achievement was as great as Susanne Knauths Langer's, kept on as a tutor at Radcliffe/Harvard for over fifteen years and finally, during the 1950s, awarded the traditional professorship at a school for women, Connecticut College. Two of Langer's distinguished works on aesthetics: *Feeling and Form* (1953) and *Problems of Art* (1957), appeared to enhance her earlier systematic work on intuitive creative force. There was nothing "feminine" about the way Langer structured her ideas, but her efforts to understand the nature of beauty, a sphere traditionally assigned to women, might well have earned the "trivial" label so often issued by American male academics in their judgment of women's work. How many scholars during the 1950s would have respected her attempts to analyze the nature of the dance?[24]

Much more "masculine" were the concerns of Hannah Arendt's great political-philosophical works, which also appeared during the decade. *The Origins of Totalitarianism* (1951) and *The Human Condition* (1958) led to her becoming the first woman full professor at Princeton in 1959.[25] Although Arendt would be justly challenged by Adrienne Rich in 1976 for not making women's contributions more visible, it seems clear that Arendt herself invites the dialogue with brave and imaginative women that Rich demands. If, "to read such a book by a woman of large spirit and great erudition can be painful because it embodies the tragedy of a female mind nourished on male ideologies,"[26] Arendt's personal struggle to grasp deep moral issues, on her own terms, nevertheless suggests a more independent female mind than Rich is willing to concede. In 1954 Arendt also lectured at the New School on American traits she considered "totalitarian": "conformism" led the list, along with identifying individuals with their work; and concentration on achievement and success. She believed finally, she said, that nonconformism was the *sine qua non* of real achievement.[27] It would not be hard to identify the values of such a speech with the value system that sustained many women who remained outside competitive power structures at that time.

Women like Hannah Arendt, who identify more with other professionals than with other women, nevertheless sometimes help redefine the conventional standards of their fields.

American institutions during the 1950s were reluctant to encourage women by rewarding their achievements. Richard Chase observed in 1950 that Ruth Benedict, in spite of many distinguished anthropological publications, "was, absurdly, only an Associate Professor." He understood the value of her commitment to women and outsiders as providing a certain clarity and intensity to her work. And characteristic of the legitimate contemporary respect for generalists was Chase's praise for her professional heresies in seeing "the problems posed and discussed in the Humanities closer to those in Anthropology than the investigations carried out in most social sciences."[28] The tendency of the most interesting women to reject narrowly professional specialization worked against them in most institutional settings.

Although Cecilia Payne-Gaposchkin, an authority on variable stars, was happy in 1956 to be made the first woman full professor at Harvard promoted through the ranks, she was then fifty-six years old and had been working in astronomy since the 1920s. Other women scientists of distinction received less recognition. Mary Peters Fieser, who published a definitive monograph on steroids in 1959, based on ten years of research, and also coauthored four books on organic chemistry with her husband, Louis, during the decade, remained a Research Associate in Chemistry; he was given an endowed professorship.[29]

Gerty Cori had shared the Nobel Prize for biochemistry with her husband in 1947—which should have guaranteed greater encouragement for women in the world of science. But Rosalyn Sussman Yalow was urged to spend time learning secretarial skills to underwrite her graduate training. She was only the second woman, by 1945, to get an engineering Ph.D. at Illinois. Fulfilling the dream of her immigrant father, Yalow worked committedly during the 1950s at the Bronx VA hospital on the idea of radioimmunoassay, which would win her the Nobel Prize in nuclear medicine in 1977. Hardly a feminist, Rosalyn Yalow nevertheless took advantage of the Nobel podium to speak about the position of women in science:

We still live in a world in which a significant fraction of people, including women, believe that a woman should not aspire to achieve more than her male counterparts and particularly not more than her husband. We cannot expect in the immediate future that all women who will seek it will achieve "equality of opportunity." But if women are to start moving toward that goal, we must match our aspirations with the competence, courage, and determination to succeed, and we must feel a personal responsibility to ease the path for those who come after us. The world cannot afford the loss of the talents of half its people if we are to solve the problems that beset us.[30]

A few other women also accomplished remarkable work in spite of broad indifference or hostility. Barbara McClintock's sophisticated work on genetic mutations in corn, published in 1953, was dismissed at the time as incomprehensible by a number of prominent scientists. Awarded the Nobel Prize in her eighties in 1983, McClintock would have to be defined as a scholar whose private intellectual satisfactions meant infinitely more than the fame brought by longevity. Because "her vision of biological organization was too remote from the kinds of explanations her colleagues were seeking" they ridiculed her semi-mystical "feeling for the organism." "Reason and experiment," she told Evelyn Fox Keller, "do not suffice." Decrying the arrogance of fellow scientists, McClintock insisted on greater reverence for nature's ways. "History will record her as the originator of new and very much more subtle and complex genetic theories that are as yet only dimly understood," noted Matthew Meselson. Not a feminist, McClintock, as Keller describes her, nevertheless believed that an intellectual woman can influence knowledge as "a maverick and a visionary."[31]

Chien-Shiung Wu, an experimental physicist who helped overthrow the law of parity, became the first woman given an honorary science degree by Princeton in 1958. Like Yalow, a mother of two, Chien-Shiung Wu took note of the failure of the scientific establishment to foster the work of women. In a conference held at MIT on "Women and the Scientific Professions" in 1964, she criticized the "tradition" that scientific and technical fields in this country were predominantly male. Inspired by Marie Curie and Lise Meitner, she too insisted that the scarcity of women in science represented "a terrible waste of potential talent." And she concluded with a social question that remained unanswered: "In our present society of plenty and proficiency, is it too much to provide excellent professional child care during the day so that mothers . . . can work in their chosen field?"[32]

Statistics from the 1950s were grim. Between 1950 and 1960 the number of women in engineering declined from 1.2 percent to 0.8 percent; in the sciences from 11 percent to 9 percent. In industrial and scientific technology the number of women dropped from 18 percent to 12 percent. We had to confront the reality that in earth science, chemical, metallurgical, metal, mining, and civil engineering, there were fewer women in 1960 than in 1950. By 1960, only 7 percent of the physicians and surgeons employed in the United States were women.[33] The 5 percent drop in Ph.D.s since the 1920s affected every field. Too many women had gladly stepped aside during the decade, as Betty Friedan had done, to allow returning veterans from World War II their choice of positions.

The women who remained in science relied on different methods of survival. Working as a research assistant with one's husband became a traditional path to intellectual fulfillment at the university level. Esther Lederberg was still another woman who worked in her husband's lab on the genetic research that won him the Nobel Prize.[34] Emma Carr, a chemist who did distinguished work in spectroscopy, and Ann Haven Morgan, whose fieldbooks became classics for many American naturalists, followed the second path to self-esteem and creativity—they taught in a woman's college, Mount Holyoke. The 1950s were the last decade for such colleges to boast of predominantly female faculties. By the 1980s Mount Holyoke would remain a rare specimen of a woman's college; yet its tenured faculty by 1983 was 70 percent male.

Other women scientists managed to play more direct roles in society. Leona Baumgartner, who had become associate chief of the Children's Bureau in 1949, took over as Commissioner of Health in New York City in 1951 and did a remarkable job to improve both health education and public services on an enormous scale. Elise Strang L'Esperance, whose idea for cancer prevention clinics had become an accepted part of our system of preventive medicine, was made a full professor at Cornell in 1950, the same year she received the Elizabeth Blackwell award. Pauline Mack directed a staff of sixty-five at the Ellen H. Richards Institute in projects related to the chemistry of everyday living. She translated woman's traditional nurturant role into the first scientific comprehensive program in human nutrition research.

In new fields, where tradition had not yet solidified, women could also excel. Maria Telkes, a physical chemist, became a pioneer in research on solar energy for heating purposes. In 1950 she was the principal speaker at an MIT forum on "Space Heating and Solar Energy." At a time when there was little interest in such projects, Telkes was encouraged by two other women, Eleanor Raymond, an architect, and Amelia Peabody, a Boston sculptor, who provided funds to build an experimental solar house, which was working successfully in 1950.[35]

Similarly, Mina Rees, a mathematician, also a dean at Hunter College, proved herself ahead of the times in her understanding of high-speed computer engineering. Having worked for the Office of Naval Research during World War II, Rees acquired an international reputation and remained in demand as a consultant. Later, as Dean of Graduate Studies at City University, Rees managed to get babysitting funds for her married graduate students. Herself unconventionally married at age fifty-three, Rees understood that childcare centers where a scientist could "leave her child with confidence" were still a *vision* by 1964, and that the adjustment of working hours and place of work to motherhood has been achieved "only in a few instances."[36]

In spite of the declining number of women engineers, Beatrice Hicks founded and became first president of the Society of Women Engineers in 1952, when there were fewer than sixty members. By the time Hicks took part in a 1955 Columbia University forum on "Careers for Women in Engineering," there were several hundred more. The most famous woman engineer of the decade, Lillian Gilbreth, an efficiency expert, had written four books on scientific management before receiving an award in 1951. She continued to lead an active consulting life into her seventies, as celebrated for rearing twelve children as for her efficiency schemes.[37]

Some scholars concerned themselves with analyzing what was happening to women in the 1950s. Mirra Komarovsky, head of the Sociology Department at Barnard, collected facts on *Women in the Modern World* (1953), concluding how essential it was for women to fulfill themselves as they enriched their families. Komarovsky not only studied her own students but extended her research beyond the professional class to try to understand *Blue Collar Marriage* (1962). Thoughtful social analysts like Helena Lopata *(Occupation Housewife)* and Jessie Bernard *(Remarriage, A Study of Marriage)* began to look more closely at woman's role as mother during this decade.[38]

In an age so productive of babies, it was natural that a few women child-rearing experts also achieved national prominence. Frances Ilg and Louise Ames joined Arnold Gesell to produce extensive catalogs of the worst traits normal children might display between birth and adolescence. Eleanor Glueck, a research assistant, joined her professor husband in collecting an enormous amount of material on "delinquent" juveniles; and Dr. Nina Ridenour, director of education at the National Institute of Mental Health, took steps to make preventive medicine—social psychiatry—a part of our greater awareness of the sources of all mental illness. Dr. Martha May Eliot became chief of the Children's Bureau in 1951; and her old friend Ethel Dunham, who had devoted years of research to the needs of premature infants, received the Pediatric Society's highest award in 1957; Helen Taussig worked on "blue babies" and alerted many pregnant women to the dangers of thalidomide. Before the decade was over, marriage counseling would become a scientific pursuit for gifted women like Emily Mudd, and so would sex therapy; Masters and Johnson set up their laboratory in 1958–59. Although the number of women pursuing conventional science dropped drastically, the few who remained left a noticeable impact on American life.[39]

Margaret Mead, our best-known woman anthropologist, had returned to the South Pacific to document the many changes in the culture she had earlier seen as primitive. In 1956 she published *New Lives for Old: Cultural Transformation—Manus—1928-1953*, celebrating the capacity of human beings to adapt and modify their traditions. Seeing the mid-twentieth century as "an emergency for humankind," Mead urged the full use of all human abilities everywhere. She wanted people to modify the institutions and customs they already had, not to waste time dreading apocalypse or dreaming of utopia.[40]

The mother of one child, Mead herself seemed to thrive on the kind of adaptation she believed essential to ensure women's contribution to the melting-pot ideal by popularizing the values of different cultures and ethnic groups. Legislative insurance of equal opportunities for education and for work followed naturally the anthropological assurance that races and sexes were equally capable. If our society could not rid itself of racism, ageism, and male chauvinism it was not because of, but in spite of, the messages of the anthropologists.[41]

Another remarkable woman—both artist and scientist—would have an equally important impact on future legislation and leave a lasting mark on the way we perceive our environment. Rachel Carson impressed the entire world with the grace and precision of her prose in *The Sea Around Us* in 1951. In the years following her literary success, she gathered the materials for and attempted to publish parts of *Silent Spring*, which would first appear as a *New Yorker* series in the early 1960s. These books, along with *The Edge of the Sea* (1955) and *Under the Sea Wind* (reissued in 1952) and *The Sense of Wonder* (1956), derived from an article to help children experience nature, remain examples of the best science writing American society has produced.[42]

Writing had always been important to Carson; she took pleasure in interpreting complex ideas for a broad audience, a choice possibly related to her early realization that women were not welcomed in the world of professional science. Encouragement by a few important teachers, however, was sustaining enough to enable her to become one of two women biologists hired by the Bureau of Fisheries. But she never stopped writing. By 1949 Rachel Carson was both biologist and chief editor of the publications of the United States Fish and Wildlife Service. "Rarely," the *New York Times* reviewer of *The Sea Around Us* noted, "does the world get a physical scientist with literary genius."[43]

Inspired by her own mother to appreciate the mystery of nature, Carson would expand our understanding of the world to include "mother sea" as well as mother earth. A woman who wept at the glorious profusion of silver mullet darting toward the sea, she wanted to share her intense pleasure with everyone. Unfortunately, Carson had to come to terms also with the technological destruction of the environment she confronted daily in her work at the Fish and Wildlife Service.

Appalled in 1953 when Eisenhower's Secretary of the Interior, Benton McKay, an automobile salesman indifferent to environmental issues, fired the courageous conservationist Albert Day as Director of the Fish and Wildlife Service, Rachel Carson wrote an irate letter to the *Washington Post*. It was "one of the ironies of our time," she noted, "that while concentrating on the defense of our country against enemies from without, we should be so heedless of those who would destroy it from within."[44]

An article in *Holiday* magazine in 1957 on the seashores, which provided the peace and spiritual refreshment so hard to achieve in most of our civilization, concluded with the warning that such shores were fast disappearing. More than once Carson would urge the need to set aside "some wilderness areas of seashore where the relations of sea and wind and shore—of living things and their physical world, remain as they have been over long vistas of time in which man did not exist." She urged us to consider finally "in this space-age universe, the possibility that man's way is not always best." The understanding of the world that she demanded was based on an almost religious awe:

It is possible to compile extensive lists of creatures seen and identified without having once caught a breath-taking glimpse of the wonder of life. If a child asked me a question that suggested even a faint awareness of the mystery behind the arrival of a migrant sandpiper on the beach of an August morning, I would be far more pleased. . . .[45]

Although *The Sea Around Us*—translated into thirty-two languages—became a best-seller for eighty-six weeks and won the National Book Award in 1951, when Carson turned her attention to the dangers of pesticides she was treated by editors and fellow scientists as simply another hysterical woman. What she had begun to question, as Paul Brooks, her friend and biographer, pointed out, was "the basic irresponsibility of an industrialized, technological society toward the natural world."[46] Many power groups in the 1950s tried to keep her message from being heard; they refused to accept the validity of the dangers she had taken such care to document. The same women's magazines that had printed her essays of appreciation on nature would not touch her essays of concern about its future— for fear of alarming their readers. Even the *Readers' Digest*, which had earlier shown interest in the problem, refused to honor a commitment to publish an abridged version of *Silent Spring*.

Not a crusader by temperament, Rachel Carson took comfort from the many scientists she knew (often requesting anonymity) who helped her gather the necessary facts; and from the many ordinary human beings who noticed changes in the environment they loved. It was her friend Olga Huckins's eloquent 1958 letter to the *Boston Herald* about the numbers of dead songbirds resulting from mosquito spraying in Duxbury, Massachusetts, that inspired Carson's total commitment to clarifying what the *indiscriminate* use of pesticides was doing to the natural world. Carson wrote Brooks: "I think I let you see last summer what my deeper feelings are about this when I said I could never again listen happily to a thrush song if I had not done all I could."[47]

Silent Spring would later be compared to *Uncle Tom's Cabin* and *The Rights of Man* in the impact it had on the mind and actions of the twentieth century. There can be no question that it was a book that forced the powerful to reevaluate their behavior. By 1963 there would be a Pesticides Committee set up in the Office of Science and Technology to assess the risks involved in using poisons and to certify safety *before* their first use. Some people would continue to insist that the careless use of chemicals was a greater danger to the world than radioactivity.

Concern for environmental dangers to human health was a part of Rachel Carson's reality long before she learned that she herself had cancer. Before she died in 1964 at the age of fifty-six, she clarified the vision that sustained her: "In each of my books I have tried to say that all the life of the planet is interrelated, that each species has its own ties to others, and that all are related to earth."[48] Disturbed at how far human beings had gone in their abuse of the planet, she concluded that it was valid to wonder if any civilization could wage war against the natural world and retain the right to be called civilized. "By acquiescing in needless destruction and suffering," she wrote, "our stature as human beings is diminished."[49]

Although Rachel Carson's enemies tried to discredit the quality of her science, history has reinforced its substance. And many Americans continue to enjoy the seashore lands added to the national-park system in the decade following her tributes to the sea and its edges. That a passionate commitment to life distinguished her from many fellow scientists seems clear. Such commitment may not necessarily be feminine, any more than her literary gift (Thoreau's *Journal* remained at her bedside). But there can be little doubt that Carson belongs with an extraordinary group of American heroines who work in a male world yet manage to shape it on their own terms. She used her talents and knowledge, as many women attempted to do during the 1950s, not for personal success in the world of men but to make the world a better place to live in.

Like some contemporary fiction writers, Carson's vision reached beyond the details of the natural to express a mystical dimension essential to her definition of self. The narrow professional world that had intimidated her had not been able to limit what she felt free to express. And human beings all over the earth profited from her repeated insistence that "the pleasure, the values of contact with the natural world are not reserved for the scientist." Her civilized accept-

ance of her own death as part of the cyclical refrain of nature contributed a deeper dimension to an age so often described in terms of its
material triumphs and anxieties. "It is good to know that I shall live
on," Rachel Carson wrote, "even in the minds of many who do not
know me and largely through association with things that are beautiful and lovely."[50]

Chapter Eleven

Conclusion

The achievements of American women during the decade of the 1950s, as we have seen, would be distinguished on many lists of twentieth-century accomplishments. What is most remarkable is that such contributions continued during a period that gave women almost no institutional encouragement to develop their gifts. The 1950s—a period of high birth rate—seen as an era of conformity and stalemate for women, must also be regarded as a period of personal growth, if not as a time of social or political gain. Women during the 1950s failed to see themselves politically as women and to value what could be gained by feminist consciousness or by gender-group awareness; but many nonetheless managed to assert themselves as human beings, and many extended traditional feminine concerns into a mechanized society that appeared to be growing less and less human. They were the individuals Gayle Graham Yates left out of her summary of contemporary feminist ideology, but paid tribute to as "the many women who have not been overtly feminist but who have advanced the cause of women's freedom by their social, educational, or literary contributions."[1] These were women who did not want to identify with men. In a culture that grows out of the tensions between group differences and mainstream success, many American women of the 1950s made the most out of being outsiders.

Against the background of fear that shaped so much of the opinion of the decade, they attempted to establish connections with richer realities. As artists, dancers, singers, actresses, and writers—and as mothers—they added much to the quality of life, if not to their own power in the world.

Personal authenticity characterized the strong-minded who rarely saw themselves as the victims Betty Friedan described. "We were that generation called 'silent,'" wrote Joan Didion about the 1950s; "but we were silent neither as some thought, because we shared the period's official optimism nor as others thought, because we feared its official repression." Social action, Didion continued, seemed a way of "escaping the personal, of masking for a while that dread of the meaningless which was man's fate."[2] That women at the time would have identified with *man's* fate, in the broadest human sense, was certain; that they would often have seen motherhood as a con-nection with the continuation of what was meaningful in life should not be hard to understand. "We were the last generation to identify with adults," Didion remarked—in notable contrast with the free-wheeling males who were her contemporaries—taking comfort in the idea that "we would survive outside history."[3]

Women who had come of age in earlier, more encouraging times continued to contribute much to the 1950s in the way of example and inspiration. Many of the larger number of women college stu-dents then actually heard lectures by Eleanor Roosevelt or Margaret Mead; they had posters of Georgia O'Keeffe's art shows on their walls and they saw Martha Graham dance. A number of gifted young women who felt alone or exceptional or stultified in some di-rections nevertheless eventually managed to flower on their own terms. Their egos had somewhere along the line been given enough reinforcement to enable them to continue to develop as individuals. The same *Ladies' Home Journal* that published story after story of sen-timental domesticity in the 1950s also published minor poems by Sylvia Plath and Adrienne Rich, thereby encouraging voices that would soon grow loud in other arenas. The *summa* Betty Friedan got from Smith College must have enabled her to believe in her capabil-ities enough to face the first rejections of *The Feminine Mystique*.[4]

Other distinguished women found individual support or mentors in a world that was not openly hospitable to their gifts. The biographies of Rosalyn Yalow and Rachel Carson suggest how important encouragement by teachers and co-workers was in sustaining their research. Women like Helen Frankenthaler and Flannery O'Connor found strength in the smaller communities of artists who shared enthusiasm for and understanding of what they were trying to do. The complexity of the decade makes it difficult to define women entirely by domesticity. If teenage girls rarely met women of achievement who also had children, American newspapers and magazines during the 1950s could not ignore the vast range of women's accomplishments. And the work of individual women during this period must ultimately be regarded as shaping the feminist awareness of the second half of the twentieth century.

As the many women whose main concern was child-rearing began to confront the forty years ahead after their last child was in school, they became more aware of the complexity of women's aging. They began to notice the middle-aged and older women Margaret Mead talked about in a 1950s speech at the New School—the women our society attempted to ignore. Not only did women appear capable of leading more than one life at a time, as the mothers reentering the labor force began to demonstrate, but they also seemed able to lead one life after another. Mead pointed out that older women might represent flexible change in a civilization that appeared all too fatalistic and mechanical.[5]

Grandma Moses and Eleanor Roosevelt were frequently in the news. Other women who had always been visible did not seem to retire. Margaret Sanger at seventy-two worked on the International Planned Parenthood Federation; Edna Ferber wrote the best-seller *Giant* at the age of seventy-seven; Mary McLeod Bethune, also in her seventies, flew off to Liberia to attend the second inaugural of William Tubman's presidency. We did not have to wait for Imogen Cunningham's collection of photographs of people who lived into their nineties, or for the popularization of the seasons of life, to realize that women often demonstrated amazing vitality in old age in spite of the fact that our youth culture refused to acknowledge their needs and contributions.[6] These "new old ladies" made hope available to many young women who had sacrificed conventional careers.

In any civilization that sustains the vital tradition of personal dissent that Richard Chase had celebrated in the 1952 *Partisan Review* survey of "Our Country and Our Culture," the women who continued to create their own definitions of success need to be honored.

Many bright women who gave up seeking careers of obvious power but found other ways to assert their values at the same time that they tended their families are deserving of more attention.

Typical of such were two remarkable women, a mother and daughter whose works influenced great numbers of Americans in the decades to come. Theodora Kroeber and Ursula Le Guin exemplify the vitality that flourished behind the more restrictive mentality of the 1950s; both became enormously popular writers. Le Guin represented the young woman who was honing her talents along with raising her children; Kroeber, the older woman who had given her youth to her family and her energies to helping a brilliant husband. During the 1950s no one knew either of these women for their writings, but they were working steadily and imaginatively on their own terms. By 1970 *Ishi in Two Worlds* and *The Left Hand of Darkness*[7] would become part of a canon of minor classics that play an important role in American life outside the mainstream of conservative academic taste. What is especially interesting about both writers is their implicit criticism of the conventional world of power. Their ability to describe and imagine value systems that differed from contemporary power structures may well have derived from their personal choices in life, as much as from their extensive experience with other cultures.

In the broadest sense the 1950s may finally be seen as the most active period of consciousness raising for modern American women; women pushing baby carriages still may have time to think. Many individuals worried about making better use of their lives. It was, after all, during this period that Betty Friedan, with three small children of her own, devised the questionnaire she sent out to Smith graduates that exposed the "feminine mystique" and led ultimately to the formation of the National Organization for Women in the 1960s. That hordes of women responded with enthusiasm when her book finally appeared in 1963 may be a testimony against *any* simplistic vision of American women's lives. Already in the 1950s popular magazines had begun to look at women's growing discontent: *McCall's* published "The Mother Who Ran Away" in 1956, and "Is Boredom Bad for You?" in 1957; by 1959 *Redbook* was speculating on "Why Young Mothers Are Always Tired."[8] And Marya Mannes found a smaller audience for continued protest in the *Reporter*. But consciousness is not change, and it would be inaccurate to infer that most women in the 1950s were able to challenge society's indifference to their abilities. Individual awareness did little to undo the institutional narrowmindedness and the bombardment by media images that reinforced women's low self-esteem. Although greater consciousness of the developmental stages of life sustained those women who looked forward to starting new careers after their children were gone, the institutions they had to deal with were not similarly enlightened. Patterns of seniority in business, politics, law, medicine, and the university often made it impossible for women to reenter the world of work at levels that allowed for significant achievement. And older women, as Alice Rossi noted, were specifically valued in the labor force as an "important reservoir for assistants and technicians and the less demanding professions."[9] They were rarely considered for positions that demanded creative contributions or decision-making.

In the sciences, as Rossi also pointed out, taking time out from work, or working part time, could be particularly damaging intellectually. Rossi confronted the painful truth that the making of outstanding contributions was considerably reduced when women were "enticed to believe that withdrawal from the labor force in their twenties, followed by part-time employment in their forties was the modern panacea to the conflict in women's roles." Putting families first, as most women did in the 1950s, appeared to be incompatible with high-level scientific achievement. Unfortunately, Rossi did not go on to define in detail how society should implement the need for "a more basic change in the relations between men and women"[10] to enable women's ideas to have greater impact on the scientific professions.

Individual solutions to the problem of when or whether to have children, and how to cope with them, prevailed. Women who came from recent immigrant backgrounds, which accepted training in science as a class advantage, seemed to have fewer qualms about whatever decisions they made. Nobel Prize winner Gerty Cori had set an example earlier by having her only son at the age of forty; Rosalyn Yalow made use of live-in childcare until her son was nine. Barbara McClintock and Rachel Carson, on the other hand, chose not to marry at all.

In 1957, when Carson, fifty years old, adopted her deceased niece's five-year-old son, she found the new commitment curtailing time for writing. Her response to the demands of nurturing, typical of some women's ability to turn responsibility to pleasure, was to write for her own child. "Help Your Child to Wonder" was published in 1956 in the *Woman's Home Companion*.[11] This essay on nature, like Margaret Mead's and Eleanor Roosevelt's writing for the public, was an effort to identify the concerns all women shared. Having experienced conventional hostility from narrower professional worlds, such women often chose not to identify with professional men but to address larger audiences. In writing for mothers on the importance of teaching children about the wonders of nature, Carson may have contributed much to the shaping of future environmentalists.

But turning responsibilities into pleasures was not as easy for the average woman with a minimal education, and even less institutional backing. The report on American women handed to President Kennedy to honor Eleanor Roosevelt's birthday in 1963 realistically described how many areas of women's lives had fallen short of fulfillment during the previous decade. When both political parties supported the Equal Rights Amendment in the platforms of 1952 and 1956, it was not with any special feminist awareness but rather with a growing concern for fair play—and in order to gain new votes. That women were discriminated against in a variety of areas under law was clear. The Internal Revenue Act of 1954 would not even allow full-time working mothers any tax deductions for childcare. Unable to get credit, to buy houses or insurance, to make contracts, even in some places to retain their personal earnings, women would have to wait until "sex" was only half-seriously added to Title VII of the 1964 Civil Rights Bill as a legitimate category for discrimination before they could presume to function as equals with men. Although the ERA twice passed the Senate during the decade, it included the Hayden rider, intent on maintaining extra rights and "preferential" treatment, thereby denying women access to many jobs.[12]

The 1963 report *American Women*, created out of a growing awareness by the end of the 1950s that we were neglecting a tremendous resource, was significantly ignored by the Kennedy adminstration which had solicited it. Changes involving the definition of the family in American life are not easy to implement. The strong traditions of English common law, as Leo Kanowitz would adequately demonstrate in *Women and the Law: The Unfinished Revolution* (1969), continued until the mid-1960s to deprive married women of many of their rights. Social-security payments, for example, were able to discriminate against married women who worked by singling out the "primary breadwinner" as the source of payments, discounting entirely women's contributions. Widows' benefits lagged far behind what their husbands would have received.[13]

Not until the 1957 Civil Rights Act were women even eligible to serve on all federal juries, and three southern states even then denied them jury duty in state trials. As late as 1963, twenty-six states exempted women from jury service for reasons not available to men, resulting in the denial to other women of the judgment by peers so essential to democracy. In 1962 there were still no women judges on either the Supreme Court or the Federal Court of Appeals; there was one woman judge on the United States Customs Court and one on the Tax Court; of 307 federal district judges only two were women.[14] Such a scarcity of women in the judiciary may well have made the treatment of rape victims and prostitutes unduly harsh.

Women law students represented only about 3 percent of the total during this decade, when nine out of ten large law firms refused even to interview women lawyers and smaller firms often demanded stenography with the law degree.[15] In 1957 the Harvard Law School dean invited the twelve women students to a "welcome" dinner, at which he spoke of having opposed the admission of women to the law school—begun in the early 1950s—and regretted that women would be taking the place of men who could work more steadily. Young lawyers conditioned to expect such hostility and discrimination against women in the practices of their own profession could hardly have been expected to recognize the many discriminatory acts against all women in the society as a whole.

American Women commended the work of civic and community women's groups for focusing public attention on "the problem of discrimination based on sex" and urged the continuation of their work. A "Know Your Rights" pamphlet was recommended to help women become more alert to their legal position. "There exist," noted the commission with suitable tact, "laws and official practices which treat men and women differently and which do not appear to be reasonable in the light of the multiple activities of women in present-day society."[16] By the end of the 1960s the multiple activites of women would include advocacy for themselves. When they began to work together to represent numbers instead of individuals, some of the institutions that thwarted their development would begin to change. The ideas that their advocacy would work for nonsexist education and counseling, availability of every category of work with access to higher level positions, equality of rights under the law, including equal pay for equal work, concern for maternity and childcare, and also involvement in the responsibility for women's rights all over the world had, however, been simmering in the minds of American women over a long period of time.

Perhaps witnessing the bravery of black women in the mid-1950s taking action as a group against the inequality all blacks had endured for so long in the South helped many white women to confront the inequities they also shared as women in a society that promised so much. Individual achievement finally mattered less when women realized how much of it stemmed from lucky opportunities rather than from any societal commitment to helping women fulfill their potential as human beings. Although 1950s white women lacked a similar movement to interpret their growing discontents as collective phenomena, they had already begun to produce a number of feminist leaders. Women like Mary Eastwood of the Justice Department and Catherine East of the Women's Bureau, and Dorothy Haener of the United Auto Workers, were waiting behind the scenes to help Betty Friedan form the National Organization for Women in the mid-1960s.[17]

Fifties "feminism," never so labeled, was for the most part a social ideal, the antecedent of that androgynous feminism that expects men to be more like women, not women to be more like men. Its vision of reform contained the hope that *all* work might be redefined or shared. As Margaret Mead declared in a 1956 speech at the Cooper Union, "we can, if we wish, move away from the situation where it is perfectly clear what man does and what woman does." She concluded that we had already "moved a little away from this single solution. And we can move farther."[18]

In a decade characterized as "affluent," "fabulous," "crucial," and "fearful," another apt adjective must also be "wasteful." Official policies everywhere continued to diminish young women coming of age. By refusing to acknowledge, like the Harvard Law School dean, that the benefit to society of different viewpoints might justify a sacrifice of work hours or warrant the restructuring of institutions, we condoned a greater waste of talent than of time. With few exceptions during the 1950s, middle-class women who wanted children had to sacrifice their careers—in spite of all the women's college propaganda that they could and should have both. The presence of superwomen did little to bring about the accommodations necessary to help the majority of women use their talents. What is most amazing is that so many survived in spite of the hostility of the times toward their intellectual advancement. Adaptable and resourceful, the women turned in upon themselves often achieved remarkable distinction on their own terms in the arts and in literature; and many were able to find lasting satisfaction in doing volunteer work designed to improve the quality of our environment and the availability of all culture. Even Betty Friedan would finally feel the need to pay tribute to the "pioneer egos" of many women volunteers who developed strengths without the supporting structures society offered men.

Often a great writer succeeds in shaping a metaphor that captures the spirit of an age better than any compilation of statistics or list of achievements. Katherine Anne Porter's too-neglected story "Holiday," conceived in the feminist 1920s but finally finished and published in 1958, might play such a role. It presents, from an outsider's viewpoint, a vision of an American farm family, flourishing economically, commonsensical and hard-working, and reproducing many beautiful children. Karl Marx is the thriving capitalist father's favorite after-dinner reading.

The narrator, depressed as Ishmael when she arrives on their Texas farm for her vacation, comes to respect the vitality of this beautiful clan. But it is the misshapen servant Ottilie, who cannot talk, who teaches her most. Ottilie, she discovers, is also a member of the family. In fact, she is "one of its most useful and competent members." Though her head waggles, her arms hang loose, and her speech amounts to grunts, no one feels sorry for her. She plays an important role: "Three times a day she spread the enormous table with solid food, freshly baked bread, huge platters of vegetables, immoderate roasts of meat, extravagant pies, strudels, tarts—enough for twenty people." The storyteller sees Ottilie finally as "the only individual in the house." It is this "shattered being that was a woman" who reminds us in her grief over the loss of her mother, and in her final affirmative liberation, that we are all "equally fools of life, equally fellow fugitives from death."[19] If the speechless Ottilie must join the parade of freaks and eccentrics that so often dominate the literature of the 1950s, she does so with intense humanity; her acceptance of life is what we remember.

Women, particularly, must celebrate those writers like Meridel LeSueur, Kay Boyle, and Lillian Smith, who remind us of how much the society we live in needs improvement, but they reinforce their own value also by remembering that we "exist on half a dozen planes in at least six dimensions and inhabit all periods of time at once," as Katherine Anne Porter wrote Josephine Herbst. When we "ignore too much," she concluded, we make a fatal mistake.[20] To ignore the complexity of 1950s women because society did so little to reinforce their strengths might well be fatal to a more complex view of American feminism.

In the 1960s American women would finally find their voices. They put aside their ambivalence about sharing the world of men and they demanded equal access to professional opportunities and positions of power in business and government. When the National Organization for Women framed its statement of purpose in 1966, its leaders disclaimed the individuality that had characterized the previous decade. "Above all, we reject the assumption that [women's] problems are the unique responsibility of each individual woman, rather than a basic social dilemma which society must solve."[21] Whether women might also pay a price for such social advancement was not at issue; it was more important for women to realize that they no longer had to deal with their problems alone. The new feminists saw clearly that although society may gain a great deal from the presence of gifted outsiders, it also loses what these outsiders can contribute to the powerful institutions that shape American life.

Notes

Chapter One

1. Quoted in Eric Goldman, *The Crucial Decade—and After: America, 1945-1960* (New York, 1960), p. 235.
2. David Caute, *The Great Fear: The Anti-Communist Purges under Truman and Eisenhower* (New York, 1978).
3. Lewis Mumford, *In the Name of Sanity* (New York: Harcourt Brace, 1954), p.155.
4. Douglas T. Miller and Marion Nowak, *The Fifties: The Way We Really Were* (Garden City, N.Y., 1975), pp. 344, 371.
5. See William E. Leuchtenburg, *A Troubled Feast: American Society Since 1945* (Boston, 1983), updated, p. 108.
6. Ibid., p. 29; a useful bibliography on McCarthyism appears in Allen J. Matusow, *Joseph R. McCarthy* (Englewood Cliffs, N.J., 1970).
7. Stephen E. Ambrose, "The Ike Age," *New Republic*, 9 May 1981, p.33.
8. See Michiko Kakutani, "Hellman-McCarthy Libel Suit Stirs Old Antagonisms," *New York Times*, 19 March 1980.
9. James B. Conant, "The Superintendent Was the Target," *New York Times Book Review*, 29 April 1951, pp. 1, 27.
10. Quoted in Goldman, *Crucial Decade*, p. 215.

11. William Phillips and Philip Rahv, eds., *The New Partisan Review Reader 1945–1953* (New York: Harcourt Brace, 1953), p. vi.

12. Goldman, *Crucial Decade*, p. 250

13. Ibid., pp. 252, 253.

14. Quoted in Caute, *Great Fear*, p. 68.

15. Quoted in Miller and Nowak, *Fifties*, p. 406.

16. Ibid., p. 39.

17. Goldman, *Crucial Decade*, p. 322.

18. Ibid., p. 335.

19. Quoted in Leuchtenburg, *Troubled Feast*, p. 99.

20. McLean Hospital Annual Report (Belmont, Mass., 1977), p. 14.

21. Miller and Nowak, *Fifties*, p. 139.

22. Ibid., p. 395.

23. Ibid., p. 7.

24. Herbert J. Gans, *The Levittowners: Ways of Life and Politics in a New Suburban Community* (New York: Vintage Books, 1967), p. 417.

25. Miller and Nowak, *Fifties*, p. 9.

26. Ibid., p. 85.

27. Ibid., p. 87.

28. Will Herberg, *Protestant—Catholic—Jew: An Essay in American Religious Sociology (1955–60)* (Garden City, N.Y.: Doubleday, 1960 ed.), p. 102.

29. Quoted in Miller and Nowak, *Fifties*, p. 8.

30. Leuchtenburg, *Troubled Feast*, p. 65.

31. For a provocative discussion of the playboy culture, see Barbara Ehrenreich, *The Hearts of Men: American Dreams and the Flight from Commitment* (Garden City, N.Y.: Anchor, 1983); Wertham quoted in Miller and Nowak, *Fifties*, p. 408.

32. Morris Dickstein, *The Gates of Eden: American Culture in the Sixties* (New York, 1977), p. ix.

33. Richard Chase, "Our Country and Our Culture" (part 3), *Partisan Review*, September–October 1952, pp. 567, 569.

Chapter Two

1. Mary Ritter Beard, *Woman as Force in History: A Study in Traditions and Realities* (New York, 1946); Betty Friedan, *The Feminine Mystique* (New York, 1963).

2. See Caute, *Great Fear*, p. 118; Carol Hurd Green; "Ethel Rosenberg," in *Notable American Women: The Modern Period*, vol. 4, ed. Barbara Sicherman and Carol Hurd Green (Cambridge, 1980). Henceforth cited as *NAW*.

3. *New York Times:* Meyer, 7 February 1954; Tuve, 13 April 1951; Markham, 9 April 1953; Maki, 28 February 1952; Betty Miller Unterberger, "Esther Brunauer," in *NAW*, vol. 4.

4. Joseph P. Lash, *Eleanor: The Years Alone* (New York, 1972), p. 287.

5. Eve Merriam, *After Nora Slammed the Door: American Women in the 1960s: The Unfinished Revolution* (Cleveland: World, 1964), p. 135.

6. Dickstein, *Eden*, p. 37.

7. Sylvia Plath, "Nick and the Candle Stick," in *Ariel* (London: Faber & Faber, 1965), p. 40.

8. Norman Podhoretz, "The Know-Nothing Bohemians," *Partisan Review*, Spring 1958, p. 307; Jack Kerouac (Sal's Aunt), *On the Road* (New York: Viking Press, 1955); Norman Mailer, "The Homosexual Villain," *Advertisements for Myself* (New York: Signet, 1959); Leslie Fiedler, quoted in Godfrey Hodgson, *America in Our Time, From World War II to Nixon: What Happened and Why* (New York: Vintage Books, 1978), p. 312. See also Ehrenreich, *The Hearts of Men*, an imaginative interpretation of male anxieties in the 1950s.

9. Dickstein, *Eden*, p. 50.

10. See Milton Meltzer, *Dorothea Lange: A Photographer's Life* (New York: Farrar, Straus & Giroux, 1978), for a discussion of "The Family of Man."

11. See Simon Frith, *Sound Effects: Youth, Leisure and the Politics of Rock 'N' Roll* (New York: Pantheon, 1981); Charles T. Brown, *The Art of Rock and Roll* (Englewood Cliffs, N.J., Prentice-Hall, 1983); Greil Marcus, *Mystery Train: Images of America in Rock 'N' Roll Music* (New York: E. P. Dutton, 1982. I am indebted to Neil Leonard for sharing his jazz library.

12. Sally Placksin, *American Women in Jazz: 1900 to the Present: Their Words, Lives and Music* (New York: Seaview Books, 1982).

13. Agnes de Mille, *Dance to the Piper* (Boston: Atlantic Monthly Press, 1951); *And Promenade Home* (New York: Da Capo, 1980).

14. See Brandon French, *On the Verge of Revolt: Women in American Films of the Fifties* (New York: Ungar, 1978); Molly Haskell, *From Reverence to Rape: The Treatment of Women in the Movies* (New York: Penguin, 1974); Marjorie Rosen, *Popcorn Venus: Women, Movies and the American Dream* (New York: Coward, McCann & Geohegan, 1973).

15. French, *On the Verge*, p. 154.

16. Haskell, *Reverence*, pp. 275–76.

17. An excellent summary of work on women in popular culture is Katherine Fishburn, *Women in Popular Culture: A Reference Guide* (Westport, Conn., 1982). Another useful book is Kathryn Weibel, *Mirror, Mirror: Images of Women Reflected in Popular Culture* (New York: Anchor Books, 1977). Because women rarely identify with the power elite, popular culture plays a significant role in defining their self-images.

18. *TV Guide*, 24–30 January 1976; 7–13 February 1976.

19. Nancy Norton, "Mildred (Babe) Didrikson Zaharias," in *NAW*, vol. 4.

20. *New York Times* 8 December 1951; Mary Lyman, "Clarissa Atkin-

son," in *NAW*, vol. 4; Dorothy Bass, "Georgia Elma Harkness," in *NAW*, vol. 4.

21. Elinor Goulding Smith, "Won't Somebody Tolerate Me?" *Harper's Magazine*, August 1956, pp. 36–38; Mundell *New York Times*, 30 March 1952.

22. See Paul Boyer, "Minister's Wife, Widow, Reluctant Feminist: Catherine Marshall in the 1950's," *American Quarterly*, Winter 1978, a perceptive appraisal of Marshall as the dutiful wife of the 1950s who flourished after her husband's death.

23. *New York Times*, 2 March 1956.

24. Robert T. Handy, "Edith Lowry," in *NAW*, vol. 4; Arnold Shankman, "Dorothy Rogers Tilly," in *NAW*, vol. 4; Virginia Foster Durr Papers, Schlesinger Library, Cambridge, Mass; I am grateful to Lucy Hackney also for information about Virginia Durr; and to Mrs. Durr herself for a telephone interview.

25. Sherry Ortner, "Is Female to Male as Nature Is to Culture," in *Woman, Culture, and Society*, ed. Michele Zimbalist Rosaldo and Louise Lamphere (Stanford: Stanford University Press, 1974), a classic. Douglas T. Miller and Marion Nowak: *Fifties*, documents the activity precipitated by nuclear anxiety. See also Schlesinger Library biography files.

26. Hall, *New York Times*, 18 February 1959; James Reed, "Katherine Dexter McCormick," in *NAW*, vol. 4.

27. Knox, *New York Times*, 29 March 1952.

28. Oettinger, Papers unprocessed, Schlesinger Library, Cambridge, Mass.

29. Horney, *New York Times*, 3 October 1958; Baumgartner, biography file, Schlesinger Library, *New York Times* passim; Wallace, *New York Times*, 8 March 1956; Campbell, *New York Times*, 1 February 1950; Raymond J. DeMallie, "Ella Deloria," in *NAW*, vol. 4.

30. *New York Times*, 13 December 1951, speech by E. C. Lindeman.

31. ER, *New York Times*, 14 February 1959.

32. William L. O'Neill, *Everyone Was Brave: The Rise and Fall of Feminism in America* (Chicago, 1969).

33. League, *New York Times*, 20 April 1958.

34. June Sochen, *Movers and Shakers: American Women Thinkers and Activists 1900–1970* (New York: Quadrangle Books, 1973).

35. Lucia Bequaert, *Single Women: Alone and Together* (Boston: Beacon Press, 1976), p. 217.

36. Lorena Hickok and Eleanor Roosevelt, *Ladies of Courage* (New York: G. P. Putnam, 1954).

37. Quoted in William H. Chafe, "Eleanor Roosevelt," in *NAW*, vol. 4.

38. Adlai E. Stevenson, *New York Times* 7 June 1955.

39. *New York Times* 7 March 1956; 1 December 1958; on 30 January

1959 the *New York Times* also noted that women venturing into engineering "may expect to find prejudice and obstacles in their way."

40. See Frank Stricker, "Cookbooks and Law Books: The Hidden History of Career Women in Twentieth Century America," in *A Heritage of Our Own*, ed. Nancy F. Cott and Elizabeth H. Pleck (New York: Touchstone Books, 1979), as well as Friedan, *Mystique*, pp. 141, 312. A *New York Times* 24 April 1957 report of a YWCA survey of 8,000 women in twenty-nine states found most content, but those over thirty-five wanted more education in order to be independent.

41. *New York Times*, 25 October 1957, Report of Council on Manpower.

42. *New York Times*, 26 January 1956.

43. *New York Times*, 26 June 1952. This group consistently supported the ERA and better jobs for women.

44. See Alice Kessler-Harris, *Out to Work: A History of Wage Earning Women in the United States* (New York: Oxford University Press, 1982), pp. 207–10, 305–6.

45. Leslie Gould and Carol Hurd Green, "Mary Heaton Vorse," in *NAW*, vol. 4.

46. See, *NAW*, vol. 4; also, *Current Biography: Who's News and Why* (New York, 1950–59).

47. Ibid.

48. Weibel, *Mirror, Mirror*, p. 217.

49. Friedan, *Mystique*, p. 67.

50. Quoted in Paul Brooks, "Rachel Carson," in *NAW*, vol. 4.

51. Evan S. Connell, Jr., *Mrs. Bridge* (New York: Viking Press, 1958).

Chapter Three

1. Talcott Parsons, "Age and Sex in the Social Structure of the United States," in *Essays in Sociological Theory* (Glencoe, Ill.: Free Press, 1949), p. 223.

2. Rona Jaffe, "A Real-life Class Reunion," *Ladies' Home Journal*, June 1980, p. 142.

3. Friedan, *The Feminine Mystique*. This book defined the restrictions of the 1950s for the new generation of feminists.

4. Ibid., p. 142.

5. See "Alma Mater, Where Are You? The Door Is Closed and I Can't Get In": Continuing Education I, Elizabeth Lawrence Cless, and Continuing Education II, Eugenia Oster Kaledin, *Radcliffe Quarterly*, June 1971; see also Berenice Brown Cronkhite, *Graduate Education for Women: The Radcliffe Ph.D.: A Report by a Faculty-Trustee Committee* (Cambridge, Mass., 1956), p. 82. Although some effort was extended to allow advanced graduate

students to do part-time work, the concern here is to keep out part-time "less serious" Ph.D. candidates.

6. Friedan, *Mystique*, p. 319.

7. Gerda Lerner, *The Majority Finds Its Past: Placing Women in History* (New York, 1979), p. xix; During the 1950s Lerner wrote a musical, *Singing of Women*, with Eve Merriam: "I always was a writer. It was as good an education as any for becoming a specialist in the history of women" (p. vii).

8. Ibid., p. 148.

9. Friedan, *Mystique*, p.327.

10. Eleanor Roosevelt, Papers (FDR Library, Hyde Park, New York), include a number of tributes to Marie Souvestre, such as *Look* magazine article, May 1951. See also *Autobiography* (New York: Harper, 1961).

11. Mary McCarthy, "The Vassar Girl," in *On the Contrary: Articles of Belief, 1946–1961* (New York: Farrar, Straus & Cudahy, 1961), p. 210; first published in *Holiday* magazine.

12. Ibid., p. 214.

13. Ibid.

14. Friedan, *Mystique*, p. 137; *It Changed My Life: Writings on the Women's Movement* (New York, 1976) pp. 103–4.

15. Adrienne Rich, "Taking Women Students Seriously," in *On Lies, Secrets, and Silence: Selected Prose 1966–1978* (New York: W. W. Norton, 1979), p. 238.

16. Ibid.

17. Ashley Montagu, *The Natural Superiority of Woman* (New York: Macmillan, 1952). Montagu argues that woman's superiority is self-evident; society need make no accommodations to child-rearing needs.

18. Lynn White, Jr., *Educating Our Daughters* (New York, 1950). The most extensive response to White is in Mirra Komarovsky, *Women in the Modern World: Their Education and Their Dilemmas* (Boston: Little, Brown, 1953).

19. White, *Educating*, pp. 53–54.

20. Ibid., pp. 60–61.

21. Friedan, *Mystique*, p. 150.

22. See Commission on Education for Women Papers, Schlesinger Library, Radcliffe College, Cambridge, Mass. Among the publications produced were *Women in the Defense Decade*, 1951; *How Fare American Women?*, 1955; *The Education of Women: Signs for the Future*, 1957; "The Economic Strength of Business and Professional Women," 1954; "Potentialities of Women in the Middle Years," 1955; "The Present Status of the Women's College," 1958.

23. *New York Times*, 1 October 1951.

24. "Three Noted Feminine Educators Caution That First Duty Is to Children," *New York Times*, 29 January 1950; 25 January 1950.

25. Letter from Florence L. C. Kitchelt, *New York Times*, 7 October 1951.

26. Kluckhohn, *New York Times*, 25 January 1950.

27. I am indebted to Ida Fisher Davidoff for providing information about her own life. Another example of an energetic older woman, Davidoff commuted from Connecticut to Philadelphia at the age of fifty-one in order to get training in the new field of marital counseling. Her own research with May Elish Markewich, "The Post-Parental Phase in the Life Cycle of Fifty College-Educated Women," unpublished dissertation, Columbia Teachers College, 1961, throws light on how a number of women coped with limited opportunities.

28. Richard Brown of the Newberry Library, Chicago, and Barbara Silverstein of New Rochelle, New York, provided information about Alice Cook; see also *New York Times*, 17 November 1955.

29. *New York Times*, 8 January 1953.

30. *New York Times*, 7 June 1955.

31. *New York Times*, 4 January 1959.

32. Mabel Newcomer, *A Century of Higher Education for Women* (New York: Harper & Bros., 1959), discussed in Friedan, *Mystique*, pp. 338–39.

33. Friedan, *Mystique*, pp. 338–39.

34. Donlon and Roberts quoted in *The Education of Women—Signs for the Future*, ed. Opal D. David (Washington, D.C.: American Council on Education, 1957), p. 115; the ambivalence of the culture left the commission relatively powerless; its decision to gather "more facts" would benefit few women during the 1950s.

35. See *Report of the Committee on Education* to the President's Commission on the Status of Women, Mary I. Bunting, chairman, October 1963; also, Nancy Frazier and Myra Sadker, *Sexism in School and Society* (New York: Harper & Row, 1973).

36. *American Women*, report of the President's Commission on the Status of Women 1963, p. 10.

37. Ibid., p. 13.

38. Ibid., p. 14.

39. Ibid., p. 15.

40. Friedan, *Mystique*, pp. 173–74.

41. Margaret Mead, *Male and Female: A Study of the Sexes in a Changing World* (New York, 1949); *New Lives for Old: Cultural Transformation—Manus, 1928–1953* (New York, 1956); ed., *Writings of Ruth Benedict: An Anthropologist at Work* (Boston: Houghton Mifflin, 1959). Mead was criticized by Diana Trilling in *Claremont Essays* (New York: Harcourt, Brace & World, 1964), pp. 56–64; and by Friedan in *Mystique*, pp. 120–30. (See Chapter 6).

42. Mead, *Male and Female*, p. 381.

43. Mead, "American Man in a Woman's World," *New York Times*, 10 February 1957.

44. Mead, *Ruth Benedict* (New York: Columbia University Press, 1974), p. 14.

45. *Writings of Ruth Benedict*, p. 140; "I wanted so desperately to know how other women had saved their souls alive" (p. 519).

Chapter Four

1. William Chafe, *The American Woman: Her Changing Social, Economic and Political Roles, 1920–1970* (New York, 1972), p. 218.

2. National Manpower Council, *Womanpower in Today's World: A Statement with Chapters by the Council Staff* (New York: Columbia University Press, 1957).

3. National Manpower Council, *Work in the Lives of Married Women* (New York: Columbia University Press, 1958).

4. Robert Smuts, *Women and Work in America* (New York: Columbia University Press, 1959), p. 48.

5. Esther Lloyd-Jones, head of guidance at Teachers College, Columbia University, quoted in *Work in the Lives of Married Women*, p. 28.

6. Ibid.

7. Erwin Canham, introd. to *Womanpower in Today's World*, p. 4.

8. Ibid., p. 125.

9. Chafe, *American Woman*, p. 218.

10. Ibid., p. 219; *The World Almanac and Book of Facts for 1959*, ed. Harry Hansen (New York: World Telegram, 1959), records a 40 percent increase in part-time workers between 1950 and 1957, p. 258; employment agencies for such work, such as *Kelly Girls*, sprang up in the 1950s, when for the first time in 1956 white-collar workers outnumbered blue.

11. *Womanpower*, pp. 192, 207.

12. *New York Times*, March 27, 1955; *Womanpower*, p. 122; see also *Life* 24 December 1956, "Women Hold Third of Jobs," pp. 30–35. The article emphasizes compassion and tolerance of repetition as keys to the low-level jobs women held.

13. *Womanpower*, p. 121.

14. Ibid., p. 132.

15. Ibid., p. 102.

16. Ibid., pp. 227, 233.

17. Report of the President's Commission on the Status of Women, *American Women* (Washington, 1963). p. 35.

18. Philip S. Foner, *Women and the American Labor Movement: From World War I to the Present* (New York: Free Press, 1980), p. 497.

19. For a summary of women's role in the war, see Susan M. Hartmann, *The Home Front and Beyond: American Women in the 1940s* (Boston: Twayne, 1982), pp. 71–101, 222–23.

20. Canham, introd. to *Work in the Lives of Married Women*, p. 8.

21. Sheldon and Eleanor Glueck, *Unraveling Delinquency* (New York: Commonwealth Fund, 1950), was simplified as *Delinquents in the Making:*

Paths to Prevention (New York: Harper & Brothers, 1952). Another book by the Gluecks, *Predicting Delinquency and Crime* (Cambridge: Harvard University Press), appeared in 1959; Miller and Nowak, *Fifties*, pp. 280–87, throws light on this phobia.

22. *Work in the Lives of Married Women*, p. 113.

23. Ibid.

24. Ibid., p. 134.

25. Ibid., p. 151.

26. David C. McClelland and others, *The Achievement Motive* (New York: Appleton, Century, Crofts, 1953).

27. *Womanpower*, p. 147.

28. Ibid., p. 327.

29. Ibid.

30. *Work in the Lives of Married Women*, p. 147.

31. Ibid., p. 196.

32. *The World Almanac 1959*, pp. 654–56; the average allotment was $30 per recipient per month including the parent or other relative with whom the child was living. "In only a few states is this form of assistance to women responsible for dependent children substantial enough to constitute a genuine alternative to employment." (*Womanpower*, p. 341).

33. *Womanpower*, p.349; Gayle Graham Yates, *What Women Want: The Ideas of the Movement* (Cambridge, 1975), pp. 44ff.

34. Sydney Herbert Ditzion, *Marriage, Morals, and Sex in America: A History of Ideas* (New York: Bookman Associates, 1953), p. 410.

35. Yates, *What Women Want*, p. 54.

36. See Foner, *Women and the American Labor Movement*, pp. 482–84. See also Kessler-Harris, *Out to Work*, pp. 305–6, 315–17.

37. Theodore Caplow and Reece J. McGee, *The Academic Marketplace*, with a foreword by Jacques Barzun (New York: Basic Books, 1959), p. 166.

38. Mrs. Roosevelt's shift, an important example of her individualism ignored in many biographies, was published in the *New York Times*, 2 January 1953. That she had been considering the issue for several years is also evident in her "My Day" columns (see chapter 5).

39. *New York Times*, 15 January 1950: Goldman said, "her most important job was the rearing of three daughters"; 23 September 1958: Rinehart "placed her home and family interests first, and thought of herself as "fiercely a mother."

40. Reka Hoff, *New York Times*, 22 January 1956.

41. Bernice Fitzgibbon, *New York Times*, 28 January 1956; YWCA pamphlet, 1956.

42. *Current Biography*, 1957.

43. Tom Mahoney, "Dorothy Shaver," in *NAW*, vol. 4.

44. *New York Times*, 6 December 1958.

45. *NAW*, vol. 4, p. 146.

46. *McCall's*, 6 January 1958.

47. Magazine circulation statistics can be found year by year in the *World Almanac and Book of Facts*.

48. Tom Mahoney, "Margaret Rudkin," in *NAW*, vol. 4.

49. *American Women*, chart 13, p. 38.

50. *New York Times*, 21 February 1952.

51. *New York Times*, 22 February 1952; 26 January 1956; 25 October 1957.

52. Ruth Schwartz Cowan, "Lillian Gilbreth," in *NAW*, vol. 4.

53. *New York Times*, 7 December 1958; Mead, *New York Times*, 16 November 1956.

54. Mirra Komarovsky, *Blue Collar Marriage*, with the collaboration of Jane H. Phillips (New York: Random House, 1964).

55. Lillian Breslow Rubin, *Worlds of Pain: Life in the Working-Class Family* (New York: Basic Books, 1976), p. 103.

56. Eli Ginzberg, *Human Resources: The Wealth of a Nation* (New York: Columbia University Press, 1958), p. 23.

57. Ibid., p. 60.

58. Ibid., pp. 164, 165.

59. Ibid., p. 170.

Chapter Five

1. "Women's Bureau Reports Credit Women for Republican Victory," *New York Times*, 23 April 1953; "Did Women Elect Ike?", *U.S. News and World Report*, 8 May 1953; see also Roosevelt and Hickok, *Ladies of Courage*, pp.19, 32–34.

2. See Susan Ware, *Beyond Suffrage: Women in the New Deal* (Cambridge, Mass.: Harvard University Press, 1981).

3. Ibid., p. 18.

4. Margaret Chase Smith, in Peggy Lamson, *Few Are Chosen: American Women in Political Life Today* (Boston: Houghton Mifflin, 1968), p. 16.

5. Roosevelt and Hickok, *Ladies of Courage*.

6. Oveta Culp Hobby, biography file, Schlesinger Library, Cambridge, Mass.; Harry Hurt, *Texas Monthly*, October 1978, p. 240.

7. See Susan Brownmiller, *Shirley Chisholm: A Biography* (Garden City, N.Y.: Doubleday, 1970).

8. *Ladies' Home Journal* advertisement in *New York Times*, 1 October 1951.

9. Maurine Neuberger, introd. to Lamson, *Few Are Chosen;* local magazines and newspapers should become a rich source of documentation for women's involvement in grass-roots politics during this period: Carmen Frederickson, "Agricultural Change in Davis County" (Logan Utah Experiment Station News, 1953); "Cincinnati Women Ring Doorbells—or How

One Woman Got into Local Politics," *National Civic Review*, March 1953; E. T. Connel, "Women Run the Rascals Out of Gary," *America*, May 1950; "A Woman for President," *New York Times*, 27 May 1956; "Some Women Who Won Tell How to Run," *Women's Home Companion*, July 1955; "If Women Were in Control," *Ladies' Home Journal*, October 1950; "The Woman Voter," *Spectator* 6 January 1956; "Congress Women," *Life* 17 January 1955. See also Jane Fishburn Collier, "Women in Politics," in *Woman, Culture and Society.*

10. Lamson, *Few Are Chosen*, p. xxiii; Roosevelt and Hickok, *Ladies of Courage*, p. 149.

11. Roosevelt and Hickok, *Ladies of Courage*, pp. 9, 176–77.

12. Ibid., p. 143.

13. Jacqueline Van Voris, "Perle Mesta," in *NAW* vol. 4, pp. 470-71.

14. Roosevelt and Hickok, *Ladies of Courage*, pp. 128–30.

15. Lamson, *Few Are Chosen*, p. 219.

16. Millicent Fenwick, *New York Times Magazine*, 27 June 1982.

17. Eleanor Roosevelt Papers, Franklin D. Roosevelt Library, Hyde Park, New York. Interview with Malcolm Muggeridge, BBC, 9 March 1955; earlier opinion cited in a paper given by Ann Davis at the Fifth Berkshire Conference on Women's History, Vassar College, 19 June 1981.

18. See *NAW*, vol. 4; Vera Micheles Dean, *Foreign Policy without Fear* (New York: McGraw Hill, 1953); Dean also wrote *How to Make Friends for the U.S.* (New York: Foreign Policy Association, 1952); *The Nature of the Non-Western World* (New York: New American Library, 1957); *New Patterns of Democracy in India* (Cambridge, Mass.: Harvard University Press, 1959); *Europe and the United States* (New York: Knopf, 1950).

19. Minnie Fisher Cunningham, in *NAW*, vol. 4; Virginia Foster Durr Papers at Schlesinger Library, Radcliffe College, Cambridge, Mass.; Dorothy Rogers Tilly, *NAW*, vol. 4. Warine Walker in *Current Biography*, 1957.

20. *Current Biography*; Roosevelt and Hickok, *Ladies of Courage;* Vassar College, *Alumnae News*, Spring 1983.

21. Quoted in Constance Smith and Anne Freedman, *Voluntary Associations: Perspectives on the Literature* (Cambridge, Mass.: Harvard University Press, 1972), p. 107.

22. *Forty Years of a Great Idea: The League of Women Voters in the United States*, pub. 226 (Washington, D.C.: LWV, 1960), p. 20. See also *League of Women Voters*, 5 vols. (Ann Arbor, Mich.: Survey Research Center, 1956–58).

23. *Forty Years*, p. 24.

24. Mary Bunting, introd. to Herta Loeser, *Women, Work and Volunteering* (Boston: Beacon Press, 1974), p. xiii.

25. Ibid., p. xi.

26. Betty Friedan, *It Changed My Life*, p. 103.

27. Eleanor Roosevelt Papers, Hyde Park: "What Are the Motives for a Woman Working When She Does Not Have to for Income?" (*Charm*, Jan-

uary 1955). An excellent survey of Roosevelt's attitude toward women's work is Marque-Luisa Miringoff, "Eleanor Roosevelt: Women and Work, Considerations for the 1980's" (Hyde Park: publication of Eleanor Roosevelt's Val-Kill, 1981).

28. Eleanor Roosevelt, "What Are the Motives?"

29. Ibid.; see also Joseph P. Lash, *Years Alone*, pp. 220–23. This book is essential to understanding the final decades of Eleanor Roosevelt's life.

30. Eleanor Roosevelt papers, Hyde Park; Tamara Hareven, *Eleanor Roosevelt: An American Conscience* (Chicago: Quadrangle Books, 1968), p. 240.

31. Oral History Interview Marietta Tree (Emily Williams, 28 January 1980), Hyde Park; Stevenson quoted in William Chafe, "Eleanor Roosevelt," *NAW*, vol. 4, p. 601; Truman quoted in Lash, *Years Alone*, p. 219.

32. Eleanor Roosevelt papers, Hyde Park: *London Sunday Times*, typescript, pp. 5, 6.

33. Eleanor Roosevelt papers, Hyde Park. Although not completely cataloged, the "My Day" columns are all available in the Roosevelt Archives; Lash, *Years Alone*, pp. 258, 261.

34. Eleanor Roosevelt papers, Hyde Park: "My Day," 8 January 1959; 23 January 1959; 31 January 1959.

35. Eleanor Roosevelt papers, Hyde Park: "My Day," 29 January 1959; 24 January 1958; 30 January 1959.

36. Eleanor Roosevelt papers, Hyde Park: "My Day," 14 January 1959; 5 March 1958.

37. Lash, *Years Alone*, p. 51; Eleanor Roosevelt papers, "My Day," 20 May 1959; see also "Eleanor Roosevelt and the International Human Rights Movement," paper presented at Fifth Berkshire Conference of Women by M. Glen Johnson, Vassar College, Poughkeepsie, N.Y.

38. Oral history interview with Marietta Tree.

39. See chapter 4 for a discussion of the work of the Commission on Women.

40. These letters are included with the Eleanor Roosevelt papers at Hyde Park; oral history interview with Marietta Tree.

41. Eleanor Roosevelt, *It Seems to Me* (New York: W. W. Norton, 1954), p. 55.

42. Eleanor Roosevelt papers, Hyde Park, "My Day," 25 May 1951.

43. "Education and Changes in the Status of Women," *Bryn Mawr Alumnae Bulletin:* oral history interview with Anna Rosenberg Hoffman, 13 October 1977, Hyde Park.

44. Eleanor Roosevelt papers, Hyde park: "Why I Am Opposed to Right to Work Laws," *AFL-CIO Federationist*, February 1959.

45. Eleanor Roosevelt papers, Hyde Park: "Gains for Women," Barnard College Bulletin, 1954.

46. Eleanor Roosevelt papers, Hyde Park: "Address to the National Council of Women," 1960.

Chapter Six

1. National Manpower Council, *Work in the Lives of Married Women*, introd. Erwin Canham (New York: Columbia University Press, 1958), p. 14.

2. See *NAW*, vol. 4; also *Current Biography*.

3. Richard Hofstadter, *Anti-Intellectualism in American Life* (New York: Knopf, 1963), p. 432.

4. Elizabeth Hardwick, "The Subjection of Women," in *A View of My Own: Essays on Literature and Society* (New York: Ecco Press, 1982), p. 168.

5. Marion K. Sanders, *Dorothy Thompson: A Legend in Her Time* (New York: Avon Books, 1973), p. 347.

6. Mari Sandoz, *Cheyenne Autumn* (New York: McGraw Hill, 1953); *The Buffalo Hunters: The Story of the Hide Men* (New York: Hastings House, 1954); *The Cattlemen: From the Rio Grande across the Far Marias* (New York: Hastings House, 1958); *Crazy Horse: The Strange Man of the Oglalas* (New York: Knopf, 1942).

7. Mari Sandoz, *Hostiles and Friendlies: Selected Short Writings* (Lincoln: University of Nebraska Press, 1959), p. 30.

8. Theodora Kroeber recorded Ishi's life in two books: *Ishi in Two Worlds: A Biography of the Last Wild Indian in North America*, with a foreword by Lewis Gannett (Berkeley: University of California Press, 1961) and *Ishi, Last of His Tribe* (Berkeley: Parnassus Press, 1964). Such books remain eloquent comments on contemporary civilization as well as on primitive life.

9. *Southern Exposure* 4, no. 4 (Winter 1977): 44.

10. Lillian Smith, *The Journey* (Cleveland: World Publishing, 1954), p. 7.

11. Ibid., p. 38.

12. Quoted in *Saturday Review of Literature*, 22 October 1966, p. 47.

13. Ibid.

14. Quoted in Judith Nies, *Seven Women: Portraits from the American Radical Tradition* (New York: Viking Press, 1979), p. 262.

15. Dorothy Day, *The Long Loneliness* (New York: Harper & Row, 1952).

16. Quoted in Nies, *Seven Women*, p. 317.

17. See Mary McCarthy, *On the Contrary*.

18. Ibid., "No News, *or*, What Killed the Dog," pp. 39, 40, 42.

19. Ibid., "The Contagion of Ideas," pp. 47, 49, 54.

20. Ibid., "Artists in Uniform," p. 66.

21. Ibid., "Up the Ladder from Charm to Vogue," p. 179.

22. Ibid., pp. 178, 187, 190.

23. Ibid., "The Vassar Girl," p. 210.

24. Ibid., "Tyranny of the Orgasm," p. 172.

25. Marya Mannes, TV reviews, *Reporter Magazine*, 20 January 1953; 2 February 1954.

26. Marya Mannes, *Out of My Time* (Garden City, N.Y.: Doubleday, 1971), pp. 219–20, 216; TV reviews, *Reporter*, 27 April 1954; 17 November 1955; 8 June 1954.

27. Mannes, *Out of My Time*, p. 250.

28. Mannes, TV reviews, *Reporter*, 22 September 1955; 31 March 1956; 22 March 1956.

29. Ibid., 9 August 1953; 17 February 1953; 23 September 1954.

30. Ibid., 17 February 1953; 5 January 1954; 23 September 1954; 8 March 1955.

31. Marya Mannes, "The Case of the Two-headed Woman," *More in Anger* (Philadelphia: Lippincott, 1958).

32. Merriam, *After Nora Slammed the Door*, pp. 63, 72; Mannes, *Out of My Time*, p. 234.

33. Mannes, *Out of My Time*, p. 233.

34. Mannes, "Personal Heresies," in *More in Anger*, pp. 154–59.

35. Diana Trilling, "Liberal Anti-Communism Revisited," *We Must March My Darlings: A Critical Decade* (New York: Harcourt Brace Jovanovich, 1971), pp. 41–67; Lillian Hellman, *Scoundrel Time* (Boston, 1976; Bantam ed., 1976, introd. Garry Wills).

36. Trilling, "On the Steps of Low Library," in *We Must March*, p. 153.

37. Hellman, *Scoundrel Time*, p. 27; Trilling, *We Must March*, p. 49.

38. Trilling, *We Must March*, p. 51.

39. Trilling, "The Other Night at Columbia: A Report from the Academy," in *Claremont Essays* (New York: Harcourt Brace & World, 1964), pp. 305–18.

40. Trilling, "The Moral Radicalism of Norman Mailer," in *Claremont Essays, p. 195*.

41. Trilling, "The Death of Marilyn Monroe," in *Claremont Essays*, p. 233.

42. Trilling, "Women's Liberation," in *We Must March*, pp. 193, 282.

43. Trilling, "Men, Women, and Sex," in *Claremont Essays*, pp. 51, 50, 58.

44. Ibid., p. 53.

45. Ibid., pp. 61, 56–57.

46. Diana Trilling, "Are Women's Colleges Really Necessary?", *Reporter*, 30 October 1951, pp. 38–40.

47. Stephen Spender, review of *Janet Flanner's World (1932–1975)*, *New York Times*, 18 November 1979.

48. Janet Flanner (Genêt), *Paris Journal 1944–1965*, ed. William Shawn (New York: Harcourt Brace Jovanovich, 1965; Harvest ed., 1965), pp. 120, 121.

49. *Janet Flanner's World: Uncollected Writings, 1932–1972*, ed. Irving Drutman; introd. William Shawn (New York: Harcourt Brace Jovanovich, 1979), p. 316.

50. William Shawn, introd. to *Janet Flanner's World*, p. xiv.

51. See Margaret Supplee Smith, "Aline Milton Bernstein Saarinen," in *NAW*, vol. 4. For a broader picture of how women use the arts as a means to interpretive power see Claire R. Sherman, ed., with Adele M. Holcomb, *Women as Interpreters of the Visual Arts* (Westport, Conn.: Greenwood Press, 1981).

52. Aline B. Saarinen, *The Proud Possessors* (New York: Random House, 1958).

53. Anne Morrow Lindbergh, *Gift from the Sea* (New York: Random House, 1955); twentieth anniversary ed. with an afterword by the author (Vintage Books, 1975), p. 134.

Chapter Seven

1. Virginia Woolf, "Professions for Women," in *The Death of the Moth and Other Essays* (London: Hogarth Press, 1947), pp. 149, 151.

2. Katherine Ann Porter, "Holiday," in *The Collected Stories of Katherine Anne Porter* (New York: Harcourt, Brace & World, 1965); "Noon Wine: The Sources"; "Ole Woman River," in *The Collected Essays and Occasional Writings of Katherine Anne Porter* (New York: Seymour Lawrence/Delacorte Press, 1970), pp. 467, 271; Donald Sutherland wrote Porter, 4 June 1953: "There has never been a woman critic."

3. Porter, "Ole Woman River," pp. 281, 280.

4. Porter, interview with Barbara Thompson, *Writers at Work, Paris Review Interviews Second Series*, introd. Van Wyck Brooks (New York: Viking, 1963), pp. 147, 148.

5. Porter, "Flannery O'Connor at Home," in *Collected Essays*.

6. Joyce Carol Oates, afterword to Harriette Arnow, *The Dollmaker* (New York: Macmillan, 1954; Avon Books, 1954), pp. 601, 605.

7. Arnow, "Washerwoman's Day," *Southern Review 1* (1936); Olsen, *Tell Me a Riddle* (Philadelphia: Lippincott, 1961).

8. Spencer, quoted in *Contemporary Authors* vols. 1–104 (Detroit, 1965), p. 1278.

9. Elizabeth Janeway, "Women's Literature," in *Harvard Guide to Contemporary American Writing*, ed. Daniel Hoffman (Cambridge, Mass.: Harvard University Press, 1979), p. 355.

10. Flannery O'Connor, quoted in "The Fiction Writer and His Country," in *Mystery and Manners: Occasional Prose*, selected and edited by Robert and Sally Fitzgerald (New York: Farrar, Strauss & Giroux, 1969), pp. 26, 30.

11. Eudora Welty, "Must the Novelist Crusade," in *The Eye of the Story: Selected Essays and Reviews* (New York: Random House, 1979), pp. 147, 150, 156.

12. Welty, "Writing and Analyzing a Story," "Place in Fiction," in *The Eye of the Story;* Elizabeth Evans, *Eudora Welty: Criticism and Interpretations* (New York: Ungar, 1981), p. 5; "The Eye of the Story," p. 40.

13. *The Complete Poems of Emily Dickinson,* ed. Thomas H. Johnson (Cambridge, Mass.: Harvard University Press, 1955).

14. Hortense Calisher, *Tale for the Mirror, Novella and Other Stories* (Boston: Little, Brown, 1962), pp. 288, 94, 100, 287, 283.

15. Grace Paley, *The Little Disturbances of Man: Stories of Men and Women in Love* (New York: Viking, 1959, Plume 1959), jacket blurbs.

16. Paley, "An Interest in Life," in *Little Disturbances,* p. 81.

17. Tillie Olsen, *Silences* (New York: Delacorte Press/Seymour Lawrence, 1978), p. 222.

18. See, Meridel LeSueur, *Ripening. Selected Work, 1927–1980,* ed. with an introd. by Elaine Hedges (Old Westbury, N.Y.: Feminist Press, 1982); Blanche Gelfant, *New York Times* book review, 4 April 1982.

19. Elinor Langer, "Josephine Herbst," in *NAW,* vol. 4; also, *Josephine Herbst: The Story She Could Never Tell* (Boston: 1984).

20. Kay Boyle, *Fifty Stories: From 1927 through 1966, Chosen by the Author* (New York: Doubleday, 1980); *The Smoking Mountain: Stories of Postwar Germany* (New York: McGraw Hill, 1958).

21. Boyle, "Begin Again," "Frankfurt in Our Blood," "Lovers of Gain," in *Fifty Stories.*

22. Boyle, "The Lost," in *Fifty Stories;* "Report from Lock-Up," in *Four Visions of America* (Santa Barbara: Capra Press, 1977); *Contemporary Authors* (1960), p. 162.

23. Jean Stafford, *The Catherine Wheel* (New York: Harcourt Brace, 1951); *The Interior Castle,* including *Children Are Bored on Sunday* (New York: Harcourt Brace, 1953).

24. Shirley Jackson, *Life among the Savages* (New York: Farrar, Straus & Young, 1953); *Raising Demons* (New York: Farrar, Straus & Cudahy, 1957); Jean Kerr, *Please Don't Eat the Daisies* (Garden City, N.Y.: Doubleday, 1957); Phyllis McGinley, *The Province of the Heart* (New York: Viking, 1959).

25. Mary McCarthy, interview with Elisabeth Niebuhr, *Writers at Work: Paris Review Interviews,* second series, introd. Van Wyck Brooks (New York: Viking, 1965), p. 300.

26. Metalious, *Guinness Book of World Records* (1973), p. 165; see also Maria Karagianis, "Remembering Grace Metalious," *Boston Globe Magazine,* 20 September 1981.

27. Elizabeth Stevenson, *Henry Adams* (New York: Macmillan, 1956).

28. Latham, in *Twentieth Century Children's Writers,* ed. D. L. Kirkpatrick (New York: St. Martin's Press, 1978), p. 734.

29. Ibid., p. 993.

30. Dorothy Sterling, quoted in *Third Book of Junior Authors,* ed. Doris

de Montreville (New York: H. W. Wilson, 1972), p. 278. I am indebted to Polly Welts Kaufman of the Boston school system for information about these authors.

31. Marchette Chute, *Shakespeare of London* (New York: E. P. Dutton, 1949); *Stories from Shakespeare* (Cleveland: World Publishing, 1956).

32. Ursula Le Guin, *The Left Hand of Darkness* (New York: Ace, 1969), translated into fourteen languages by 1980. In her introduction Le Guin asserts that we are already psychologically androgynous.

33. Madeleine L'Engle, quoted in *Twentieth Century Children's Writers*, p. 760.

34. See Leslie Fiedler, *Freaks: Myths and Images of the Secret Self* (New York: Simon & Schuster, 1978).

35. James Merrill, "Elizabeth Bishop (1911–1979)," *New York Review of Books*, 6 December 1979; Robert Pinsky, "The Idiom of a Self: Elizabeth Bishop and Wordsworth," *American Poetry Review*, January/February 1980. The forthcoming work of Gertrude Reiff Hughes will identify Bishop with a feminist custodial tradition.

36. Moore quoted in Howard Nemerov, ed., *Poets on Poetry* (New York: Basic Books, 1966), pp. 15, 157.

37. Theodore Roethke and Adrienne Rich, statements on reissue of Louise Bogan, *The Blue Estuaries: Poems 1923–1968* (New York: Ecco Press, 1977).

38. Quotations on May Sarton and Barbara Howes in *Contemporary Authors*.

39. Muriel Rukeyser, *Collected Poems* (New York: McGraw Hill, 1978), Kay Boyle quotation on jacket; "F. O. M.," p. 406.

40. Adrienne Rich, "When We Dead Awaken: Writing as Revision," in *On Lies*, pp. 40-41; "Aunt Jennifer's Tigers," *Poems: Selected and New 1950-1974* (New York: Norton, 1975), p. 4.

41. Rich, "Snapshots," in *Poems*, p. 50.

42. Janeway, "Women," in *Harvard Guide*, pp. 372–74.

43. Denise Levertov, *Light Up the Cave* (New York: New Directions, 1981), p. 86.

44. Quoted in Janeway, "Women," in *Harvard Guide*, p. 359, from *With Eyes in the Back of Our Heads* (1959); Denise Levertov, *The Poet in the World* (New York: New Directions, 1973), p. 106.

45. Not visible in the 1950s, Di Prima published her work in 1975: Diane Di Prima, *Selected Poems 1956–1975* (Plainfield, Vt.: North Atlantic Books, 1975); of the Beats, Joyce Glassman said: "The women were there as onlookers. . . It was a very masculine aesthetic." Barry Gifford and Lawrence Lee, *Jack's Book: An Oral Biography of Jack Kerouac*, (New York: Penguin, 1979), p. 236. See also Joyce (Glassman) Johnson, *Minor Characters* (Boston: Houghton Mifflin, 1983), a vivid and poignant picture of the 1950s.

46. Harold Clurman, quoted in *Contemporary Dramatists*, ed. James Vinson (New York: St. Martin's Press, 1951), p. 365.
47. Lawrence Graver, "Carson McCullers," in *NAW*, vol. 4, p. 444.
48. Lorraine Hansberry, *A Raisin in the Sun* (New York: New American Library, 1958), pp. 26, 38.
49. Ann Douglas, "Dorothy Parker," in *NAW*, vol. 4, p. 524.
50. Olsen, *Silences*, p. 10.

Chapter Eight

1. Quoted in Leuchtenburg, *Troubled Feast*, p. 98.
2. Gallup Survey 529K, analyzed in Nelson Polsby, "McCarthyism as a Republican Phenomenon," in Matusow, *Joseph R. McCarthy*, pp. 148–56.
3. Lerner, *The Majority Finds Its Past*, pp. 74-75.
4. *New York Times*, 6, 9, 10 December 1955.
5. Louise Meriwether, *Don't Ride the Bus on Monday: The Rosa Parks Story* (Englewood Cliffs, N.J.: Prentice Hall, 1973), unpaged.
6. Quoted in *New York Times*, 11 December 1956.
7. Rosa Parks, interview with Marcia Greenlee, 22 August 1978, Black Women's Oral History Project, Schlesinger Library (Cambridge, Mass.).
8. E. D. Nixon; quoted in Howell Raines, *My Soul Is Rested: The Story of the Civil Rights Movement in the Deep South* (New York: Penguin, 1977), p. 51.
9. Lucy, quoted in *New York Times*, 28 February 1956.
10. *New York Times*, 26 February 1956.
11. *New York Times*, 25 February 1956.
12. *New York Times*, 8 March 1956.
13. *New York Times*, 3 March 1956.
14. Shirley Chisholm, 1970 speech to 91st Congress Hearings, at Conference on Women's Employment; quoted in Gerda Lerner, ed., *Black Women in White America* (New York, 1972), pp. 352–57.
15. *NAACP Annual Bulletin*, 1957, p. 22.
16. *New York Times*, 23 September 1957.
17. *New York Times*, 11 May 1958.
18. *New York Times*, 10 September 1957.
19. *New York Times*, 9 September 1957.
20. Herbert H. Denton, "Little Rock Nine Recall School Segregation Battle," *Washington Post*, reprinted in *Boston Globe*, 10 September 1982.
21. *Crisis: A Record of the Darker Race*, April 1959, p. 209.
22. Lerner, *Black Women*, p. 274.
23. Howard Zinn, "A Case of Quiet Social Change," *Crisis*, October 1959, p. 475.

24. Stanley Edgar Hyman and Ralph Ellison, "The Negro Writer in America: An Exchange," *Partisan Review*, Spring 1958.

25. Ibid., p. 205.

26. Quoted in Lawrence Levine, *Black Culture and Black Consciousness: Afro-American Folk Thought from Slavery to Freedom* (New York: Oxford University Press, 1977), p. 185.

27. Taylor, quoted in *New York Times Magazine*, 28 June 1980, p. 31.

28. Elizabeth Hardwick, *Sleepless Nights* (New York: Vintage Books, 1980), p. 36.

29. Billie Holiday with William Duffy, *Lady Sings the Blues* (New York: Doubleday, Lancer, 1956), p. 8.

30. Quoted in John Chilton, *Billie's Blues: The Billie Holiday Story 1933–1959* (New York: Stein & Day, 1975), p. 158.

31. Ibid., p. 171.

32. Ibid., p. 238.

33. Quoted in Seymour Gross and John Edward Hardy, eds., *Images of the Negro in American Literature* (Chicago: University of Chicago Press, 1966), p. 131.

34. James Baldwin, introd. to Robert Nemiroff, *To Be Young, Gifted and Black: Lorraine Hansberry in Her Own Words* (Englewood Cliffs, N.J.: Prentice Hall, 1969), p. x.

35. Ibid., p. xiii.

36. Ibid., p. 115.

37. Ibid., p. xvi.

38. Robert Nemiroff, *The 101 "Final" Performances of Sidney Brustein: Portrait of a Play and Its Author* (New York: New American Library, 1966), p. 181.

39. Baldwin, *To Be Young*, p. xiv.

40. See Mary Helen Washington, ed., *Black-Eyed Susans: Classic Stories by and about Black Women* (Garden City, N.Y.: Anchor, 1975); *Midnight Birds: Stories of Contemporary Black Women Writers* (Garden City, N.Y.: Anchor, 1980).

41. See *I Love Myself When I Am Laughing: A Zora Neale Hurston Reader*, ed. Alice Walker, introd. Mary Helen Washington (Old Westbury, N.Y.: Feminist Press, 1979).

42. Gwendolyn Brooks, *Report from Part One: An Autobiography* (Detroit: Broad Side Press), p. 16.

43. Ibid., p. 21.

44. Gwendolyn Brooks, "Sadie and Maud," in *Selected Poems* (New York: Harper & Row, 1963), p. 9.

45. Brooks, *Report*, p. 14.

46. Nikki Giovanni, *Gemini: An Extended Autobiographical Statement on My First Twenty Five Years of Being a Black Poet in America* (New York: Bobbs-Merrill, 1971; Penguin, 1976), p. 45.

47. Brooks, *Selected Poems*, pp. 82, 87, 89.

48. Jacket quotation, *Maud Martha* (New York: Harper & Bros., 1953), paperback ed.

49. Mary Helen Washington, introd. to *Black-Eyed Susans*, pp. xiii, xiv.

50. For an insightful analysis of black domestics in literature see Trudier Harris, *From Mammies to Militants* (Philadelphia: Temple University Press, 1982).

51. Brooks, *Selected Poems*, p. 93.

52. *Maud Martha*, p. 180.

53. *Report*, pp. 178–79.

54. *Miami Herald*, 27 March 1950, quoted in Robert Hemenway, *Zora Neale Hurston: A Literary Biography* (Urbana: University of Illinois Press, 1977), p. 325.

55. Ibid., pp. 327, 334.

56. Ibid., p. 331.

57. Ibid., p. 329.

58. Ibid., p. 332.

59. William Bradford Huie, *Ruby McCollum: Woman in the Suwannee Jail* (New York: E. P. Dutton, 1956).

60. Hemenway, *ZNH*, p. 348.

61. Pauli Murray, *Proud Shoes: The Story of an American Family* (New York: Harper & Row, 1956), p. vii.

62. Ibid., p. viii.

63. Moms Mabley, quoted in Levine, *Black Culture*, p. 365.

64. Eugenia Collier, "Foreword" to Ora Williams, *American Black Women in the Arts and Sciences: A Bibliographic Survey* (Metuchen, N.J.: Scarecrow Press, 1973), p. vi.

65. Giovanni, *Gemini*, pp. 12, 144.

I am indebted to Ehrai Adams of Hopkinsville, Kentucky for reading an early version of this chapter.

Chapter Nine

1. *The Potential of Women*, ed. Seymour M. Farber and Robert H. L. Wilson (New York: McGraw Hill, 1963), part of series called *Man and Civilization* sponsored by the University of California, San Francisco Medical Center; *Health Progress in the United States 1900–1960: Report of the Health Information Foundation*, ed. Odin W. Anderson and Monroe Lerner (Chicago: University of Chicago Press, 1963) p. 95; see also Irma H. Gross, *Potentialities of Women in the Middle Years* (East Lansing: Michigan State University Press, 1956).

2. Edmund W. Overstreet, "Biological Make-Up of Women," in *The Potential of Women*, p. 22.

3. Eleanor Maccoby, "Women's Intellect"; Esther Peterson, "The Impact of Education"; Marya Mannes, "The Problems of the Creative Women," included in *The Potential of Women*.

4. James C. Doyle, "Unnecessary Hysterectomies: Study of 6,248 Operations in Thirty Hospitals during 1948," *Journal of the American Medical Association*, 31 January 1953.

5. A. W. Diddle et al., "Gynecological Surgery in Five Non-teaching Hospitals," *Obstetrics and Gynecology*, February 1953. See also Barbara Seaman, *Free and Female* (New York: Coward, McCann & Geoghegan, 1972); and Gena Correa, *The Hidden Malpractice: How American Medicine Mistreats Women* (New York: Jove/HBJ Books, 1978), popular studies of women's health based on research.

6. See Rose Kushner, *Why Me?* (Philadelphia: Saunders Paperbacks, 1980), for a thorough discussion of breast surgery.

7. Boston Women's Health Book Collective, *Our Bodies, Ourselves: A Book By and For Women* (New York: Simon & Schuster, 1971), reflects women's reaction to the authoritarian attitudes of doctors in previous decades.

8. Gena Correa, *The Hidden Malpractice*, pp. 15, 16; Correa suggests readers study later congressional hearings on the oral contraceptives (January, February, March 1970).

9. "Therapeutic Abortion: A Problem in Law and Medicine," *Stanford Law Review 417*, 1959. Quoted in Leo Kanowitz, *Women and the Law: the Unfinished Revolution* (Albuquerque: University of New Mexico Press, 1969), pp. 26, 258.

10. Ibid., p. 243.

11. Calderone Papers, Schlesinger Library for the History of Women, Cambridge, Mass.; letter to Howard Taylor, M.D., 6 May 1957.

12. Corea, *Hidden Malpractice*, chapter 10; for a radical reaction see Mary Breasted, *Oh! Sex Education!* (New York: Praeger, 1970).

13. "Cruelty in Maternity Wards" ed. Gladys Denny Shultz, *Ladies' Home Journal*, May 1958, p. 44.

14. Ibid.

15. Ibid., p. 154.

16. *Ladies' Home Journal*, December 1958, pp. 59, 58, 139.

17. Helene Deutsch, "Delivery" (vol. 2, *Psychology of Women*); *Women: Body and Culture: Essays on the Sexuality of Women in a Changing Society*, ed. with an introd. by Signe Hammer (New York: Harper & Row, 1975); see Richard W. and Dorothy C. Wertz, *Lying-In: A History of Childbirth in America* (New York: Free Press, 1977), for a general survey of birth practices.

18. See Nancy Pottishman Weiss, "Mother, the Invention of Necessity: Dr. Benjamin Spock's *Baby and Child Care*," *American Quarterly*, Winter 1977.

19. Jessie Bernard, *The Future of Motherhood*, chapter 3, "Non-Motherhood" (New York: Dial Press, 1974).

20. Marynia Farnham and Ferdinand Lundberg, *Modern Woman: The Lost Sex* (New York, 1947) Farnham was the psychiatrist; Lundberg, a journalist.

21. Ibid., p. 370.

22. "The Lost Sex," in *The Way of Women*, ed. J. E. Fairchild (New York: Sheridan House, 1956), pp. 31, 37. In 1955, 34.7 percent of women with children were in the labor force; 16.2 percent had preschool-age children.

23. For a useful historical presentation of this dilemma, see Carl Degler, *At Odds: Women and the Family in America From the Revolution to the Present* (New York, 1980).

24. Inge Broverman et al., "Women and the Criteria of Mental Health," in *Readings on the Psychology of Women*, ed. Judith Bardwick (New York: Harper & Row, 1972), p. 300, a key document in understanding women's socialization.

25. Paul Goodman, *Growing Up Absurd: Problems of Youth in the Organized System* (New York: Random House, 1960); Abraham Maslow, *Motivation and Personality* (New York: Harper & Row, 1954); Gordon Allport, *Becoming: Basic Considerations for a Psychology of Personality* (New Haven: Yale University Press, 1955); Erving Goffman, *The Presentation of Self in Everyday Life* (Garden City, N.Y.: Doubleday, 1959); *Asylums: Essays on the Social Situations of Mental Patients and Other Inmates* (Chicago: Aldine, 1961).

26. Alfred C. Kinsey, *Sexual Behavior in the Human Female*, by the staff of the Institute for Sex Research, Indiana University (Philadelphia, 1953); see also Regina Markell Morantz, "The Scientist as Sex Crusader: Alfred C. Kinsey and American Culture," *American Quarterly*, Winter 1977.

27. Edmund Bergler, M.S., and William S. Kroger, M.D., *Kinsey's Myth of Female Sexuality: the Medical Facts* (New York: Grune & Stratton, 1954), p. 141.

28. See Anne Koedt, "The Myth of the Vaginal Orgasm," in *Radical Feminism*, ed. Anne Koedt et al. (New York: Quadrangle Books, 1973); Alex Shulman, "Organs and Orgasms," in *Woman in Sexist Society*, ed. Vivian Gornick and Barbara K. Moran (New York: Basic Books, 1971).

29. For a historical examination of the woman doctor's status in America, see Mary Roth Walsh, *"Doctors Wanted: No Women Need Apply"* (New Haven: Yale University Press, 1977).

30. Mary Howell, oral history interview with Regina Morantz, in *Collection on Women in Medicine*, Medical College of Pennsylvania (Schlesinger Library).

31. Dr. Margaret A. Campbell (Mary Howell), *Why Would a Girl Go into Medicine? Medical Education in the U.S.: A Guide for Women* (Old Westbury, L.I.: Feminist Press, 1973).

32. Mary Howell, interview with Gena Corea, in *Hidden Malpractice*, pp. 62–63.

33. Mary Howell, Unprocessed Papers, Schlesinger Library.

34. Janet Travell, *Office Hours: Day and Night* (New York: NAL, 1971).

35. United States Departments of Labor and Health, Education and Welfare, *Health Careers Guidebook*, 1955; *Progress in Health Services*, 1956 (Washington, D.C.: United States Government Printing Office).

I am grateful to Carol Nadelson for having taken time to read and discuss this chapter.

Chapter Ten

1. Laurie Lisle, *Portrait of an Artist: A Biography of Georgia O'Keeffe* (New York: Washington Square Press, 1980), p. 348.

2. Eleanor Munro, *Originals: American Women Artists* (New York, 1979), pp. 202, 245, 484; see also tribute to Nevelson, *New York Times*, 16 July 1979; and Hilton Kramer, "Nevelson: Her Sculpture Changed the Way We Look at Things," *New York Times Magazine*, 30 October 1983.

3. Mitchell, quoted in Munro, *Originals*, p. 245.

4. Irving Sandler, *The New York School: The Painters and Sculptors of the Fifties* (New York: Harper & Row, 1978), p. 37.

5. Hartigan quoted in Cindy Nemser, *Art Talk: Conversations with 12 Woman Artists* (New York: Scribners, 1975), p. 167; Hartigan, Sandler, *New York School*, p. 115. Hartigan called herself "George" in her 1951 show as a gesture of identity with George Sand and George Eliot.

6. Mitchell, in Munro, *Originals*, p. 203.

7. Irving Sandler gives a good general picture of the abstract-expressionist movement, but the women involved have to be studied as individuals. Eleanor Munro's *Originals*, Cindy Nemser's *Art Talk*, and Lynn F. Miller and Sally Swenson, *Lives and Works: Talks with Women Artists* (Metuchen, N.J.: Scarecrow Press, 1981), provide valuable insights into the artists' lives.

8. Lee Krasner, quoted in *New York Times* article on East Hampton, by Michiko Kakutani, 7 June 1981.

9. De Kooning quotation in "The Fifties: Aspects of Painting in New York" (Washington: Hirshhorn Museum and Sculpture Garden, Smithsonian Institution, 22 May–21 September 1980), brochure.

10. Neel, quoted in Nemser, *Art Talk*, p. 134; see also Patricia Hills, ed., *Alice Neel* (New York: Harry N. Abrams, 1983), a survey of Neel's achievements.

11. Munro, *Originals*; Nemser, *Art Talk*.

12. Otto Kallir, *Grandma Moses* (New York: Harry N. Abrams, 1973); *New Yorker*, 23 December 1961.

13. Martin Duberman, *Black Mountain: An Exploration in Community* (New York: Dutton, 1972), pp. 53–56.

14. See Roger Copeland, Dance Review, *New York Times*, 18 April 1982.

15. Ibid.

16. Don McDonagh, *Martha Graham* (New York: Praeger, 1973), pp. 12, 297; jacket quotation from *New York Times*.

17. Margaret Bourke-White, *Portrait of Myself* (New York: Simon & Schuster, 1963), pp. 303, 308.

18. Judy Dater, *Imogen Cunningham: A Portrait* (New York: New York Graphic Society, 1979), p. 14; Imogen Cunningham, *After Ninety* (Seattle: University of Washington Press, 1977).

19. Berenice Abbott, interview with John Russell, *New York Times*, 16 November 1980.

20. *Diane Arbus* (Millerton, N.Y.: Aperture Monograph, 1972).

21. Annie Gottlieb, introd. to *Women See Women*, ed. Cheryl Wiesenfeld, Annie Gottlieb, et al. (New York: Thomas Y. Crowell, 1976), p. iv.

22. Susan Sontag, *On Photography* (New York: Dell, 1973), p. 4.

23. Eve Arnold, *Flashback: The 50's* (New York: Knopf, 1978).

24. Susanne Knauths Langer's list of publications is so distinguished that her failure to achieve any professorial rank at Harvard must be seen as a patent example of prejudice. *Feeling and Form: A Theory of Art* (New York: Scribners, 1953); *Problems of Art* (New York: Scribners, 1957); also *Reflections on Art: A Source of Writings by Artists, Critics, and Philosophers* (Baltimore: Johns Hopkins Press, 1958).

25. Hannah Arendt, *The Origins of Totalitarianism* (New York: Harcourt, Brace, 1951); *The Human Condition* (Chicago: University of Chicago Press, 1958).

26. Adrienne Rich, "Conditions for Work: the Common World of Women," in *On Lies*, p. 212.

27. Arendt, quoted in Elisabeth Young-Bruehl, *Hannah Arendt: For Love of the World* (New Haven: Yale University Press, 1980), p. 210. At a conference on feminist thinking (University of Pennsylvania, 8 April 1984) Young-Bruehl remarked that Arendt's philosophical preference for human relationships over abstract truth also distinguished her from most political theorists.

28. Richard Chase, "Ruth Benedict, the Woman," *Columbia University Forum*, Spring 1950, pp. 19, 22.

29. *Current Biography*, 1950–1959; *Modern Scientists and Engineers*, 3 vols., ed. Sybil Parker (New York: McGraw Hill, 1980); *NAW*, vol. 4.

30. "Rosalyn Yalow," *Current Biography*, 1978, p. 460; I am indebted to Dr. Yalow for providing materials about her life.

31. Evelyn Fox Keller, *A Feeling for the Organism: The Life and Work of Barbara McClintock* (New York: W. H. Freeman, 1983) pp. xiii, xiv, 201; Matthew Meselson quoted on p. xi.

32. Chien-Shiung Wu, in *Women and the Scientific Professions*, ed. Jacquelyn A. Mattfeld and Carol G. Van Aken (Cambridge, Mass.: MIT Press, 1965), pp.47-48.

33. Ibid., p. 48, jacket; Betty Friedan, *Mystique*, notes, pp. 338–39; see also Mary Roth Walsh, *"Doctors Wanted: No Women Need Apply"* (New Haven: Yale University Press, 1980). There are slight variations in statistics depending on how the figures are organized, but the truth they present is clear.

34. I am indebted to Ruth Hubbard for helping to clarify this pattern. Indispensable to an understanding of these problems is also the bibliography of the book she edited with Mary Sue Henifin and Barbara Fried, *Biological Woman—The Convenient Myth* (Cambridge, Mass.: Schenkman Publishing, 1982).

35. Leona Baumgartner Papers, Schlesinger Library, Radcliffe College, Cambridge, Mass.; *NAW*, vol. 4; *Current Biography*, 1950.

36. Rees, quoted in Mattfeld and Akens, *Women and the Scientific Professions*, p. 35.

37. Beatrice Hicks, *Contemporary Biography*, 1955; "Lillian Gilbreth," in *NAW*, vol. 4.

38. Mirra Komarovsky, *Women in the Modern World* (Boston: Little, Brown, 1953); *Blue Collar Marriage*, with Jane H. Philips (New York: Random House, 1964); Helena Lopata, *Occupation Housewife* (New York: Oxford, 1971); Jessie Bernard, *Remarriage, A Study of Marriage* (New York: Russell & Russell, 1956).

39. Some books that grew out of the decade's needs include Arnold Gesell, Frances Ilg. Louise Ames, *Child Development: An Introduction to the Study of Human Growth* (New York: Harper, 1949); Eleanor and Sheldon Glueck, *Delinquents in the Making: Paths to Prevention* (New York: Harper, 1952); Nina Ridenour, *The Children We Teach* (New York: Mental Health Materials Center, 1957); Emily Mudd, *Practice of Marriage Counseling* (New York: Association Press, 1951).

40. Mead, *New Lives for Old*, p. 25.

41. Another important woman anthropologist of the 1950s was Ruth Underhill, who contributed to our understanding of Native Americans with *Red Man's America: A History of Indians in the United States* (Chicago: University of Chicago Press, 1953), and *Here Come the Navaho: A History of the Largest Tribe in the United States* (United States Indian Service, 1952).

42. Rachel Carson, *The Sea Around Us.* (New York, 1951); *The Edge of the Sea* (Boston: Houghton Mifflin, 1955); *Under the Sea Wind: A Naturalist's Picture of Ocean Life* (New York, 1952); *The Sense of Wonder* (New York: Harper & Row, 1956); *Silent Spring* (Boston, 1962).

43. Quoted in Paul Brooks, *The House of Life: Rachel Carson at Work; with Selections from Her Writings Published and Unpublished* (Boston, 1972), p. 140.

44. Ibid., p. 155.

45. Carson quoted in Philip Sterling, *Sea and Earth: The Life of Rachel Carson* (New York: Crowell, 1970), p. 146.

46. Brooks, *House of Life*, p. 293.

47. Carson letter, ibid.

48. Carson, quoted in Frank Graham, Jr., *Since Silent Spring* (Boston: Houghton Mifflin, 1970), p. 63.

49. Carson, quoted in Brooks, *House of Life*, p. 316.

50. Ibid., pp. 325, 323.

Chapter Eleven

1. Gayle Graham Yates, *What Women Want*, p. viii.

2. Joan Didion, *The White Album* (New York: Simon & Schuster, 1979), p. 206.

3. Ibid.

4. Betty Friedan, *It Changed My Life*, pp. 38–39, 245.

5. Margaret Mead, New School speech, *New York Times*, 9 March 1950.

6. Imogen Cunningham, *After Ninety*, introd. Margaretta Mitchell (Seattle: University of Washington Press, 1977).

7. Theodora Kroeber, *Ishi and Two Worlds: A Biography of the Last Wild Indian in North America* (Berkeley: University of California Press, 1961); Ursula Kroeber LeGuin, *The Left Hand of Darkness* (New York: Ace Publishing, 1969).

8. "The Mother Who Ran Away," *McCall's*, April 1956; "Is Boredom Bad for You?", *McCall's*, April 1957; "Why Young Mothers Are Always Tired," *Redbook*, September 1959.

9. Alice Rossi, "Barriers to the Career Choice of Engineering, Medicine, or Science," in *Readings on the Psychology of Women*, ed. Judith M. Bardwick (New York: Harper & Row, 1972), p. 78.

10. Ibid.

11. Rachel Carson, "Help Your Child to Wonder," *Woman's Home Companion*, 1956.

12. Yates, *What Women Want*, pp. 46–50; see also Leo Kanowitz, *Women and the Law: The Unfinished Revolution* (Albuquerque: University of New Mexico Press, 1969), chapters 4 and 5.

13. *American Women*, Report of the President's Commission on the Status of Women, 1963, p. 42.

14. Ibid., p. 46.

15. Marguerite Wycoff Zapoleon, *The College Girl Looks Ahead to Her Career Opportunities* (New York: Harper, 1956), p. 192.

16. *American Women*, p. 44.

17. Friedan, *It Changed My Life*, pp. 111, 116.

18. Mead, Cooper Union Speech published in *The Way of Women*, ed. J. E. Fairchild (New York: Sheridan House, 1956), p. 23; Mead enjoyed challenging stereotypes. See also "One Vote for This Age of Anxiety," *New York Times Magazine*, 20 May 1956; and "American Man in Woman's World," *New York Times Magazine*, 10 February 1957.

19. Katherine Anne Porter, "Holiday," in *Collected Stories* (New York: Harcourt, Brace, Jovanovich, 1969), pp. 428, 421, 435.

20. Porter, letter to Herbst, in Joan Givner, *Katherine Anne Porter: A Life* (New York: Simon & Schuster, 1982), p. 72.

21. NOW statement of purpose in Friedan, *It Changed My Life*, p. 128.

Essay on Sources

T o find out what women were doing and how they were envisioned during the 1950s I first read extensively in the *New York Times*. The *Times's* well-designed indexes on issues related to women and children as well as the newspaper's frequent references to women in all fields made such work rewarding. Public utterances of worthies like Margaret Mead and Eleanor Roosevelt, consistent advocates of cultural pluralism, reveal private strengths along with social attitudes. Although the *Times's* coverage of American life as a whole may be limited because of its New York perspective, I found its coverage of the civil-rights activities in the South during the 1950s especially good.

In order to get a sense of the political background of the period I relied on Eric Goldman's *The Crucial Decade—and After: America, 1945–1960* (New York: Vintage, 1960) and William E. Leuchtenburg's *A Troubled Feast: American Society Since 1945* (Boston: Little, Brown, 1983), solid liberal interpretations of the contemporary events. A more radical book, *The Fifties: The Way We Really Were*, by Douglas T. Miller and Marion Nowak (Garden City, N.Y.: Doubleday, 1975), was useful for the sheer quantity of facts it offers. Although Miller and Nowak's interpretations often seem glib and patronizing about people who lived through the 1950s, I sympathize with their open anger. They are the only historians of this period who consider women worth writing about at any length. Another radical text, Marty Jezer's *The*

Dark Ages: Life in the United States 1945–1960 (Boston: South End Press, 1982), simply sees women as overwhelmingly oppressed. This book is useful as a record of the early roots of 1960s protest movements. It may be inevitable that historians of the media age overuse advertising images to define the entire society.

David Caute's *The Great Fear: The Anti-Communist Purges under Truman and Eisenhower* (New York: Simon & Schuster, 1978) provided a detailed account of the paranoia of the times, and Allen J. Matusow's *Joseph R. McCarthy* (Englewood Cliffs, N.J.: Prentice-Hall, 1970) filled in details about the life of the man whose spirit dominated the decade. Lillian Hellman's *Scoundrel Time* (Boston: Little, Brown, 1976) captured the mood of the period with literary grace and sustained outrage and Victor Navasky's *Naming Names* (New York: Viking 1980) recorded the intensity of emotion involved in defining loyalties. For a sense of intellectual attitudes, I used the *Partisan Review* articles "Our Country and Our Culture" (September—October 1952) and Morris Dickstein's chapter on the 1950s in *The Gates of Eden: American Culture in the Sixties* (New York: Basic Books, 1977). Although not mentioned in my text, books I also profited from reading are: John Kenneth Galbraith's *The Affluent Society* (Boston: Houghton Mifflin, 1958), William H. Whyte's *The Organization Man* (New York: Simon & Schuster, 1956), and Paul Goodman's *Growing Up Absurd: Problems of Youth in the Organized System* (New York: Random House, 1960). These books simply tend not to see women as a separate presence in American life; the concept of gender was not part of the consciousness of the 1950s. A ten-page bibliography at the end of the Miller and Nowak book was useful for general background information.

Published historical material about women in the 1950s is hard to find, suggesting how essential it may be to expand the criteria we use to record women's behavior. Gerda Lerner's valuable book *The Majority Finds Its Past: Placing Women in History* (New York: Oxford University Press, 1979) helped me to focus on what materials women's history might include; I also profited from her work on black women, *Black Women in White America* (New York: Pantheon, 1972). No work on this decade can ignore the writing of Betty Friedan. Although *The Feminine Mystique* (New York: Norton, 1963) is the book that defines women's lives from after World War II until the 1960s, Friedan's second book, *It Changed My Life: Writings on the Women's Movement* (New York: Random House, 1976), may be more important in helping to see the 1950s in clearer perspective. Friedan is another social critic who, I believe, makes too much of media images. My own point of view derives also from Mary Ritter Beard's *Woman as Force in History: A Study in Traditions and Realities* (New York: Macmillan, 1946), a text concerned with the complex nature of women's indirect power more than with women's absence in the institutional world. A number of other books not mentioned in the text have influenced my thinking about woman's values. Chief among these are:

Carolyn Heilbrun's *Reinventing Womanhood* (New York: Norton, 1979); Adrienne Rich's *Of Woman Born: Motherhood as Experience and Institution* (New York: Norton, 1976); Elizabeth Janeway's *Man's World, Woman's Place: A Study in Social Mythology* (New York: Morrow, 1971) and *Powers of the Weak* (New York: Knopf, 1980); Jean Baker Miller's *Toward a New Psychology of Women* (Boston: Beacon Press, 1976); and Carol Gilligan's *In a Different Voice* (Cambridge,: Harvard University Press, 1982). The danger to individual women implicit in separate male—female value systems must be understood as clearly as the worth of such systems to society as a whole. What may be defined as a different set of priorities could become an excuse for keeping women out of institutional power structures.

More concretely embedded in the writing are references from Katherine Fishburn's *Women in Popular Culture: A Reference Guide* (Westport, Conn.: Greenwood Press, 1982), a thorough, intelligent survey of every kind of popular image. I looked into some magazines like the *Ladies' Home Journal* and *Life*, which attempted a number of analyses of new social patterns such as "Changing Roles in Modern Marriage" (24 December 1956). Works concerned with the specific achievements of women in special fields, such as Eleanor Munro's *Originals: American Women Artists* (New York: Simon & Schuster, 1979), receive some critical attention in chapter endnotes.

Along with a new edition of Eleanor Flexner's 1959 classic on women's political rights, *Century of Struggle: The Woman's Rights Movement in the United States* (Cambridge,: Belknap Editions, Harvard University Press, 1975), for linear historical background concerned with women's behavior and goals, I used Carl Degler's *At Odds: Women and Family in America From the Revolution to the Present* (New York: Oxford University Press, 1980), William L. O'Neill's *Everyone Was Brave: The Rise and Fall of Feminism in America* (Chicago: Quadrangle Books, 1969), and Gayle Graham Yates's *What Women Want: The Ideas of the Movement* (Cambridge,: Harvard University Press, 1975). Indispensable to an understanding of woman's economic position during this period are William Chafe's two books: *The American Woman: Her Changing Social, Economic and Political Roles 1920–1970* (New York: Oxford University Press, 1972) and *Women and Equality: Changing Patterns in American Culture* New York: Oxford University Press, 1977). The books that dictated woman's role at the time, Lynn White, Jr.,'s *Educating Our Daughters* (New York: Harper & Bros., 1950), and Marynia Farnham and Ferdinand Lundberg's *Modern Woman: The Lost Sex* (New York: Harper & Bros., 1947), remain essential to an understanding of the attitudes of the decade; as does the more liberating Kinsey report on women, *Sexual Behavior in the Human Female* (Philadelphia: Saunders, 1953).

United States government publications published in 1963 by the Kennedy Commission under the general heading *American Women* were useful guides to the defects of the previous decade. The commission appointed subgroups that produced surveys of women's education, civil and political rights, social insurance and taxes, employment opportunities, and volunteer work, and studies of the way women were portrayed by the media. Models of clarity and insight, these publications exemplify the careful thinking available at the end of the 1950s, as well as the paradox that the commission's recommendations, even by the mid-1960s, were largely unheeded. Private foundation reports on what was happening to women during the 1950s were also helpful. The National Manpower Council with Columbia University published three valuable books on women's employment: *Womanpower in Today's World* (1957), *Work in the Lives of Married Women* 1958), and *Human Resources: The Wealth of a Nation* (1958). The Commission on Education for Women also produced a number of useful papers and pamphlets during the 1950s analyzing the need for change, such as *How Fare American Women?* (1955) and *The Education of Women: Signs for the Future* (1957). These papers and publications are accessible at the Schlesinger Library, Radcliffe College, Cambridge, Massachusetts.

Assessments of the valued contributions of many individual women can be found in *Notable American Women: The Modern Period*, volume 4, edited by Barbara Sicherman and Carol Hurd Green (Cambridge,: Harvard University Press, 1980); *Current Biography* (New York: H. W. Wilson, 1950–60); and *Contemporary Authors* (Detroit: Gale Research Co., 1965). The Schlesinger Library also contains unpublished materials on the lives of Leona Baumgartner, Mary Calderone, Virginia Foster Durr, Betty Friedan, and Mary Howell. There too, I read an interview with Rosa Parks included in the Black Women's Oral History Collection. At Vassar College, Poughkeepsie, New York, I consulted the papers of Ruth Benedict.

Information on the three most influential women of the decade is available both in books and in archives. Indispensable as an introduction to Eleanor Roosevelt's work during these years is Joseph P. Lash's *Eleanor: The Years Alone* (New York: Norton, 1977). Useful also for understanding Roosevelt's attitudes during the 1950s are two papers: Marque-Luisa Miringoff's "Eleanor Roosevelt: Women and Work, Considerations for the 1980's" (Hyde Park, N.Y.: Val-Kill Publications, 1981); and M. Glen Johnson's "Eleanor Roosevelt and the International Human Rights Movement" (presented at Fifth Berkshire Conference on the History of Women, Vassar College, 1981). The Franklin D. Roosevelt Library at Hyde Park, New York, houses Eleanor Roosevelt's papers, magazine articles, and speeches, as well as a complete set of "My Day" columns. There too, researchers can find transcripts of a number of oral history interviews with Eleanor Roosevelt's family and friends, and with colleagues who worked with her at every period of her life. Margaret Mead's publications for intelligent nonprofessional readers are the most valuable sources for her ideas during this decade. *Male and Female: A Study of the Sexes in a Changing World* (New York: Morrow, 1949) and

New Lives for Old: Cultural Transformation—Manus 1928–1953 (New York: Morrow, 1956) are more rewarding than subsequent autobiographical writing. A memorial volume, *American Anthropologist* 82, no. 2 (June 1980), provides a useful introduction to Mead's anthropology. In view of ongoing controversies concerning Margaret Mead's scientific contributions, it may be important to note that although her personal American papers are in the Library of Congress, her anthropological papers on different cultures remain with those of other workers at the Institute for Intercultural Studies where they are open to expected revisions and modifications. Because she was a gifted writer, able to suggest the mystery as well as the mechanics of nature, Rachel Carson should also first be measured by her own books: *The Sea Around Us* (New York: Oxford, 1951), *Under the Sea Wind: A Naturalist's Picture of Ocean Life* (New York: Oxford, 1952), and *Silent Spring* (Boston: Houghton Mifflin, 1962). A short biography, additional writings, and a useful bibliography are included in Paul Brooks's *The House of Life: Rachel Carson at Work* (Boston: Houghton Mifflin, 1972). Imaginative thinking on Carson appears most recently in the unpublished work of Vera Norwood of the University of New Mexico, Albuquerque: "Rachel Carson and the American Environment" (paper presented at the meetings of the American Studies Association, Philadelphia, 1983). Carson's papers are at the Yale University Library, New Haven, Connecticut.

Opinions of many culture critics consulted are written into the text as well as into the endnotes. I make no pretense of either objectivity or omniscience. My own brand of liberal feminism makes me regret not being able to include more women and not having space to say more about the many who are barely mentioned—more than I regret not having a neat feminist theory. The book is meant to provoke students to ask more questions about a rich but neglected period in the lives of American women.

Index